Children at Sea

For Piers
with love

Children at Sea

Lives Shaped by the Waves

Vyvyen Brendon

PEN & SWORD
HISTORY

First published in Great Britain in 2020
and reprinted in 2021 by
Pen & Sword History
An imprint of
Pen & Sword Books Ltd
Yorkshire – Philadelphia

ISBN 978 1 52677 242 8

A CIP catalogue record for this book is
available from the British Library.

Typeset by Mac Style
Printed and bound in the UK by
CPI Group (UK) Ltd, Croydon, CR0 4YY

Pen & Sword Books Limited incorporates the imprints of Atlas,
Archaeology, Aviation, Discovery, Family History, Fiction, History,
Maritime, Military, Military Classics, Politics, Select, Transport,
True Crime, Air World, Frontline Publishing, Leo Cooper,
Remember When, Seaforth Publishing, The Praetorian Press,
Wharncliffe Local History, Wharncliffe Transport, Wharncliffe True
Crime
and White Owl.

For a complete list of Pen & Sword titles please contact

PEN & SWORD BOOKS LIMITED
47 Church Street, Barnsley, South Yorkshire, S70 2AS, England
E-mail: enquiries@pen-and-sword.co.uk
Website: www.pen-and-sword.co.uk

Or

PEN AND SWORD BOOKS
1950 Lawrence Rd, Havertown, PA 19083, USA
E-mail: Uspen-and-sword@casematepublishers.com
Website: www.penandswordbooks.com

Contents

List of Illustrations

The author thanks the following for kind permission to reproduce pictures in their care: The National Library of Australia, Plate 2; The State Library of New South Wales, Plates 4, 5 and 6; Coram in the care of the Foundling Hospital, Plate 11;The Royal Institution of Cornwall, Plate 9; Royal Museums Greenwich, Plate 22; Charles Dickens Museum, Plates 24 & 25; Barnardo's, Plate 27; Anjo Kan, Dreamstime.com, Plate 32.

Acknowledgements

This voyage of discovery could not have been accomplished without the support of a willing crew, to whom I owe my thanks.

I am especially grateful to those who helped to salvage some of these children at sea by supplying me with valuable source material. Alison Duke of the Foundling Museum gave me a transcript of George King's autobiography and allowed me to see the battered original. Othnel Mawdesley's journal was kindly lent to me by Bridget Somekh, whose ancestor, Lieutenant Mitchell, was his companion in captivity. Anthony Barlow, a descendant of William and Charles Barlow, entrusted me with vital correspondence about William's death. Megan Parker of Barnardo's put me in touch with Ada Southwell's Canadian grandson, Chris Beldan, who generously sent me letters, photographs and the results of his own research. He and members of his family have encouraged and endorsed my telling of Ada's story.

My course has been guided by the expert staff and volunteers of museums and archive collections: Angela Broome and Michael Harris of the Royal Cornwall Museum in Truro; Paul Cook of the Paper Conservation Studio at the Caird Library; Amanda Martin of the Isles of Scilly Museum; Louisa Price of the Charles Dickens Museum; and knowledgeable teams at Chatham Historic Dockyard, the National Archives, the London Metropolitan Archives and the Oriental and India Office Collections.

Others have been generous with their time and expertise by answering queries and providing references: Christopher Andrew, Roger Banfield, Michaela Ann Cameron of the University of Sydney, Kevin Egan, Vic Gatrell, Pat Gillibrand, Katie Herbert of Penlee House Gallery, Jackie Millen, Katherine Moulds of the Caird Library, Colin Mumford, Jennifer Murphy of the Representative Church Body Library in Dublin, Stephen

Taylor, John Tyler and Phoebe Wyss. My brother Rod Davis and cousins, Diana Page and Ruth Vickery, aided me in the quest for family records.

It has been exciting to visit places associated with these young sailors, often in the company of obliging friends and relations. Georgie, Gayle and Lucas Brendon accompanied me to St Agnes Lighthouse and other Scillonian sites. Beau, Sonny and Anya Brendon explored Portsmouth Harbour with me. Judith Findlay has been my travelling companion on expeditions to Penzance, Chester, Broadstairs, Ramsgate, Chatham and the Cove of Cork. On my behalf, Rupert and Christine Brendon spent an extremely hot day at Williamstown cemetery in South Australia, where they identified and photographed the grave of Captain Charles Davis. My husband Piers has accompanied me throughout the whole enterprise, often bringing his own sharp pen and sword to my aid.

The publication of the book was made possible by the enthusiastic efforts of my agent Laura Morris. The friendly efficiency of Claire Hopkins, Lori Jones, Karyn Burnham, Emily Robinson, Rosie Crofts and Laura Hirst has made it a pleasure to work with Pen & Sword Books.

Every effort has been made to trace copyright holders for images and text used in the book. The publishers welcome information on any attributions which have been omitted.

Introduction: A Historian at Sea

This book tells eight stories of lone boys and girls crossing the seven seas. They travelled as slaves, convicts, sailors or migrants, cast adrift from what Samuel Taylor Coleridge called their 'sweet birth-place', to live among strangers. 'Alone on a wide, wide sea', far from any kind of child protection, they faced storms and calms, disease and abuse, piracy and war, as well as hazards of the imagination – 'the curse in a dead man's eye', or a vision of 'a thousand thousand slimy things ... upon the rotting sea'.[1]

I was drawn to this subject by a strong affinity for the sea. During the first four years of my life my father, Royer Davis, was serving with the Royal Naval Volunteer Reserve (RNVR). Of course, I didn't understand then the danger he was in as he escorted supply ships across the Arctic Sea to Russia on the Murmansk Run, though I was perhaps conscious of my mother's anxiety. He survived the fury of the elements and of German attacks – though he would never afterwards speak of those times. Some of my contemporaries also braved the perils of wartime oceans as they were evacuated from beleaguered Britain to the safer shores of America and the Dominions. But I survived the bombs which fell on Exeter and Plymouth to spend my childhood on Devon's coast, roaming the cliffs and beaches close to the village where Coleridge spent his early years.

Sometimes I would listen to my grandfather, Harold Davis, tell of his boyhood in the Isles of Scilly. He liked to show me a photograph taken in the 1870s of his father, Captain Charles Royer Davis, who poses with three of his brothers. He told me that they were all merchant sailors who had been apprenticed at about the age of 14, taking one of the few opportunities for employment available on the Isles, where their father was Keeper of St Agnes Lighthouse. Seated beside Charles are Edwin and John, both Master Mariners like himself. Their hard years of seafaring had clearly aged them and it is difficult to believe that they were all under

35. Behind them is their teenage brother Samuel, still a fresh-faced cabin boy. The picture was apparently taken in Calcutta, where they had met by a remarkable coincidence: their separate vessels had been forced to take refuge in the port from storms in the Bay of Bengal. The bare floorboards and background suggest to me now that the picture was taken not in a studio, but in the Sailors' Home overlooking the Hooghly River which provided temporary board and lodging for the officers and crew of the British Merchant Marine.

The photograph was precious to Grandpa because it was the last one taken of a father he never knew. In November 1877, Charles was given command of the sailing ship *Macduff* for a voyage from Melbourne to London. *Macduff* belonged to a fleet of wool clippers bound for South Australia around the Cape of Good Hope, carrying passengers who were replaced by cargoes of wool for the journey back to Britain around Cape Horn. These 'rolling kings', as the sea-shanty dubbed them, were famed for their great speed and demanded great navigational skill from the captain.[2] Their long voyages were fraught with danger, as the recent experiences of this very ship illustrate. On the outward voyage earlier in 1877 it had been quarantined as a result of eight cases of smallpox (including that of the captain); it had collided with a fishing smack in the English Channel; and it had lost a sailor who fell overboard. Charges were brought against her captain, T.T. Watson, both for not halting his ship when 'cries of distress were heard' from the fishing boat, and for not taking 'the proper steps to save the lost man's life'.[3] All these 'worrying cases' appeared in the Melbourne press, which reported that they had rendered the wretched man 'almost entirely imbecile', with the result that he was superseded by Charles for the return journey.[4]

In July 1878 27-year-old Captain Davis was appointed to take the ship back to Melbourne with thirty-one passengers 'in most superior accommodation'.[5] This sixteen-week voyage was to be his last. Davis family tradition recounts that as the ship approached Melbourne in early October along the notorious 'shipwreck coast' of western Victoria, he 'fell overboard, was saved by his crew but died the next day on board his vessel'.[6] My own research reveals a less dramatic story. The *Melbourne Argus* reports the passage as 'comparatively uneventful', apart from the serious illness of Captain Davis: 'Rapid consumption appears to have set in and marked him for its own.' On reaching Melbourne he was 'in a very weak and exhausted condition' and died on board *Macduff*. His death certificate confirmed a diagnosis of 'phthisis pulmonalis', a condition no doubt exacerbated by a life spent in vessels 'swept from end to end by every roaring sea'.[7] The newly constructed telegraph line soon took the sad news back to the Scillies, where 'great sympathy' was expressed for his young widow Ambrosine and baby son Harold, who had been born a few months before his father's departure for Melbourne. Charles was buried in Williamstown Cemetery on Hobson's Bay, where all the vessels 'hauled their flags at half-mast in memory of the deceased', and the gravestone 'erected by his fellow shipmasters and other friends as a token of respect' can still be seen.[8] Charles is also commemorated on his mother's weathered headstone in St Agnes churchyard close to the island's rocky shore.

Edwin and John Davis survived Charles but both were subsequently shipwrecked, the former off India in 1881 and the latter off Beachy Head in 1889. No longer would Edwin's intrepid wife Janie be able to join her husband whenever he was in a European port, 'generally taking one of the children'.[9] Two more of the lighthouse keeper's seven sons had already perished at sea, Thomas and the youngest, Lewis, who was drowned on his first voyage after leaving school at 14. The only two sons to escape a marine death were his first-born, William, and cabin-boy Sam, both of whom abandoned seafaring and took up their father's profession, thus helping to prevent the loss of other sailors' lives.

Apart from the photograph and family legends passed down through the generations, the evidence for this story is sparse. There are apprenticeship indenture papers, grave inscriptions, newspaper reports and registers of deaths at sea, but the Davis family wrote no memoirs and preserved no letters. In any case, it is always difficult to research maritime lives and deaths in those days since 'seamen were not documented'.[10] They carried no passports and they were not usually included in census returns or parish death registers. If they died on a voyage their bodies would often be washed up on some other shore 'without a grave, unknell'd, uncoffin'd and unknown',[11] as Byron put it, while families simply knew that sons, brothers and husbands failed to return from their mysterious watery world. Added to this elusiveness is the problem of discovering how children thought and felt at a time when they were supposed to be seen and not heard. Thus I found myself a historian at sea, grasping at such flotsam and jetsam as came my way to recreate the lives and deaths of Keeper Davis's sons. Nevertheless, I was inspired to investigate further tales of those who embarked as children on voyages which would shape the rest of their lives.

Brine was evidently in the blood of those born and bred in a lighthouse, yet no one in Britain lives more than sixty miles from the sea. 'Men and sea interpenetrate', wrote Joseph Conrad in 1898 'the sea entering into the life of most men … in the way of amusement, of travel, or of bread-winning.'[12] And it has always seeped into the lives of British children, dreaming of watery adventures as they read exciting maritime tales like Defoe's *Robinson Crusoe*, heard tell of mermaids and leviathans, wore sailor suits, launched toy boats, explored rock-pools and built sand-castles on the beach. In her memoir of a childhood spent on the Great Western Beach at Newquay Emma Smith describes an ocean as 'ever-present and omnipotent as God … both feared and loved, as God is supposed to be feared and loved; endlessly interesting in its unchanging changeability; always, inevitably there.'[13] Charlotte Runcie's memories of Scottish seaside summers put her, too, in awe of the 'delicate and powerful' element 'forming the weather, the place we evolve from, providing everything the planet needs for life'. Wherever she lived, the sea was always calling her back.[14]

Sometimes children fell victim to this 'greedy god' who had to be 'appeased with regular doses of sacrificial souls'.[15] On any West Country shore in earlier centuries, children ran the risk of being kidnapped by Barbary pirates to become white slaves across the Mediterranean in North Africa, and to feel all their lives 'the pull of captor society', even if they were rescued.[16] At the same time, British slavers sailed from Western ports to capture multitudes of African children for the trans-Atlantic trade. There were further hazards for youngsters in all the coastal towns and villages of Britain. They could be spirited off across the Atlantic as indentured labourers, press-ganged into the Royal Navy as cabin boys and powder monkeys, or lured, like the young Walter Raleigh in the iconic Millais painting, by 'tales of wonder' told by old sailors.[17] Juvenile law-breakers were frequently incarcerated in prison hulks off the coasts of Britain before being transported over the seas. Long after this practice died out, so-called 'charities', Dr Barnardo's being the best known, continued to supply young labourers to the colonies. Until 1967, 'waifs and strays' were gathered up from the streets of Britain's cities for long sea migrations, from which they rarely returned. The offspring of more affluent families were piloted by requirements more of their own (or their parents') choosing. Aspiring naval officers were meant to join a ship by the time they were 14, and children from sultry parts of the Empire were ensconced in Britain's bracing boarding-schools by the age of 7 or 8.

All the subjects of my stories were born in Georgian and Victorian times, when the sea was still the key element of Britain's national existence, vital to defence, commerce, culture and empire. This meant, of course, that I could not interview them as I did some of the Raj children and prep school pupils who featured in my previous books.[18] In two cases, however, such oral history had already been created. In 1807 the musician Joseph Emidy told his 18-year-old flute pupil, James Silk Buckingham, about his extraordinary journey from slavery in Brazil through forced labour in the British navy to an independent and settled life in Cornwall. Buckingham later included this story in his autobiography along with his own maritime adventures. Growing up in Falmouth in the 1790s with a 'strong and unconquerable predilection for a sealife', Buckingham had served on several Lisbon-bound packet-boats while still a boy. By the time he was 10 he had engaged in smuggling, got dead drunk on sweet Portuguese wine at the hands of the 'rough wag' of a boatswain, been held in 'painful captivity' aboard a French privateer, and fallen in love with a dark-eyed Spanish señorita. It was only his experience as a 15-year-old volunteer in the Royal Navy which put him off the sea. After witnessing such common naval practices as a mutineer hanged by the yard-arm, and a deserter flogged to death, he jumped ship and was lucky enough to escape recapture by the press-gang.[19] His own background gave Buckingham a particular interest in his music tutor's life story, but he was told no details of Emidy's abduction from Africa, transportation in a slave ship and bondage in a Portuguese colony, experiences too painful to recount in the course of a flute lesson. I have had to reconstruct them from ample documentation about the infamous system, including the reminiscences of other young victims. It was also important to modify

Buckingham's rather distorted account of Emidy's service with the Royal Navy by comparing it with naval records. The musician's later career was easier to trace, as he was frequently mentioned in Cornish newspapers and memoirs.

Child migrants were not much more likely than slaves to tell their own stories. They usually repressed in adulthood the pain and humiliation of being separated from their families and despatched abroad. Thus Barnardo's child, Ada Southwell, did not reminisce about her transatlantic transition from East End kid to Canadian indentured servant, which can only be reconstructed from the charity's sparse and closely guarded records, and the correspondence of a conscientious older sister. After Ada's death, however, her Canadian husband told an attentive daughter about his life and marriage, unwittingly revealing some of the effects the childhood severance had had on his wife.[20] By such indirect and chancy means a child's voice can sometimes echo down the generations.

The least distinct voices are those of child convicts transported to Australia. After all, the whole point of choosing this newly-discovered penal destination was its distance from the civilised world. These unwanted subjects would find it all but impossible to communicate with their disgraced families and disgraceful companions, let alone to make the return journey. They could simply be forgotten. In recent years, however, historians and descendants have tried to discover what lives the convicts made for themselves in their new world – but it's not easy. Early Australian records of births, marriages and deaths are patchy and unreliable. Accounts by the marines who guarded the convicts rarely mention convicts' names, let alone record their feelings or reactions to their plight. And the prisoners themselves did not have the leisure and materials or, in many cases, the ability to write their own history. Thus it is has been especially difficult to reconstruct the fortunes of a young first-fleet passenger such as Mary Branham. The full story of her loves and losses may never be salvaged.

In the case of four of my five naval subjects, however, I discovered a treasure trove. Marine Private George King wrote an autobiography, a much rarer achievement for one of his lowly rank than for the young gentlemen of the upper decks.[21] It recounts his experiences as a Coram boy, a Trafalgar man, and an old salt. Restrained and literate though it is,

I had to make sure that he was not spinning a series of sailors' yarns, by comparing his tale with ships' musters, captains' logs and contemporary accounts. Similar sources helped to authenticate the careful diary kept by Midshipman Othnel Mawdesley when he was taken prisoner off the Spanish coast two years after the Battle of Trafalgar. Mawdesley did not, however, write of his Chester childhood, which could only be reconstructed through sites in this well-preserved city, and documents in its Record Office. Another find was the huge correspondence of the Barlow family, carefully gathered by Sir George Barlow, a high-ranking and long-serving officer of the East India Company, and preserved now in the India Office Library. The collection includes the juvenile and adult letters of William and Charles, his two sailor sons, often bearing signs of their salty passage and hardly read since they were first opened by their recipients. The wayward William wrote sketchily and inaccurately only when he felt obliged to, while his serious brother maintained an earnest and informative correspondence with his adored father and sisters – yet both collections have their own historical value.

So it's all the more of a pity when family correspondence is destroyed. In 1860 Charles Dickens made a bonfire at Gad's Hill of all the letters he had ever received from his family and friends. They included those written by his sons from their boarding school over the Channel in Boulogne, and from the more distant parts to which they were dispatched in their later boyhood. The only son who joined the Royal Navy was Sydney, whose shipboard letters went up in flames with the rest, leaving the historian with only his father's responses. Fortunately, Dickens wrote so much and so well that I have been able to build up a picture of Sydney as a boy and as a young man. Certain characters in the novels, for example, throw up a flare which helps to illuminate his tempestuous passage from cherished 'Little Admiral', to a wretched son denied access to the paternal home.

Such sea-changes took place in the lives of all the youngsters whose further careers are traced in this book. As children they were more vulnerable than their older shipmates, susceptible to bullying and easily led astray. On some, however, youth bestowed the vitality to face danger in embattled and stormy waters, the adaptability to join 'the brotherhood of the sea', and the optimism to face an uncertain future on distant strands. For them, 'the good, strong sea, the salt, bitter sea' could represent, as it did for Joseph Conrad's character Marlow, 'the endeavour, the test, the trial of life'. Others, like a ship's boy he observed, 'wept as if his heart would break' at 'the weirdness of the scene', and might never recover from an untimely voyage away from home and family.[22] Ashore or afloat, such a traveller would remain 'all at sea'.

Chapter 1

Mary Branham and the Young Convicts of the First Fleet 1787

A mong the 778 convicts who embarked on the six small, crowded ships prepared to transport them to Botany Bay in 1787, there were at least fourteen girls and twenty-five boys aged 18 and under. There may well have been more, but few records of prisoners' ages were kept, nor was there any attempt to accommodate youngsters separately. Their juvenile status more often emerges from London court records made during brief trials for theft and larceny, which had usually taken place in 1783–4. In some cases the children themselves gave evidence, affording us a last chance to hear their voices before they disappeared across the seas.

Mary Branham (or Bramham), accused in December 1784 of stealing clothes and taking them to the pawnbroker, simply stated that she had 'nothing to say'. It was her mother who revealed that she was not yet 14 and had been 'deluded', or seduced, away from home six weeks earlier so that she 'knew nothing of her till she was found at the prosecutor's house'. Meanwhile, two witnesses gave Mary 'a very good character as a very dutiful child'.[1] Boys facing similar accusations were more often vociferous in their own defence. John Owen, for example, who was 14 when charged with stealing a case of knives and forks, tried to explain why he had been running through a field in Haggerston on the afternoon of his arrest: 'I was taking a walk round, and some boys came up to me and said there was a mad bull and presently a gentleman pursued me and took me back.' He claimed that the young girl who identified him had been 'persuaded to it'.[2]

Two more 14-year-olds, George Robinson and John Nurse, were indicted with their 16-year-old friend, George Bannister, for stealing clothes worth 4*s* 10*d*. They had been arrested among some willows by the Thames, but all three produced stories to explain why they had been there. Robinson said that he was delivering a message for his mother who took in needlework when: 'I wanted to ease myself … and I was just buttoning up my breeches.' Nurse claimed that he had been 'sent of an errand over Chelsea-bridge' and was sheltering from the snow and rain: 'They came and took hold of me and threatened to chuck me into the Thames.' Bannister's defence was that he was on his way to look after his mother's ass and running to keep warm when a woman cried out 'Stop thief': 'A little time after two men came and fetched me out.'[3]

Despite such pleas, which may or may not have been genuine, all these children were summarily convicted and sentenced to seven years' transportation. If the value of the stolen goods had been more than 40 shillings, or if the theft had been accompanied by violence or breaking into a property, the penalty would have been death. Thus Mary Branham just missed the gallows because goods she had stolen were estimated to be worth 39 shillings, a valuation which may have been prompted by a sympathetic judge's recognition of her obvious vulnerability. A similar instance was that of 14-year-old Francis Gardener, charged with stealing twenty bushels of coal from a boat on the Thames. Examining this young sailor who had come home from the sea to find that 'both father and mother were dead', the judge did not award a death sentence, even though the boat had been broken into. Gardener's accomplice, a 'young fresh boy' whose father pleaded that he was 'led astray by other people', was let off on condition that his family sent him away to the East or West Indies.[4] In the case of three other young lads, James Pulet, Nicholas English and Peter Woodcock, the value of a stolen watch was reduced in court from 50 to 39 shillings on the grounds that it was 'an old watch and worth little more than the silver'.[5]

Even when imposed, a death sentence on juveniles was very often commuted to transportation. Thus Joseph Tuso, a 'little thief' of 14 who said he had nobody to call in his defence 'but a poor father', was sentenced to death in July 1784 for highway robbery, only to be told the following February that he was not to be hanged, but 'transported for life to Africa'.[6] Such a reprieve was naturally a great relief to convict, family and friends – but transportation nevertheless carried a great stigma, as is illustrated by the case of Hetty Sorrel in George Eliot's *Adam Bede*, set in 1799. Her escape from the hangman's noose occurs in a dramatic scene where the local squire gallops to the steps of the public scaffold, 'carrying in his hand a hard-won release from death' for the 17-year-old dairymaid he has seduced and whose baby she has killed. Instead Hetty will suffer the 'wretched fate of being transported', while her guardian uncle and aunt must endure the disgrace of having 'them belonging to us as are transported o'er the seas'.[7]

Until the Declaration of Independence in 1775, it was Britain's American colonies that had received such convicts in their thousands. Transatlantic banishment was clearly impossible during the ensuing six-year war, and in 1783 the new United States refused to take any more of the felons, whom Benjamin Franklin compared to rattlesnakes. Even so, a desperate British government tried to reinstate this convenient dumping ground for its unwanted subjects. The *Mercury* set sail for Georgia in 1784 with about 200 prisoners on board, including 13-year-old shoemaker James Grace, and 10-year-old chimney-sweep John Hudson. When the ship was taken over by a group of convicts during a storm off the Devon coast both boys escaped in a small boat, but they and all the other transportees were soon recaptured and transferred to a prison-ship anchored off Plymouth. Here they stayed while the Home Office tried to make new arrangements to relieve its overcrowded hulks and gaols.

Some inmates had already been sent to the west coast of Africa which more commonly served as a source of slaves for Britain's transatlantic trade. Even though over half the convicts died of malaria and other tropical diseases within weeks of landing, judges continued to specify Africa in transportation sentences, as the case of Joseph Tuso shows. Mary Branham was also intended for these dying grounds, for her name appears along with those of other young prisoners in lists prepared for Africa-bound ships in 1785.[8] But this voyage was never made; in the meantime the Home Secretary, Lord Sydney, had had another idea.

It came from American-born James Matra, who had served as a midshipman on Captain James Cook's first voyage of exploration on HMS *Endeavour* in 1768–71. Cook had charted the unknown east coast of Australia, naming the place of their first landing 'Botany Bay', because of the amazing plants found by his naturalists, and the region as a whole 'New South Wales'. Matra's original suggestion that American Empire Loyalists should find asylum there was transformed into a Home

Office scheme for a new penal colony in a land recommended for 'the fertility and salubrity of the climate'. An even greater advantage was 'the remoteness of its situation (from whence it is hardly possible for persons to return without permission)'. Its unexplored hinterland and treacherous coastline would make New South Wales 'a great outdoor prison'.[9]

*   *   *

The King's Speech of 1787 accordingly announced that Botany Bay would receive 'a number of convicts in order to remove the inconvenience which arose from the crowded state of our gaols', and the Royal Navy was put in charge of preparing a fleet for the longest voyage ever undertaken by so large a group to so unknown a destination. It was almost as though they were going into outer space.

Between January and April of that year, over 500 male, and nearly 200 female, prisoners emerged from city gaols and floating hulks to be conveyed to the coast in carts and crowded on to six specially commissioned merchant ships. Most of the young lads already mentioned embarked on the all-male *Scarborough* and *Alexander* transports. Among others who joined them were Francis and Thomas Mclean, brothers given a commuted death sentence in 1784 when aged 15 and 16 for stealing, with force and arms, cutlery and clothes valued at over 60 shillings. Also on his way to seven years transportation was 15-year-old Charles McClellan, convicted of pickpocketing just ten pence.

The sexually-mixed convict cargo of the *Friendship* was carefully recorded in the journal of Marine Lieutenant Ralph Clark. On his list were Hudson and Grace, the two young boys who had escaped from the *Mercury* three years earlier, as well as John Wisehammer and William Brice, sentenced to seven years transportation as young teenagers in 1785 for stealing, respectively, 'a bladder of snuff' and a looking glass.[10] The *Charlotte* also held a mixture of male and female convicts, but no identifiable youngsters.

The remaining two transports were set aside for female prisoners, some of whom were still girls. Ann Mather, for example, was embarked on to the *Prince of Wales* two weeks after her trial for clothing theft, during which she described herself as 'an unfortunate girl, away from my mother', and pleaded that the garments had been given her by 'a man in brown coat and round hat to be taken to a pawnbroker'.[11] There were so many recently convicted prisoners on this ship that they seem to have been rounded up at the last minute to make up the number of females. Among them were Phoebe Flarty and Ann Parsley, lasses who shared lodgings and habitually roamed Piccadilly selling 'matches and hat pins about the street'.[12] The last children to board were Elizabeth Youngson and her brother George, delivered by the turnkey of Lancaster gaol on 13 May. Aged about 14 and 13, they had been tried at Lancaster Castle in March for 'feloniously and violently' breaking into a silk warehouse and stealing a purse containing over 40 shillings, for which they received death sentences, commuted three weeks later to transportation.[13] It must have been because of his tender years that George was allowed to accompany his sister on the *Prince of Wales*.

The exclusively female convicts consigned to the *Lady Penrhyn* were listed by its surgeon, Arthur Bowes Smyth, who included their ages in his journal.[14] Mary Branham was now 17, as was Sarah Bellamy, a Worcestershire servant charged in 1785 with stealing money from her employer. Sarah had begged in vain 'to be publicly whipped at afternoon at the next two market days', rather than be transported for seven years.[15] The youngest girl of the first fleet was also on *Lady Penrhyn*: Elizabeth Hayward, an apprentice clog-maker of 13, had been sentenced in January 1787 for stealing a silk bonnet, linen gown and Bath cloth cloak from her employer.

During the four months which elapsed between the first embarkations and final departure, none of the convicts could imagine what lay ahead. Still in chains they were confined below decks with no headroom, little light, foul smells and only about 6ft by 18in of space per person. Some managed in these difficult conditions to write letters to friends and relations, which were collected up by marine officers. No such letters survive, but Watkin Tench, a marine lieutenant on board the *Charlotte* with the 'tiresome and disagreeable' duty of inspecting them, described their content. He found a frequent 'apprehension of the impracticability of returning home, the dread of a sickly passage and the fearful prospect of a distant and barbarous country', sentiments he dismissed as 'an artifice to awaken compassion' and encourage the recipients to send money and tobacco.[16] Clearly, he did not think convicts capable of homesickness such as that frequently expressed by his fellow officer, Ralph Clark, on leaving his wife and baby son: 'Never did a poor criminal go to meet the unknown with greater reluctance than I leave the best of women and the sweetest of boys.'[17]

By the time the fleet left Portsmouth harbour on 13 May, however, Tench had developed rather more sympathy for the 'humble, submissive and regular' prisoners in his charge and as they sailed away, he could see that some felt 'the pang of being severed, perhaps forever, from their native land'.[18] This was a more realistic account of the mood of seaborne exiles than the pious hopes voiced by judges that transportation would bring about their salvation.[19]

*   *   *

There are twenty or so eye-witness accounts of this momentous sea voyage, but none written by the convicts themselves. Nor are they often named, still less quoted, in the journals and letters of naval and marine officers, surgeons and seamen. Thus convicts' experiences can be viewed only through the eyes of their guardians who, as one transportee later wrote, had not 'tasted the bitter cup of affliction themselves', and were 'apt to view us wretched beings with more contempt than is necessary.'[20]

This particular batch of convicts was lucky, at least, in its commander, Captain Arthur Phillip, who travelled on HMS *Sirius* in company with the fleet and had been deputed to govern the new colony. He did not have a high opinion of his charges and knew some of them to be 'compleat villains', but he believed that others could 'regain the advantages and estimation in society of which they had deprived themselves'.[21] During the voyage he took great care of their health and welfare, ensuring that they received fair rations of food (but no alcohol), that they were unchained and allowed on deck once out at sea, that their quarters were kept as clean as possible and that they received medical attention. Surgeon Bowes Smyth thought this 'extream indulgence' was far more than the prisoners merited – but he had to admit towards the end of the journey that it was 'pretty extraordinary how very healthy the convicts … have been during so long a passage and where there was a necessity of stowing them thick together'.[22] Only thirty-six male and four female prisoners died between embarkation and landing, and most of these deaths occurred before the fleet sailed, as a result of an epidemic on board the *Alexander* of typhus fever brought from the gaols. This contrasts with the badly supervised second fleet of 1790 in which private contractors embarked too many prisoners, cheated them of their rations, kept them chained together and refused them access to the deck. As a result, over a quarter of the thousand or so who set off perished during that voyage.

None of the younger convicts of the first fleet died during the eight-month passage to Botany Bay but they experienced, along with their elders and indeed the ship's crew, the many trials of a long sea journey in a frail sailing ship. Changing climate conditions were perhaps the hardest to bear. In the choppy waters of the English Channel and the Bay of Biscay they suffered acute seasickness, which would be renewed later on during storms bringing additional hazards. Bowes Smyth records that violent squalls in the South Atlantic caused the ship to roll so much that 'many of the women and ship's company received bruises from falls', and no one could get any sleep. Later on, in mountainous waves off the southern coast of Australia, 'the convicts were washed out of the lower berth', and to prevent the danger of the ship being 'filled with water and sunk ... it was absolutely necessary to clap the close hatches over all the convicts'. As they neared their destination, an even more terrible storm frightened the convicts so much that 'most of them were down on their knees at prayers'.[23]

Bowes Smyth also noted that by this stage in the journey the stench on board had become so offensive that he had to keep his cabin door open to provide some air. This was not an option down on the prison decks close to the bilge water, described graphically by Robert Hughes as 'a fermenting, sloshing broth of sea water mixed with urine, puke, dung, rotting food and dead rats'.[24] And despite daily cleaning of the decks and airing of bedding the ships were 'swarming with bugges', as Lieutenant Clark complained.[25] These discomforts, probably even greater than those endured in British slums and prisons, were exacerbated as the fleet passed through the tropics and the temperature down below reached

90 or 100 degrees Fahrenheit at night. Convicts of all ages found solace where they could.

Deprived though they were of such diversions as alcohol, tobacco, friends, family and the need to support themselves, they could enjoy the innocent pleasures afforded by the exotic topography of the voyage. Flying fish came on board, sperm whales sported alongside the ships and flocks of albatross and other sea birds flew in their wake. As the fleet lay at anchor off Rio de Janeiro in the Portuguese colony of Brazil, the prisoners could not of course go ashore with the crew to catch butterflies, collect curiosities, drink tea in orange groves, watch colourful religious processions or hear bands playing in the streets. The only music they could hear came from fellow captives: 'slaves breaking out into songs of lamentation' on board a ship from the coast of Guinea which was moored close by. Still, 'the people in the guard boats would frequently amuse themselves with throwing some hundreds of oranges to the convicts on the different transports'.[26] The chief physician of Rio took pity on them, donating money 'to be expended for their use in such articles as Captain Sever should think most beneficial to them in their unhappy predicament', and some of the sailors bought 'articles for their accommodation' here and at their other ports of call, Tenerife and Cape Town.[27]

The sailors' gifts were sometimes rewards for sexual favours as there is ample evidence that prostitution flourished on board the ships containing women and girls, despite officers' attempts to clamp down on it. On 17 April, before the fleet even departed, two lieutenants inspecting the women's berths on the *Lady Penrhyn* discovered that five convicts were missing . After finding four of them in the sailors' quarters and one with the second mate, 'they ordered all the five women to be put in irons'. The sailors do not seem to have been punished on this occasion, but the second mate, who should have known better, was removed from the ship.[28] Ralph Clark reports that the *Friendship*'s seamen 'brock throu the bulkhead and had connection' with those 'damned whores the convict women of whom they are very fond', and on whose behalf they tried to procure extra provisions. He placed most of the blame on the 'abandoned' women in their care and was delighted at Cape Town when all his female charges were sent to the *Prince of Wales* to make room for sheep who would, he thought, be 'much more agreeable shipmates'.[29]

The lack of any female testimony makes it impossible to estimate the proportion of women and girls who suffered as unwilling victims of Jack Tar's 'sexual piracy'. Rape undoubtedly occurred. Modern historians judge, however, that there were often mutual benefits, with the women able to use sex 'as a commodity to survive, given the high demand for their services'.[30] There may even have been some affectionate relationships, such as those apparently formed by Mary Branham and Sarah Bellamy on the *Lady Penrhyn*. Mary's lover was William Curtis, whom some identify as the nephew of his wealthy namesake, the ship's owner Alderman William Curtis. Meanwhile, Sarah consorted with Joseph Downey. Both the seamen, judged to be 'very good men and able sailors', were promoted during the voyage to become quarter-masters, a position which gave them access to valuable commodities like tea and sugar.[31] Such comforts would have been all the more welcome when both their young sea-wives became pregnant. Sarah gave birth to a baby boy late in the voyage, helped no doubt by some of the older women and by Bowes Smyth's experience in midwifery.[32] It is more difficult to trace Mary's confinement. Among the 'children brought out and born on board ship', the surgeon listed an infant he named as John Brenham, as well as Joseph Bellamy, in both cases stressing their illegitimacy by using the mother's surname.[33] Some historians and genealogists have assumed that John was a child brought on board by Mary, but there is no other record of such an infant's existence. It is more likely that Bowes Smyth listed the names carelessly and that this baby was the offspring of William Curtis. At their baptisms, conducted by Chaplain Richard Johnson once they reached dry land, both boys were given their fathers' Christian names and surnames, as was customary in eighteenth-century families.

In caring for their new-born babies at sea, such young mothers faced even greater challenges than they would have done back in Britain. They struggled to keep their babies fed 'when breast feeding in public was not considered respectable',[34] to keep them clean on a water allowance often as low as three pints a day, to keep them healthy in crowded, wet and unventilated quarters, and even to keep them adequately covered when no one had thought of providing linen and flannel for such uses. Women on the *Lady Penrhyn*, for example, were reduced to 'plundering the sailors ... of their necessary clothes and cutting them up for some purpose of their own'.[35]

Busy and (it is reasonable to assume) happy with their motherly duties, these girls were less likely to suffer the boredom and despondency which afflicted most first fleet convicts, for whom there were none of the activity, work and schooling provided on later voyages. Some of the more skilled prisoners were employed by marine officers to wash, mend and make clothes; Lieutenant Clark, for example, had socks, gloves and trousers made by a woman he names as Mrs Hart, who is listed as a mantua maker. He also got an unnamed convict cabinet maker to construct a writing desk and a box to hold the butterflies he had caught in Brazil, both intended as presents for his beloved wife. But such employment (and presumably payment) was not likely to come the way of the young street boys aboard, most of whom had no trade. Thus they had all too much time to be corrupted by older and more experienced offenders. Some may have shared in such misdeeds as an attempted mutiny on board the *Scarborough*, as well as the regular theft, fights and abuse of officers which took place on all the ships – though the only youngster named among those punished is the highway robber John Bennett, who was 17 or 18, 'a young man but an old Rogue', in the words of Lieutenant Clark. He was flogged twice on the *Friendship*, first for breaking out of his irons and later when he was found asleep in a longboat after stealing other convicts' provisions.[36] Some of *Scarborough*'s young villains may have taken part in a happier event mentioned in the journal of Marine Private John Easty on 2 January 1788: 'This night the Convicts made a play and sang many songs.'[37]

By this time the fleet was passing through 'a tract which no other ship has gone before', and a sailor was posted all the time at the foretop masthead of *Sirius* to look out for land. On Christmas Eve, Bowes Smyth drank to the health of all his friends and relations in England: 'I never thought of [them] with such sensations as I do now, being so many thousands leagues distant.' Meanwhile Lieutenant Clark still longed for his 'beloved wife and tender Alicia', and was sure that 'never was anybody so sick of the sea' as he was. It did not seem to occur to either officer that their unwilling fellow passengers might have similar feelings, or that their 'horrid oaths and imprecations' might be an expression of despair at ever reaching dry land, let alone seeing their own families again.[38]

*   *   *

It was another month before the convicts set foot on Australian shores after a voyage of 252 days over more than 15,000 miles of ocean. Botany Bay proving unsuitable for settlement, the fleet sailed further north to land at Port Jackson, 'one of the finest harbours in the world', according to Clark. He was mightily relieved when the male prisoners disembarked on 28 January: 'I hope in God that I will have nothing to doe with them any more.' They were followed by the women on 6 February and by scenes of 'debauchery and riot' which continued all night amid the 'most violent storms of lightning, thunder and rain' that Bowes Smyth had ever seen.[39] Even the more humane Governor Phillip was shocked, warning the assembled group the next day that if the male convicts 'attempted by night to get into the women's tents there were positive orders for the sentry to fire upon them'. He also made it clear that 'stealing the most trifling article of stock or provisions should be punished with death', for he knew that the whole colony depended on existing supplies until more were sent from Britain.

Such severity was not unreasonable, for male convicts were allotted the same weekly rations as their civilian and military guards (though still minus the alcohol): seven pounds of salt beef, three pints of dried peas, seven pounds of flour, six ounces of butter and half a pound of rice, while women received two-thirds of this allowance. Anything more would have to be grown, reared, shot or caught, so that 'if they did not work they should not eat'.[40] We cannot know how Phillip's words went down with his audience for there is little evidence of how first-fleet convicts felt as they struggled to survive in the new colony. Baptism, marriage and death registers, punishment records, victualling lists, musters and land-grants reveal the fate of some transported youngsters – but only occasionally their reactions to events. We know, for example, that baby Joseph Downey did not survive for long, becoming 'the first European child to be received into Sydney's soil' after his death on 27 February 1788; but Sarah Bellamy's grief is unrecorded.[41] And we can only guess at the desolation she and Mary Branham experienced when Curtis and Downey joined the *Lady Penrhyn* for her next assignment. The two sailors left Sydney Cove on 5 May for a voyage on which North American furs and Chinese tea would replace the cargo of convicts.

Sarah, at least, had not lost her spirit as can be seen in the records of the Judge Advocate's Bench set up by Governor Phillip. The following year she was accused of making a disturbance when Marine Captain James Meredith, a friend of Lieutenant Clark, tried to force his way into the hut where she was sleeping. She cried out that 'she did not know what she had done, that he should come and disturb her peace'. The drunken Meredith would not leave, but pulled her hair and beat her through the window until the night watch came and got the intruder to leave. At the trial she protested that she was but a poor prisoner, 'determined not to put up with such unmerited behaviour from Captain Meredith or anyone else'.[42] The remarkable outcome of the case was that the charge against the convict was dismissed while the captain was reprimanded – her brave words had succeeded in defying the might of colonial power.

Before long, Sarah found happiness with James Bloodworth, a master bricklayer transported for stealing a game cock and two hens at Esher in Surrey, where he left a wife and four children. His skills were invaluable to the colony and also to his new partner, for whom he built a two-roomed house with a window and hearth in Jackson Cove. The couple had eight children, four of whom survived their early years, before Bloodworth's death in 1804. In the Female Register compiled by Rev. Samuel Marsden, minister of St John's Parramatta, Sarah is described as Bloodworth's concubine, even though the parson had to admit that 'no relationship could have been more respectable, devoted or tenacious than theirs'.[43] This is an unusually detailed story of a convicted child who grew to maturity in the hulks and on a transport ship before going on to lead a productive and fulfilled life, leaving proud Australian descendants to inherit her own red hair.[44]

It is harder to trace how Mary Branham fared. Thomas Keneally's novel *The Playmaker* imagines that in June 1789 she acted in the convicts' performance of George Farquhar's *The Recruiting Officer*, and that the play was directed by Ralph Clark. But Watkin Tench's account of this event does not name the actors or producer, and Clark's Journal for this period is missing. Still less is there evidence to bear out Keneally's racy account of Mary becoming Clark's lover during the rehearsals, one of the 'improbable incidents' which a reviewer attributed to the novelist's 'fervid imagination'.[45] It is true that in March 1790 both Mary and the lieutenant were aboard *Sirius* when it took a party of convicts to the new colony which had been started on Norfolk Island, some thousand miles distant. There is no proof, however, of Keneally's assertion that Clark 'ensured that Mary was among the convicts transported to that outstation'. Once on the island, Clark wrote in his journal of the floggings he administered to errant convicts, the birth of convicts' children, the state of the weather and the sea, his yearning for a ship to take him away from the place, and his joy when letters eventually arrived from his beloved Alicia. The journal cites many convicts by name but never mentions Mary Branham – not even when she gave birth to a baby girl on 23 July 1791. It is only the baptismal register of St Philip's church, Sydney, for 16 December which reveals that Alicia Brenham (sic) was the daughter of Ralph Clark, who had clearly betrayed the wife to whom he had sworn undying loyalty. Three days after the baptism his greatest longing was fulfilled as he left the colony for good aboard HMS *Gorgon*, leaving 'no record of his feelings at saying goodbye to Mary'.[46]

On the musters of that same ship the name William Branham appears among the children of marine officers. This can only be Mary's 4-year-old son, William Curtis, brought on board under the sponsorship of her lover. Some historians have assumed that his mother accompanied him, but this cannot be the case as neither Mary's name, nor that of baby Alicia, appears on *Gorgon*'s careful passenger lists.[47] Clark's journal, which was intended for his wife's reading, contains no reference to William, though it often records his distress about the number of children dying on the voyage. 'This hot weather is playing the devil with the children' he wrote, after about ten had been committed to the deep.[48] Young William survived all shipboard perils to be disembarked at Portsmouth on 21 June 1792, but there is no further trace of him. If he really was related to the wealthy William Curtis, who was now an MP, he may have fared well.

This is not the only puzzle surrounding this convict's child. The burial register list of St John's church in the new Parramatta settlement lists a William C. Branham for 7 December 1791, just a few days before the boy of that name was recorded on *Gorgon*'s muster list.[49] Since there were no other Branhams in New South Wales at that time there is no plausible explanation for the discrepancy, since Mary would hardly have given two living sons the same name. William C. Branham's burial record must remain a mystery; it would surely be too fanciful to picture the heartbroken mother faking the death of a child who was about to disappear across the sea.

The names of three more children on *Gorgon*'s muster suggest that it was common practice for marine officers to transport their illegitimate sons away from their convict mothers to the mother country. Robert Kellow and James Meredith, both a year old, accompanied their namesake fathers on board, leaving behind not only their mothers, but also baby sisters, all of whom would help to redress the sexual imbalance in the colony. An even younger infant present on the voyage was 2-month-old James Furzer, son of the young street-hawker Ann Parsley, and her lieutenant lover, after whom he was named. Captain Furzer (as he became) married a more respectable Ann after his return to England, but his will nevertheless made the boy a handsome bequest, to be kept in trust until he was 21 by his unmarried sister. She was to use it 'for the sole purpose of educating and cloathing my said son James in the world in such situation as his circumstances will allow'.[50]

Meanwhile, Phoebe Flarty, the 14-year-old friend with whom Ann Parsley had been tried in 1787, had been getting into more trouble. With three other girls she was accused in September 1788 of taunting Captain Robert Browne of the supply ship *Fishbourn*, calling after him as he passed the bakehouse: 'Who bottles pease soup?' and: 'Who puts their men in the coal hole?' Even though the New South Wales courts were usually 'very busy punishing insolence', all four were discharged after promising not to do it again, perhaps because they were 'little more than children'. After being moved to Norfolk Island, Phoebe received two punishments of twenty-five lashes for further youthful offences: 'allowing hogs into the garden she was tending', and 'coming into town without permission'. She subsequently returned to Sydney with two children and by the time she died in 1817 at the age of 44, she had gained her freedom, married the free settler with whom she had lived for ten years, helped him to farm his land grant of 30 acres and had about four more children.[51]

Phoebe's story is similar to that of some other transported girls. Lydia Munro, a young shoplifter with a fourteen-year sentence, was also involved in a court case when she accused a fellow convict of 'wanting to have connexion with her against her will' as she went to bathe in the sea. Although the man was initially found guilty he was later forgiven, despite clear evidence of violence, after convincing the magistrates that Lydia was known as a prostitute. She subsequently married another convict, Andrew Goodwin, with whom she was sent to Norfolk Island. By the end of the century the couple were farming a land grant of 23 acres, supporting seven children and supplying maize to the government. But in 1805 the Norfolk Island settlement was closed and most of its inhabitants were sent to establish a new colony on the virgin bush of Van Diemen's Land (now Tasmania). It was here, in Hobart Town, that Lydia reared at least nine offspring before dying as a widow of 86 at the home of one of her daughters.[52] The youngest female transportee, Elizabeth Hayward, followed a similar trajectory. Assigned for her protection to Rev. and Mrs Johnson as a house-servant, she was soon given thirty lashes for 'insolence' towards them and despatched to Norfolk Island. She went on to own a house worth £8, give birth to three children, marry a third-fleeter and settle with him on 40 acres in Van Diemen's Land. Many of her descendants served in the First and Second World Wars.[53]

By women such as these, whom officers like Clark and Bowes Smyth castigated as troublesome whores, 'meals were cooked, kitchens scrubbed and children minded. Someone was out there milking cows, nurturing chickens, turning raw materials into edible foodstuffs, making clothes, trying to make loose dirt into floors.'[54] The new colony across the seas could not have been created without them, a fact recognised by Governor Phillip when he insisted that women's rations should not be reduced as men's were when no supply ship had arrived by November 1789. 'Many of them', he explained 'had children who could well have eaten their own and part of their mother's ration, or they had children at the breast.'[55]

To the convict men and boys fell the hard physical labour of building a colony from scratch. In Port Jackson and on Norfolk Island they cleared ground, felled trees, planted crops, tended hogs, sheep and cattle, shot mutton-birds and kangaroos, caught fish, made bricks and constructed houses, hospitals, stores and wharfs – albeit with some reluctance. The penalty for idling was to be beaten into greater exertion, though such a punishment could not always be carried out. In December 1790 Lieutenant Clark sentenced John Wisehammer (who was probably now 18) to fifty lashes for neglecting his work as a carpenter on Norfolk Island;

but only eight could be administered because the surgeon 'said he could not bear more [when] he fainted away twice'. As predicted by Lieutenant David Collins, the colony's Judge-Advocate, when men's rations were reduced by a third earlier that year, labour was hardly possible 'for want of energy to proceed'.[56] Records show, however, that John survived the rigours of the early years and had settled by January 1792 on ten Norfolk Island acres, working as a baker and living with Susannah Milledge, who had arrived with a new contingent of female convicts. George Robinson was among other young men able to subsist, thanks to land and a hog granted to them on the island in return for good behaviour. James Grace got his bounty as a reward for catching mutton-birds for the community, but died prematurely in 1793.

Other young convicts fell into the category described by Governor Phillip, who 'destroy and rob in spight [*sic*] of every possible precaution', on whom punishment had no effect. He was thinking of a youth like Benjamin Ingram who had been sentenced to transportation at 15 for stealing the proverbial pocket handkerchief. He could not submit to his fate, but absconded several times into the bush and committed repeated burglaries even after his sentence had expired. After being imprisoned on Norfolk Island, he hanged himself in his cell on 26 January 1795. His short life, wrote Judge-Advocate Collins, had been one of 'wretchedness and villainy'.[57]

Charles McLellan was equally defiant in the face of his chastisers. The journal of Lieutenant Gidley King, governor of Norfolk Island, records giving the boy, whom he judged to be 14 years old, thirty-six lashes in April 1788 for stealing rum. Charles got another three dozen the following month for uttering words judged as seditious: 'If there were more convicts here, they would not submit to having their salt provisions stopped when a quantity of fish were caught.' After enduring several more lashings and a fractured skull incurred while chopping wood, the boy stole some pots and was exiled for six weeks on a barren, uninhabited island. The uncowed McLellan seems to have left the colony in 1793, by which time his seven-year sentence had expired.[58]

* * *

It is quite possible that Charles McClellan, who came from Sunderland-on-Sea, had some experience of ships and was able to work his passage home. This was certainly an opportunity taken by other young men once their sentences were over. Some convicts claimed as early as July 1789 that they had served their time, taking into account the years spent in prison before transportation. But amazingly, the relevant papers had been left behind when the first fleet sailed so that they had to wait until proof could be sent before being emancipated. Lieutenant Collins imagined that it must have been 'truly distressing to their feelings to find that they could not be considered in any other light', while Private Easty likened their plight to that of slaves, 'all the while they are in this country'.[59] For those with life sentences there was no alleviation to that bondage – and a convict like Dickens's Abel Magwitch, who dared return to 'the land which had cast him out', would be hanged if recaptured.[60] Others, however, gained their freedom when documentation – as well as eagerly awaited supplies, letters and news of the world – arrived with the second and third transportation fleets.

Thus Francis Gardener and the Maclean brothers, who had been sentenced in 1784, were able to leave New South Wales legitimately in 1791, though it is not known how they procured a passage. They were followed by other young emancipists making their way back to Britain, seeking their fortune in India or simply going to sea. Joseph Tuso, an unreformed 'great rascal', became a seaman, as did William Farley, who had served seven years for stealing sugar when he was 15. Nicholas English and the handkerchief thief, William Saltmarsh, sailed for Bengal, leaving a colony where each had received some hundreds of lashes as well as doing useful work as a wheat farmer and a cooper respectively. Like free sailors and marines before him, Saltmarsh also left a wife and baby; for them it was more difficult to escape from what one female convict described as 'our disconsolate situation in this solitary waste of the creation'.[61]

These words come from one of the very few convicts' letters which have survived. Its writer explained that she had sent it privately through a friend so that it would not be examined by an officer. Another transported correspondent, whose letter was published in the *Gazetteer* in December 1790, described the fleet's 'Crusoe-like adventures', the 'wretched situation, which has been occasioned by the miscarriage of our supplies' and the 'ardent expectations' with which they were constantly 'looking out to sea'. A marine officer conjured up the colony's far-flung isolation even more vividly: 'So cut off from all intercourse with the rest of mankind are we [that] we know not of any transaction that has happened in Europe, and are no more assured of the welfare or existence of any of our friends than of what passes in the moon.'[62] At least he knew that he would eventually leave those treacherous shores on which the *Sirius* had recently been wrecked, though the homeward journey was riskier than a modern space mission. Most convicts knew that they must live out their days as lost to their friends as to the rest of mankind. Thus Hetty Sorrel's repentant lover laments that he 'can do nothing for her all those years; and she may die under it, and never know comfort any more.' The only information that he, her family, or the reader ever receives is that 'the poor wanderer' has died 'when she was coming back to us'.[63]

In the desperate circumstances of the colony's early years, convicts rarely possessed the leisure, the materials, or the incentive to tell their stories. But from official records kept by their gaolers it is possible for historians and descendants to trace how some of them fared – and just occasionally to hear their voices. It is clear that some of the teenage pickpockets and thieves sent unwillingly across the oceans fulfilled the hopes of Arthur Phillip by gaining more 'estimation' in their new society than they might have expected in Britain. Sarah Bellamy, for example, rented out a room to an Irish convict schoolmaster so that he could teach her children to read.

Other convicts fulfilled the expectations of more cynical officers like Lieutenant Clark, who predicted on board the *Friendship* that John Bennett would come to the gallows within six months of landing at Botany Bay. After being flogged for theft in February 1788, Bennett was indeed hanged the following May for stealing bread and sugar from the *Charlotte*'s tent. Surgeon George Worgan wrote to his brother about this 'execution of a very young lad, but an old hardened offender, who, on his arrival at the fatal tree, said he was now going to suffer a death which he had long deserved'.[64] It is less clear whether Gloucestershire lads, William Okey and Samuel Davis, merited the death they met with in the same month. Having been sent into the bush with tools and tents to gather rushes, they were killed 'in a horrid manner' by aborigines' spears. Governor Phillip suspected that 'the natives were not the aggressors', and it was generally supposed that the murder was 'done through revenge for taking away one of their canoes'. If this was the case, Okey and Davis were certainly not the only white men to have frustrated Phillip's aim of cultivating the 'confidence and friendship' of Australia's native population.[65]

Very often the first-fleeters simply disappear from view. Nobody knows, for example, what happened to little John Hudson after Lieutenant Clark had him punished with fifty lashes on Norfolk Island 'for being out of his hut after nine o clock'. There is no evidence for the assumption of some historians that he was the victim of the 'unheard-of vices' which flourished on the island in the 1820s when it became a harsh penal settlement for twice-convicted men.[66] But neither is there any proof that the boy fulfilled the hopes of his judge by being saved from destruction.

The eventual fate of Mary Branham is equally obscure. She cannot be traced in any records after 1791, and nor can her daughter Alicia – but her surname appears in a puzzling entry in the registers of St Philip's church, Sydney. 'Dominic Branham' was apparently buried in 1792 and has sometimes been identified as Mary's deceased offspring. Although no mother's name is recorded it is quite possible that Mary gave birth to this short-lived son after the departure of her first-born. The only other explanation is that this entry refers to a 26-year-old Irish convict called Dominick Brennan, who arrived on the third fleet's *Queen* in September 1791 with his wife and a baby daughter. According to Governor Phillip, this ship's convicts were 'so emaciated, so worn away by long confinement, or want of food … that many of them will never recover'.[67] It is possible that Dominick was an unfortunate victim of this passage, whose name is incorrectly spelt in the register.

Whatever the truth of the matter, Mary Branham's is a sad and elusive story. The distant transportation of all these young people (and of thousands more in their wake) served the British government's purpose by getting them out of the way, out of sight and out of mind – just as it suited George Eliot to write the fallen Hetty out of her novel. The exercise was so successful that it is now very difficult for descendants or historians to find out what became of the convicts. A sea journey shaped their lives. It transported them from their country – 'for their country's good'. It exiled them from their families. It isolated them from current events in Britain and Europe. It also cut them adrift from history.

Chapter 2

Joseph Emidy c.1775–1835: Slave and Musician

The boy later known as the slave and musician, Joseph Emidy, was born in about 1775. As he later told James Silk Buckingham, he spent his early years in a small village near Africa's Guinea Coast, where British, Portuguese, French and Dutch slavers plied their flourishing trade.[1] He grew up among the sounds of Africa: the birds in the forest – warblers, fly-catchers, doves and parrots – and 'public dances accompanied by songs and music suited to the occasion'. The musicians played drums of different kinds, as well as the twenty-one-string *kora* and the *balafon*, which resembles a xylophone. Drawn to the music, he was probably taught by the men to play and was praised as a quick pupil. His was not necessarily a poor family for this was a rich and fruitful country, where corn, cotton, tobacco, spices and a variety of delicious fruits grew in abundance. His father may even have owned slaves, who had been captured in local wars or sold in punishment for crimes.[2] There is no record of the child's African name.

When he was about 8 years old he was taken from his home, captured first by men of his own complexion rather than by white traders. Most African children living anywhere near the coast were warned about *panyaring*, the systematic kidnapping of villagers to supply European slave-ships, but a dreamy young boy might well forget to keep a look-out for strangers when the adults were away working in the fields. Perhaps, like Ottabah Cugoano, the boy had strayed into the forest with his playfellows 'to gather fruit and catch birds', when he encountered a gang of ruffians who seized those who could not flee quickly enough.[3] He was then yoked with other captives into a *coffle* and taken off, soon travelling so far that he could not hope to find his way home, even if he had been able to escape. Eventually the desolate band of prisoners arrived at the seashore, and the boy saw for the first time those waters which were to play so large a part in his life, the surf sounding to his childish ears like the roar of a wild beast. He also now encountered the pale-skinned men he had heard of, the *pothos*, who were said to capture children, sail with them across the sea and feed them to demons.

For the time being the frightened child was held, along with many other Africans of different tribes and languages, in one of the large forts which lined the Guinea coast. They were herded into a pen known as a *barracoon* and watched by guards in a tower. Most of the men were chained or flung into dungeons where they often perished from disease, but children at least were allowed to run loose and play as best they could.[4] Eventually the boy was inspected as a commercial commodity – stripped of his clothes, made to jump, stretch out his arms and open his mouth to show his teeth. He was clearly judged sound and healthy, for a Portuguese trader bought him, paying his captor in such valued commodities as guns, cowrie shells, or rolls of calico. He was then branded with a hot iron bar, so that his chest would bear for the rest of his life the *carimbo* as proof of his legitimate purchase. In his case the dragon crest of the Portuguese crown and the letters of a Brazilian company were the marks of ownership though he did not, of course, understand what they signified. All he knew was the pain and humiliation he felt.

It was the practice of Portuguese slavers to give their new acquisitions a Roman Catholic baptism. While they were still in the fort all the slaves were assembled in a courtyard, where a priest passed along the lines. Through interpreters he gave each slave a new name, sprinkling salt and holy water on their tongues and telling them that they were now children of Christ, should think no more of their place of origin and 'be content'.[5] Thus was the African child baptised a Christian in words which meant nothing to him, though mention of the Holy Spirit may have reminded him of the spirits he believed to exist in the animals, trees and rivers of his homeland. He was christened Joseph, the name of the King of Portugal and also of the carpenter married to Mary, mother of Jesus.

*   *   *

The passage across the Atlantic was an experience which a slave like Joseph could never forget. He was put into a small boat and rowed out to a large vessel, looking to him like a house on the water. Thus he left the shores of Africa for the last time. Well might he suppose, as did Oloudah Equiano, that his fate was to be eaten by the 'white men with horrible looks, red faces and red hair', especially if he saw large cooking pots on the deck.[6]

Hundreds of slaves were packed on board these ships. The boys slept together deep down in the hold, stowed tightly in three tiers like books on a shelf and unable to get up without the whole section rising. The hatches were closed at night so that it became unbearably hot and a terrible stench developed. Dreadful sounds echoed around the ship: of children crying, of slaves vomiting when they became seasick, of the fights which often arose in the men's deck close by, of chains rattling, of whips cracking and of the sailors shouting in the Portuguese language which he could not then understand.

There was never enough food to go around all the slaves, even though many sickened and died during the passage and were thrown overboard. Sometimes they were fed salt meat, but usually meals consisted of boiled corn or horse beans. The scarcity of water meant that they were always thirsty and could hardly ever wash. But worse even than such physical distress was the boy's mental suffering. He must have been thinking of the family he might never again see, longing for the forests, fruits and flowers of his native village, and yearning for the music which had always been part of his life. As another Portuguese slave remembered: 'We had no one to share our troubles, none to care for us, or even to speak a word of comfort to us.'[7]

In some ways, however, the journey was easier for boys like Joseph than it was for adult men. Children were allowed to wander on the vessel by day, feeling the fresh air and the salt spray on their faces – and perhaps for this reason, the mortality rate was lower among juvenile slaves on this middle passage than among their seniors. It was exciting for them, as it was for transported young criminals, to see fishes jumping out of the water and large sea birds hovering around the ship. It was fun to play chasing games, often mimicking the slave raids which they all had cause to remember. Sometimes there might be messages to carry between the men chained below decks and the women who, like them, were unrestrained. Some of the women were kind to these lonely children but they too were melancholy, parted as they were from their husbands and offspring.[8]

The greatest consolation for Joseph was surely the music to be heard on board. The captain would sometimes have the slaves brought on deck to dance so that their limbs would not become too weak from being so long shackled. Sailors played the drum, fiddle or bagpipes and slaves were ordered to sing. But neither the captain nor any other European listener could understand the Africans' songs, which told of hunger and sickness, the fear of being beaten and sorrowful memories of their own country.[9]

* * *

It took about forty days for a ship to sail from West Africa to the coast of Portuguese Brazil, usually docking at Salvador de Bahia, the principal slave port according to the English woman Maria Graham, who observed its slave market with 'shame and indignation'.[10] For those captives who had survived the voyage it was a great relief to be on dry land again, even if their minds were still all at sea. The warm bath and nutritious food they were given before being offered for sale provided some comfort. Another former slave describes word spreading like wildfire when a slave ship came in, so that Portuguese customers would rush to inspect the 'cargo of living merchandise', selecting the pieces, the *peças*, most suitable to their needs.[11] They touched and handled them to see whether they were strong and sound of limb and might also question them to establish the level of their skills and understanding.

Most Africans transported to Brazil were bought as labour on the colony's sugar, tobacco, cotton and rice *fazendas*, or in its gold and diamond mines. Here they were subjected, notwithstanding the myth of benign Brazilian slavery, to the same brutal exploitation as prevailed in North America and the Caribbean.[12] A slightly-built 8-year-old child like Joseph is unlikely to have survived the relentless toil, inadequate housing and sparse rations to which plantation slaves were subjected.[13] But he was an intelligent lad who might have picked up enough of the Portuguese language used by the ship's crew to say his name, his approximate age, and something about his musical skills. Such proficiency was likely to impress a wealthy *senhor* looking for a personal attendant to add to the body of servants in his household and Bahia was the home of many such European immigrants, living in its multi-coloured stucco houses and worshipping in its Baroque churches. The surname of Joseph's purchaser was certainly Emidio (still quite a common name in Brazil today), the anglicised version of which became Joseph's in later life – for a slave had no surname but that of his master.

House slaves had a less arduous existence than miners or field-hands. Their work was lighter, they had shelter (if only in a cellar), they might be given cast-off clothes and they could eat the remains of food from the master's table. Joseph's duties, like those of other slaves bought as children, would change as he grew older. At first he would assist the cook in the kitchen, wait on his master in the dining room and help him in his toilette. Later on, as his understanding of Portuguese increased, Senhor Emidio might require his company in the evenings, especially if he lived alone, even using him as a partner in card games, singing and dancing. This rather familiar way of treating house slaves in Brazil convinced some contemporary visitors that they were 'indulged to licentiousness'. Thomas Lindley, a British trader detained in Bahia for over a year on a smuggling charge, was amazed to see them conversing with the master 'on the most equal and friendly terms', and even answering back. This led him to believe that slaves here were 'cheerful and content', but, of course, there was much that he did not see.[14] When no one else was present, for example, a master such as Emidio could demand physical intimacy from a house-boy (or from a young female slave), though this would be less likely if a wife came over from Portugal, imposing on the household a stricter regime of courtly Portuguese manners and elaborate religious observances.

Another penalty of a young house-slave's existence was its sheer loneliness.[15] On a plantation he would at least have had playmates after work was over and also the opportunity to take part in *batuques*, occasional communal dances accompanied by instruments improvised from gourds or hollow tree trunks. In these, wrote a French woman living in Brazil, 'negroes … forget their ills and servitude and only remember their native country and the time that they were free.'[16] In a family with children, however, a young slave was often employed to amuse the owner's offspring. This could mean that in a nursery equipped with alphabet books, a slave acquired the 'science of reading', which Fanny Kemble found to be 'much more common among negroes' than she had supposed before she went to live on her husband's Georgian plantation.[17] Thus it is easy to imagine Joseph acquiring literacy while still a slave. He also developed quite early in life the ability to play the violin, and this too may have begun in the nursery, with a child's small instrument. As was observed of him much later on, Joseph had 'extremely long, thin, fingers, not much larger than a goose quill', well suited to playing the violin.[18]

* * *

A British clergyman describing a slave market in Rio observed that 'many reach Brazil in a very rude condition and quite unable to communicate and so they remain for the rest of their lives. Others in a few years grow skilful and learn … how to make the best of their situation.'[19] Joseph clearly fell into the latter category and his master no doubt fostered skills which made him a more valuable slave. Musical aptitude was especially prized and some plantation owners even boasted slave orchestras which played 'erudite' (classical) music to their families and guests. A talented violinist like Joseph (or Solomon Northup in Jamaica) could come in very useful when 'a grand party of whites assembled'.[20] There was much wining and dining, for example, when the first convict fleet docked at Rio de Janeiro where Surgeon Bowes Smyth and marine officers 'danced to a viol played by a Negro slave' on a visit to a Portuguese collector of butterflies.[21] Occasions like these could enable Joseph to build up his repertoire with new tunes, such as the seductive love songs known as *modinhas.*

Brazilian city slaves equipped with such skills often became *prêtos de ganho*, permitted to do independent work with the obligation to give their masters part of the earnings.[22] They could put the remainder towards buying their emancipation, for in Latin-American legal codes there was 'a basic assumption … that Africans would eventually become freedmen'.[23] On expeditions out of his master's house Joseph would see such *emancipados* gathering at the fountains, selling flowers in the streets, plying their trade as barbers, or manning merchant ships. But he would be closely guarded lest he try to escape and join the communities of runaways in and around the city. Knowledge of the thumbscrew, chains, stocks and five-tailed, metal-tipped whip with which he might be punished, would make Joseph very careful not to arouse suspicion. In Bahia's main square the *pelourinho* (whipping post) reminded any slaves who might forget their place – and the square bears its name to this day.

If, as is likely, Senhor Emidio was a merchant engaged in the flourishing trade between Brazil and Portugal he would have wanted to use his slave's reading and reckoning skills in his business. Some slaves, for example, acted as clerks at the busy harbour, noting the receipt and delivery of cargoes, as Equiano did for his humane Quaker master, Robert King.[24] There they witnessed the frequent arrival of new West African slaves (known as 'guineabirds'), making up the numbers depleted by mortality rates of 10 per cent a year, low birth rates and frequent flight. Like Maria Graham in 1821, they might hear the 'poor wretches' singing 'one of their country songs in a strange land' as they came ashore.[25] And this was not the only music to be heard in the city. Bands of *barbeiros* (barber-musicians) passed through the streets on religious festival days and gave little concerts at the port whenever ships arrived or departed; slaves earned themselves a little money by playing in public; a drum and a fiddle accompanied couples dancing the popular fandango; street-sellers sang out their wares and gangs of heavily laden porters chanted 'their peculiar national songs' for the double purpose of timing their steps and aiding their endurance.[26]

The words of the songs and the styles of the dances were familiar to Joseph for they originated either from his native Guinea or from Portuguese Angola. He probably began to feel at home in Brazil in a tropical climate bearing fruit akin to that of West Africa and a culture increasingly intermixed with African traditions. Thus the gods he had known in Guinea, the *orixás*, became fused with Christian saints, the most popular being Yemanja, goddess of the waters, identified with Our Lady of the Navigators.[27] Did Joseph hope for her protection when, at some point in his late boyhood, he embarked on a ship heading into the North Atlantic Ocean?

*   *   *

With the social and political upheavals in Europe following the French revolution of 1789, a Portuguese merchant like Senhor Emidio had reason to worry about the safety of his interests in Lisbon. If he decided to move there for a period to look after his affairs, it would be natural for him to take with him a useful household slave like Joseph. But he clearly knew that the transportation of slaves to Portugal had been outlawed by a decree of 1761 declaring 'all those who arrived after that date to be free'. This meant that either before leaving Brazil or on arrival in Portugal, owners had to grant liberty to their accompanying slaves in return for a sum similar to that for which they had been purchased, reckoned by Thomas Lindley to be about £30 sterling. This entitled them to a document of manumission enabling them to 'enjoy all the rights and guarantees which the laws of our country bestow'. They would have to guard this closely lest anyone try to claim them as property, for freed slaves could be hunted down like 'stray beasts and cattle'.[28]

Whether as a free man or still enslaved, Joseph 'came to Lisbon with his owner or master', as he related to Buckingham, thus completing another lap of the Atlantic slave triangle, from the Americas to Europe.[29] This was a longer journey than the one which had taken him from Africa, lasting for about two months across notoriously turbulent waters. At least he had no cause to agonise as he had when a child, understanding now that Europeans were not devils or cannibals, oppressive though their power was. And on this passage any slaves travelling with Portuguese families were not shackled, packed into the hold or starved of food and water. In fact they often fared better than the white sailors manning the ship, who were liable to be whipped with a cat o' nine tails or sent to cling for hours at the top of a masthead. As the vessel neared the shores of Europe, Joseph might even have felt excited at the new experiences in store for him on the 'free soil' of Portugal.

Travellers approaching Lisbon from the sea were always impressed by its fine harbour on the river Tagus. Buckingham, who first arrived there as a 9-year-old sailor-boy, described it as 'one of the noblest maritime cities in the world', with 'long lines of factories and warehouses fringing the water's edge, the numerous fleet of Portuguese ships of war, large Indiamen as they were called from the Brazils, and vessels and flags of every nation crowding the stream'.[30] Other visitors admired the numerous churches, castles, villas and gardens 'of grand and beautiful appearance' on the hills rising above Lisbon. No doubt Joseph expected a fine city, for most of the Europeans he had encountered were wealthy and lived in an opulent style. But on coming ashore he witnessed, as did Buckingham and other observers, streets full of filth, offensive odours, an astonishing number of wild dogs, a multitude of beggars and many ruined buildings. Older inhabitants still related the 'dreadful scenes' of the earthquake and tidal wave which had struck Lisbon in 1755, when thousands of its inhabitants were killed and much of city was destroyed. Its 'fatal effects' were indeed still visible in many areas.[31]

But the central district where most wealthy families lived had been rebuilt, with well-paved streets, shady colonnades and stately mansions. Their capacious apartments overlooked the grand *Praça do Commercio*, in the middle of which was a new bronze statue of the former king, whose name Joseph bore. Nearby were the Royal Exchange, where merchants did business, and the riverside warehouses which housed their goods. Joseph probably helped his master at the harbour as he had done in Brazil, and attended the evenings when he received guests at home. His colour was no social handicap in Lisbon where fashionable people followed the lead of Queen Maria herself, who was often seen in public with black attendants and favourites. Indeed Joseph's presence was an asset, since he could help to provide the sort of music which Lisboans enjoyed. He was already familiar, for example, with the lilting Brazilian *modinhas* described by the music-loving writer William Beckford, who heard them sung in Lisbon, as 'the most seducing, the most voluptuous [music] imaginable, the best calculated to throw saints off their guard and to inspire profane deliriums'.[32] So useful did Joseph prove himself that he was supplied with a violin and a teacher so that he could learn to read music and improve his performance. It seemed that his fortunes were changing. As his musical proficiency and repertoire advanced he became a well-known performer, invited to play in other gentlemen's houses and at the chapel services attended 'at least once a day' by Lisbon's devout ladies.[33]

* * *

After three or four years Joseph's reputation rose so high that he was invited to join the orchestra of the Lisbon Opera, which often played before Queen Maria, famed for her love of fine music. He was so busy by now that he had probably left the Emidio household to set up home for himself. A natural area for him to choose would have been the district of Mocambo, designated for over two centuries as a 'place of refuge' for free and enslaved Africans, who preserved their own festivals, dance and music among its narrow streets.[34] Many of the small houses portrayed in the panoramic tile-panel of early eighteenth-century Lisbon had (like itself) survived the earthquake and could provide Joseph with lodgings at a rent he hoped to be able to afford from his musical endeavours.

There were plenty of opportunities in a city which abounded with music, often of a very high standard. The musicians of the Royal Chapel, for example, moved Beckford to tears and trembling by their thrilling performance of Jommelli's High Mass.[35] Players like Joseph also travelled by mule to the Queen's summer palace at Sintra to serenade the royal party in chambers painted with magpies and doves, or in scented gardens where they were accompanied by nightingales. He could also have helped to provide the 'soft strains of music' which Buckingham heard wafting from the barge taking the Queen to and from her bathing-place on the Tagus.[36] Most frequently he played the music of Mozart, Haydn and Gluck as second violin in the elegant new Royal Opera House opened by Queen Maria in 1793. All this made it possible for him to support himself without having to resort to such indignities as those observed by Beckford at a bull-feast near Lisbon: 'The band of negroes tumbled about the amphitheatre in the dress of monkeys and waggled their tails to the woeful sound of some wretched bassoons and fiddles.'[37]

There is also a chance that Joseph enjoyed his new-found freedom. On warm evenings when he had no employment he could take his fiddle to play in small neighbourhood squares. In the old Alfama district, for example, people would gather to collect water from the fountains (after which it is named), or to buy fish after the catch had come in. They would leave off their labours for a while to sing and dance, sometimes to melodies and rhythms Joseph knew from Brazil. The *batuque* and forms of the fandango such as the *lundu* and the *fofa* were especially popular with Lisboans.[38] An area where he would have felt curiously at home was Belem, where in the grounds of the royal winter palace was to be found a tropical garden. This contained plants from all over the world and also an aviary full of brightly coloured birds sent to the queen as a yearly tribute from Brazil and from Portugal's colonies in Africa and Asia. These birds had made journeys like Joseph's – though they had not gained their liberty – and as he listened to their song he might almost have fancied himself back in Africa. Less uplifting was the menagerie of foreign animals which were kept in 'pestilential filth' and supplied with such meagre rations that an old elephant, fed on 'a short allowance of cabbages', died of hunger.[39]

These gardens were often frequented by prostitutes, but it is unlikely that Joseph approached them. His experience of life had shaped a nervous youth, worried about falling into any kind of scrape, when, as Equiano found, 'no black man's testimony is admitted, on any occasion, against any white person whatever'.[40] He also had to be wary of the Inquisition which still had some power in Portugal. Beckford, for example, witnessed its agents laying hold of 'negro beldames, who retire into dens and burrows for the purpose of telling fortunes and selling charms for the ague'.[41] Black people were as much an object of suspicion as Jews, and Joseph's best course was to profess the Roman Catholic faith into which he had been baptised in Africa. But he had no reason to suspect that the greatest threat to his wellbeing would come not from the law or the church but, once again, from the sea.

*   *   *

There were always many English ships in Lisbon harbour owing to their extensive trade with Portugal and the long-standing alliance between the two countries. Since the outbreak of war between England and Revolutionary France in 1793, this naval presence had greatly increased. English officers were to be seen at concerts and in gentlemen's houses, while sailors gathered water supplies from the fountains or roamed the streets drinking and brawling. The young Buckingham, on the third of his voyages to Lisbon, also observed the Royal Navy's press-gang, 'prowling along the river and the shore, seizing all Englishmen that could be found', including some of his shipmates. The boy only escaped its clutches by running into a doorway and being hidden by some motherly Portuguese ladies.[42]

Joseph was not so lucky in his encounter with Sir Edward Pellew, the Cornish captain whose ship, the *Indefatigable*, anchored in May 1795 for extensive repairs. This renowned English seaman became a familiar sight in Lisbon over the next two months so that when he attended the Royal Opera House, Joseph could not fail to recognise him – a burly figure in all his finery and medals. Pellew enjoyed music and might have been observed beating out the notes on his knee in the manner of his fictionalised counterpart, Patrick O'Brian's Captain Jack Aubrey.[43] And he was certainly impressed by 'the energy with which the young negro plied his violin in the orchestra' – so much so that he decided to impress him into service as a fiddler, 'to furnish music for the sailors' dancing in their evening leisure'. When Joseph left the theatre later in the evening he was seized by three strong sailors, 'violin and all', carried a few streets away to the port and rowed out to the *Indefatigable*. Shocked by this story, as well as by his own narrow escape from the press-gang, Buckingham judged such kidnapping to be 'equally criminal' to slave-trading and was to campaign against the practice as a Radical MP and journalist.[44] Indeed, memories of his own childhood capture must have come flooding back to Joseph as he was once again made a prisoner.

The ship's muster book for 1795 includes Landsman Josh Emede, born in Lisbon and aged 25; despite the anglicisation of his name and the inaccuracy of his native land and age, this is obviously Joseph.[45] In addition to playing music for the sailors' entertainment, he had to perform normal naval duties in return for a wage of eighteen shillings a month. He was also provided with a hammock and clothing, or 'slops', consisting of a round hat, short blue coat and loose trousers. In vain might he have shown the papers proving that he was a free man who should not have been seized in this way. There was no means of escape as the *Indefatigable* was moored far out in the Tagus. Joseph was now a sailor and was to remain so for many a year.

The two weeks in which the ship lay at anchor gave him time to gaze longingly at the city which had been his home, thinking of the engagements which he could not now fulfil. There was no call for his fiddling while he and his shipmates performed the heavy work involved in preparing the ship to make sail. A mere landsman unfamiliar with these duties, and with the English tongue in which orders were given, was a natural butt for ribaldry from the crew, especially after they had imbibed their grog rations. Common tricks were to get the victim to turn around to be taken unawares with a pail of water landing on him, or to loosen the ties of his hammock so that it collapsed when he climbed into it at the end of the day. In Joseph's case his colour, too, made him the target of his shipmates' scorn. He remembered being 'the only negro on board ... looked down upon as an inferior being' and forced to eat his salt beef and hard biscuit alone rather than at one of the merry mess tables strung up among the guns.[46]

Once the ship sailed, however, Joseph won the sailors' 'high favour' by bringing out his violin for evenings of entertainment announced by the captain. It was not difficult for him to learn the hornpipes and reels to which they loved to dance and to accompany them in singing their favourite old sea shanties, or the new songs of Charles Dibdin, such as *The Lass that Loves a Sailor* and *The Cabin Boy*. Buckingham expresses sympathy for 'poor Emidee ... forced, against his will, to descend from the higher regions of the music in which he delighted – Gluck, Haydn, Cimarosa and Mozart, to desecrate his violin to hornpipes, jigs and reels, which he loathed and detested.'[47] In truth, the writer was more likely to be expressing his own musical tastes rather than those of a young man who had grown up among African and Brazilian rhythms, and might well have found his heart gladdened by the cheerful strains his fiddle was now sounding.

*   *   *

Joseph certainly needed consolation as he performed the arduous tasks of scrubbing the decks, hauling the guns and anchor, climbing the rigging and keeping watch at night. After living all his life in hot climates, it was hard to endure months of wet and chill in the English Channel and the Bay of Biscay. And, along with the rest of the sailors, he was often placed in grave danger by stormy seas and by England's long conflict with France and its current allies, Spain and Holland. The *Indefatigable* gave chase to many vessels with the aim of capturing them, taking them back to port and claiming the prize money from which all the crew would benefit – even landsmen like Joseph. Several French ships were seized in this way, usually without shots being fired. But all on board feared for their lives just before Christmas in 1796 off the coast of Brittany, when Pellew challenged the *Droits de l'Homme*, a powerful French ship with far more guns than his own.

A terrible battle raged for many hours during a night of heavy seas. Joseph had to take his turn on the gun deck swamped up to his waist, and also down below where the surgeon tied himself and his patients to the stanchions as he carried out amputations and other operations. Eventually the moon came out and revealed that the enemy ship had been driven on to rocks and wrecked – and that *Indefatigable* too was heading rapidly for the jagged French coast. It took many hours of struggle before she was free of danger, Pellew joining in with the crew and showing the remarkable seamanship for which he was famous. At the end of this, about twenty men were dead and the *Indefatigable* was so badly damaged that she had to limp back to her home port of Falmouth for repairs lasting several months. But this single-ship victory was hailed as a 'noble exploit', equalled by few other frigate captains.[48]

Neither the three months spent in Falmouth's crowded harbour, nor any other docking, gave Joseph the opportunity to make the acquaintance of the country he was now serving. As he later recounted, he was 'never permitted to set his foot on shore', lest he should 'escape at the first possible opportunity'.[49] In truth, he had his own cause to fear flight – that he might be mistaken for an escaped slave. Nor was his shipboard confinement unusual; so desperate was the need for men in wartime that most crew members had to stay on board while at anchor, a source of much grievance among them. The only Falmouth folk Joseph saw were the Jewish traders who came out in bumboats to sell their wares, and the women who came on board to satisfy the men's sexual demands. He might have been glad to purchase some of the pedlars' goods – they included 'old watches and seals, watch chains, rings, fancy shoes, scarlet and blue silk handkerchiefs, clay pipes and fresh food of every description' – since he had come on board with no possessions but his violin.[50] It is less likely that he had any dealings with the women of the town except in so far as they shared the hammocks of his fellows on the crowded lower deck, or danced sometimes to his fiddle.

Indefatigable was a rather quieter ship for the next two years. News came in 1797 of mutinies on board many other English vessels, but Pellew had no trouble with his crew. They were not lacking in food or drink, having been often enough in port to take on supplies, and they knew that they had won plenty of prize money. During the rest of Joseph's time on board, a good many more French or Spanish vessels were captured without blood being shed. On one occasion a French privateer was sighted while they lay off Lisbon, a poignant reminder for Joseph of better days. Less familiar was a wintry spell surveying the rocky coastlines of the Isles of Scilly. Since there was not much adventure to be had here, musicians were in demand to prevent the crew suffering boredom and taking too much grog. Careful watch had to be kept, though, for these rocky islands were a magnet for shipwrecks, despite the fires burning in St Agnes lighthouse.

Eventually, after several further successful actions, the ship headed into Plymouth harbour early in 1799, and it was here that Captain Pellew's command of *Indefatigable* came to an end. Most of his crew packed their chests or bundles, took the pay due to them and headed ashore, doubtless to spend some of their gains in carousing and debauchery. After that, many would return to the Cornish tin mines, fishing boats or farms they had come from, and to the families and friends waiting for them in Falmouth, Truro, Penryn, St Just, Probus and other West Country towns and villages.[51] Joseph was in no such position.

*   *   *

Anyone would assume, as Buckingham clearly did, that this reluctant seaman took the first opportunity to leave naval service, a belief perpetuated by Richard McGrady in his excellent account of Emidy's subsequent musical career.[52] In fact, as the naval historian Stephen Taylor has shown, 'he willingly followed Pellew to his next ship'. The muster books for *Impetueux*, of which Pellew now assumed command, list Joseph Emede (spelt in various ways) in May 1799 and in subsequent years.[53] They also indicate that he was now ranked as an able seaman, suggesting that Pellew thought highly enough of his fiddling to invite him on board *Impetueux* with promotion. This is a clue to Joseph's motives for staying on at sea. With better pay and a greater share in prize money he could hope to accumulate enough funds to set himself up as a musician in England. He might almost have been glad to be among the crew of over 600 men (which included two of Pellew's sons: Midshipman Pownoll and 14-year-old Able Seaman Fleetwood) who saw Captain Pellew piped on board to take up his new command.

Although war continued to rage over the seas, Joseph was never again in as much danger as he had been in the battle with the *Droits de l'Homme.* On this new ship he had more cause to be frightened of the crew. Many of them were Scots and Irishmen with accents barely intelligible to him. They had been together for some time and had been getting away with a fair amount of indiscipline – drunkenness, fighting and insolence towards the officers. As one of the Pellew's former crew, Joseph was naturally an object of suspicion and here again his black face would not help to make him popular. His position was made more difficult when he began to hear rumours of a plot to get rid of the new captain who had ordered a series of heavy floggings to punish rudeness and cheek. He himself had no cause to love Pellew, but it was not in his nature to be party to violence and mutiny. No doubt he tried to lie low, but this was difficult once the ringleaders started to threaten those who were unwilling to join them with a beating.

Matters came to a head while *Impetueux* was anchored off the coast of Ireland, waiting for a French invasion force which never materialised. A crowd of some 200 crew members swarmed up on to the quarter deck, demanding that they be given a boat in which to carry a letter to the commander of the fleet complaining of 'cruel usage'. When Pellew, who had emerged from his cabin in his dressing gown, demanded that they give him the letter, the tumult increased, at which the captain flew back to his cabin, returning almost immediately with a sword in his hand. With the help of his armed officers he drove the mutineers down to the gun deck, where the ringleaders made fresh attempts to incite the crew to kill the captain and seize the ship. Eventually they were overpowered and clapped in irons so that the trouble died down – but there was still a wretched atmosphere below decks with frequent brawling and 'toadies' such as Joseph being shunned or even sent to Coventry.

It was a thoroughly miserable ship which sailed off to Minorca, where a court martial was held on board another British vessel. Once the proceedings were over the crew was mustered on deck to see the three ringleaders hanged at the yardarm and their bodies committed to the deep, while the rest of the mutineers were flogged around the fleet and then dispersed to other ships. It was the sight of such cruelty which caused Buckingham to desert the navy and to campaign against such practices in later life. They must also have been thoroughly upsetting for Joseph – but again the fiddle came to his rescue. One of the captain's methods of bringing the crew together was to organise musical events, especially on moonlit nights. There were no doubt other musicians on board, an Irish piper perhaps or a Scottish fiddler, with whom he could form a little band to play for the men's dancing and accompany them in song. Seasoned performer that he was, Joseph was well able to play solo tunes from his repertoire or even of his own composition, helping this fractious crew to fall, in Pellew's words, 'as quiet as lambs'.[54]

Even so, this was never a happy ship and there were some hard times over the next two years. One winter was spent in the Bay of Biscay, plagued by icy storms, when the sailors subsisted on salt provisions. And in eight tedious months of blockading the French off Rochefort, the bored crew again resorted to drink and brawls. Great was the relief, therefore, when suddenly in October 1801, a French ship was sighted flying a flag of truce, signifying that a peace agreement had been signed. The long war, it seemed, was over.

*   *   *

Joseph's rejoicing was no doubt mixed with some trepidation. He had no idea what would become of him once he disembarked in Plymouth harbour in April 1802 after his 'seven long years' at sea.[55] He had less reason to fear the press gang now that the fighting had stopped, but cause still to dread recapture into slavery. Judge Mansfield's famous ruling of 1772 had pronounced that 'a negro cannot be taken out of the kingdom without his own consent', but it had not actually outlawed slavery.[56] Custom certainly sanctioned domestic bondage: it was not uncommon in Cornwall at this time for husbands to sell their wives in the local market.[57]

Joseph had been paid off with the rest of the crew, but he knew that it was often difficult for men of his low rank to collect the prize money due to them. To survive he must use his talents as a musician in a country where he was unknown, and whose language he spoke only as a rough sailor. He decided to make for Falmouth, perhaps remembering the obliging traders he had encountered on board *Indefatigable*. It is also likely that Pellew, a Cornishman with a fine mansion and good connections there, was prepared to vouch for his musical skills and good character. Even so, it took courage to board a packet boat around the coast to start afresh as he had once done in Lisbon.

Sailors often found it hard to settle to life on land after many years afloat, unable to sleep at night without the rhythm of the waves to lull them and missing the shipmates with whom they had shared the bond of the sea. This was no doubt true of the friendless Joseph, but there were urgent tasks to occupy him. He had to find lodgings, buy a suit of clothes to smarten up his appearance and get to know the town. It was a prosperous and bustling sea port in those days with naval frigates, mail packets, fishing craft, ferry boats, trading vessels and East Indiamen crowding the harbour. On a quayside crammed with sailors, smugglers and wealthy merchants, activity centred on the Customs House, over which presided none other than Samuel Pellew, brother of Sir Edward. In the midst of all this activity Joseph's colour would not have attracted too much attention, so that he could pluck up courage to offer his services at the grand residences around the harbour. He stood a good chance of finding work, since musicians were needed at the dinners and evening parties hosted in 'one or other of the captains' houses every evening', and at the fortnightly balls held in the Assembly Room.[58] It did not take long for him to become known, with word of his 'mysterious talent' passing from one household to another and spreading to neighbouring communities. A Camborne resident, for example, described 'this unknown Negro' as 'the most finished musician I ever heard of … a wonderful manipulator on the Violin, Cello or Viola'.[59]

He also placed advertisements in the local newspaper, offering his services as a music teacher with 'a most easy and elegant stile'. In a society where musical accomplishments were highly regarded he soon gained pupils, not only in the violin but also in the cello, piano, clarinet, flute, guitar and mandolin. One of his early pupils was the teenage Buckingham, who hoped that proficiency in the flute would be 'a most agreeable recommendation in female society'. And the 'friendly intimacy' which existed between the Pellew and Buckingham families suggests that Sir Edward had recommended 'the African negro' as a teacher.[60] Before long Joseph was embraced by the 'Gentleman Amateurs' of the Falmouth Harmonic Society, who were glad of his expertise in the concerts they held regularly in private houses and sometimes in public rooms. As early as August 1802, just four months after he had first set foot on English soil, Mr Emidy announced that he intended to give a 'Grand Miscellaneous Concert' and ball, 'under the patronage of several respectable gentlemen'; one of them was surely Sir Edward Pellew, 'around whom the social life of the place revolved'. The programme included a Violin Concerto and Mandolin Solo of his own composition and concluded with the National Anthem 'in full chorus'. Tickets were to be sold for three shillings and sixpence from his lodgings 'at Mr Hayne's'.[61] Similar events followed, including one at Mrs Hick's School Room, Falmouth, in 1806, where he was to play 'with the assistance of several Gentlemen performers and the Band of the North Devon Militia'. Thus, reports Buckingham, 'he made rapid progress in reputation and means'.[62]

He could have tapped another source of income if he encountered one of the Jewish pedlars he had met on board *Indefatigable*, since they often acted as unofficial prize agents for seamen in West Country ports. Even after paying commission and possibly being cheated during this complicated process, he would eventually stand to gain a substantial sum, maybe even 'enough to buy a cottage or some land'.[63] In all these ways and with much hard work, Joseph found that he was earning enough to support himself. His main worry arose when war against the French resumed in May 1803. His thoughts must have flown to the danger of a second impressment, making him reluctant to linger for long in the port.[64]

*   *   *

Even more remarkable than his professional development was the speed with which Joseph found a Cornish wife. He could not have had high expectations of domestic bliss when he went to live in Cornwall, knowing that there would be no women of his own complexion there and suspecting that marriage with a white woman would meet with general disapproval.[65] But through one or other of his musical activities he soon met the 22-year-old Jane Jenefer Hutchins, daughter of a local mariner.[66] Notwithstanding his lack of experience with women, he clearly wooed her successfully during his first Cornish summer. And despite his dubious origins, her father must have found him an acceptable son-in-law for they were married on 16 September 1802 in Falmouth Parish church. In the same church, the couple baptised five sons and a daughter named Cecilia, after the patron saint for music, all of whom thrived, apart from baby Benjamin who died in 1812. It was thus a family of seven which occupied the house near the market place from which Joseph conducted his growing musical enterprise.

The connection with his Hutchins in-laws was bound to help his integration into Falmouth society. Another factor in his favour was the growing liberalism of this area. Many of the merchants followed the example of the Quaker Fox family, which 'formed a complete colony in and around Falmouth', in supporting the campaign against the British slave trade.[67] They had given a favourable reception to Thomas Clarkson, one of its leaders, when he visited the town in 1789, welcomed the abolition of the trade in 1807 and went on to champion the movement against slavery in the British Empire. But above all it was music which saved this former slave and lowly sailor from being shunned by polite society; he found, as did the homesick Josef Haydn when he came to London from Austria, that its language was 'understood all over the world'.[68] Joseph's Cornish neighbours seemed to forget his colour as they danced to his minuets, learned to play under his tuition or applauded new works such as the violin concerto and rondo he composed for the King's birthday in 1810. Thus, although Emidy was probably the only black resident of the county, apart from drummers and trumpeters attached to the Royal Cornwall Militia, he found that he was accepted there.[69] This harmony is epitomised in the only surviving portrayal of him: he is pictured in an elegant drawing room, a slight figure energetically plying his bow and clearly leading a 'A Musical Club', which consists of ten ruddy Cornishmen playing wind and string instruments and a well-dressed portly observer.[70]

The vicissitudes of his life made Joseph fearful of change, a trepidation which was borne out in 1807. Buckingham had been so impressed with his teacher that he took some of his compositions to London to show to an acquaintance who arranged fashionable concerts in Hanover Square. This was none other than Haydn's patron Johann Salomon, who liked the pieces, as did a number of professional performers. But according to Buckingham, they were all of the opinion that it would be too risky to invite Joseph to present them in London where 'his colour would be so much against him'.[71] It is difficult to say whether they were right. As Joseph probably knew, some freed slaves had succeeded in London; Ignatius Sancho, for example, had gained influential patrons, enabling him to open a grocery shop, write plays, compose music and publish his *Letters* which went into five editions. While being well integrated with 'literary middling sort of people', he and his family were nevertheless 'gazed at' and abused by Londoners prejudiced against 'their woolly headed brethren', and Sancho never felt more than 'a lodger' in England – 'and hardly that'.[72] There were certainly black musicians like the one-legged Billy Waters who scraped a living by busking in the streets and taverns of London. But Billy's way of life would not have suited Joseph, who was happy to accept a handsome sum from the benefit concert of his works arranged by Salomon, while continuing to make a decent living in the sea-washed county on which he had landed.

* * *

In about 1812 the Emidy family moved away from the coast to the inland port of Truro, the county town which was sometimes known as the 'London of Cornwall'. The centre for the area's thriving tin and copper mines, it was expanding rapidly at this time and could offer Joseph even more opportunities for work at its fine Assembly Rooms and in the elegant new dwellings of Lemon Street, named after Sir William Lemon, Cornwall's Whig MP and a staunch opponent of the slave trade. Joseph was soon to be seen leading the Truro Philharmonic Orchestra in 'his usual spirited stile' at regular concerts and balls, which were 'respectably attended' by 'the beauty and fashion of Truro', often including both the Ultra-Tory Lord Falmouth and Truro's reformist MP Sir Hussey

Vivian, along with their elegant wives. Advertisements and reports in the local press show that they provided a 'judicious selection' of Baroque eighteenth-century music and newer works, including music 'composed expressly for the occasion by J. Emidy'. This ranged from full symphonies and concertos for violin, French horn or bugle to 'beautiful variations of that pleasing air *Bluebells of Scotland*', which he performed 'with a taste and effect scarcely to be expected at so great a distance from the capital'.[73] Alongside one of the concert reviews in the *Royal Cornwall Gazette* is a story which suggests the fate which might have befallen Emidy had he been less diligent and talented: 'John Pinhoe, a black man, who had been confined in the town-prison at Plymouth-Docks for a burglary, hung himself behind the door of his cell. As he was proved to be of a sane mind previous to the commission of the horrid act, the Coroner's Jury brought in a verdict of *felo de se*.'[74]

For the next twenty years or so Joseph and Jenefer lived in Charles Street, Truro, adjacent to, but much humbler than, Lemon Street. Their two- or three-bedroom terraced house accommodated not only the four children born in Falmouth, but also three more: Eliza Rose, Richard and William. It was hard work for Jenefer to keep the household going as there is no record of any servant to help her. It is not known where the children were educated, but there was a new church school in Falmouth and by the time the family moved to Truro, Joseph could afford to send them to one of its modest private academies. Nor can we tell whether the children experienced any difficulties arising from their being 'mulattoes', who were attacked by the normally radical journalist William Cobbett for stamping 'the mark of Cain' on the country 'in disregard of decency, [and] defiance of the dictates of nature'.[75] The only hint of prejudice appears in the *West Briton* in 1816, where it is reported that the oldest son Joseph, 'a mulatto boy of eleven years of age', had been accused of stealing 'a quantity of pence' from a local shop and sentenced to six months hard labour. But since Joseph (who was actually 12 at the time) admitted to the theft, for which such a punishment was not unusual, this is not proof of discriminatory treatment – indeed he was lucky not to be put on a transportation ship.[76]

The Emidy household was clearly a musical one in which the children were encouraged to sing and to play instruments. The second son,

Thomas, followed in his father's footsteps by becoming leader of a brass band, playing at traditional Floral Days, regattas and balls. Although qualified as a cabinet maker and carpenter, he is described as a musician in Census returns and published *The Royal Cornwall and Devon Artillery Quadrilles*, which he had composed and arranged for the pianoforte. An indication of Thomas's popularity in Cornwall is the report that over 3,000 people attended his funeral in Truro in 1871. The youngest child, William, is similarly listed as a Professor of Music, or as a Bandmaster in Liverpool. Cecilia lived up to her name by making her debut in one of her father's concerts where '*Robin Adair* was prettily sung by Miss Emidy and encored by the audience'. Meanwhile their brother James became a different sort of entertainer, travelling the country as a 'celebrated African rider', performing 'surprising feats' in circuses and theatres.[77]

The closest glimpse we have of domestic life in Charles Street is through the obituary and epitaph written for Richard Emidy, who died in 1837 at the age of 20 . He is described as an 'intelligent young man … the pleasure of his family circle', 'dutiful and diligent as a son and affectionate as a brother'. In the neighbourhood he was remembered especially as a 'zealous and persevering' teacher in St John's Sunday School 'where he had himself received instruction' – a reminder that this was for many children an important means of education.[78] Richard was not married, but three of his brothers had English wives and thirteen children between them. Neither Cecilia nor Eliza found a husband, but there is certainly no evidence of either being scorned, in the words of *Vanity Fair's* George Osborne, as 'a Hottentot Venus'.[79] Both went to live with their youngest brother in Liverpool, where they earned their living as dressmakers. The impression we have is of a united and industrious family, well integrated into English life and not appearing to suffer unduly from the colour of their skin.

Joseph himself continued to travel around Cornwall well into his fifties, still enjoying the 'very distinguished patronage' of Cornwall's nobility and gentry, teaching music, organising concerts and writing new compositions. Sadly, none of the scores have survived, so we cannot know whether the rhythms of Africa, the melodies of Brazil, or the sounds of the sea itself crept into his compositions. After his death in 1835 at the age of 60, his 'long and unwearied public service' was marked by concerts in Truro and Falmouth, 'for the benefit of his wife and family'.[80] He was buried in the cemetery of Kenwyn church, which served a large Truro parish, though it lacked an organ in Emidy's time – an orchestra, in which he might well have played, accompanied the choir.[81] The gravestone erected by his family rightly records his long musical career in Cornwall and the harmony with which 'he liv'd in peace with all', but incorrectly describes him as a native of Portugal. Whether by accident or design, his African origins, Brazilian enslavement, and great sea journeys are ignored, as they are in two obituaries which appeared in the local press. Thus although his 'flights of genius', 'deep musical research', and 'enthusiastic devotion to the science' are acknowledged, his triumph over obstacles and difficulties is untold. Buckingham concluded that if his colour had not been 'so much against him', he might have 'become a Mendelssohn or a Beethoven'.[82] As it was, his fiddle had saved this child at sea from the plagues of slavery, ignominy and penury which so often afflicted his race.

Chapter 3

George King 1787–1855: A Foundling at Sea[1]

L ate in the year 1787 a young woman submitted a desperate plea to the London Foundling Hospital, set up earlier in the century by a benevolent sea captain, Thomas Coram. She knew that it provided a refuge for illegitimate babies, like her 3-month-old boy, who would otherwise be castaways surviving as best they could amid the brine of social and religious prejudice. She also knew that once he was rescued she would probably never see him again, especially since so many foundling boys were 'bred to the sea'.[2]

> The Petition of Mary Miller is humbly presented which showeth that your Petitioner is a very Great Object having had the misfortune of having a Child with a young man who has quitted her and child leaving them in the most Extreme misery and not knowing where he is gone to she has no friend nor any way of maintaining herself nor Child. She humbly intreats Gentlemen that you would be graciously pleased to grant her the privilege of drawing for the benefit of your Charitable Hospital which will be a Charity of the greatest Merit being conferred upon an Object in the greatest need of Charity and who remains with all possible gratitude Gentlemen your most Grateful Petitioner.
>
> Mary Miller

Before accepting such a petition the governors always made careful inquiries to establish that the unmarried mother was worthy of their charity, one who had genuinely been misled by her lover and intended to support herself once relieved of the child. A scrawled note on the back of Mary's neatly presented document shows that they were satisfied in her case: 'The Rev. Mr Harper having recommended this Person as a proper object – Admitted to Ballot.'[3]

So it was that on Wednesday 7 November, Mary and the other successful petitioners came to the Foundling Hospital in Holborn to take part in a lottery which would determine the fate of their children. In the elegant chapel, where Coram was buried, they drew balls from a bag. A black ball meant rejection; a white one entitled them to bring their babies for admission the following Saturday; and those with a red ball could take the places of any mothers whose babies were found on inspection to be too unhealthy. Having drawn a white ball, Mary Miller brought her baby to the Hospital on Saturday 10 November to be examined for symptoms of venereal disease, scrofula, leprosy or other infectious diseases. Pronounced free of these conditions, he was taken from his mother, admitted as child number 18053, baptised and given a new name. He was royally christened George King – just as the young slave Joseph Emidy had been named after the current Portuguese monarch some years earlier. The very next day, George was sent with a full layette of warm clothes and blankets to the care of Ann Yeulet, a wet nurse in Hertfordshire, who was to be paid two shillings and sixpence a week to look after him for the next six years.[4]

All this information can be found today in the careful records of the Foundling Hospital – but George himself never learned any of it. His own version of his origins appears in the autobiography he wrote during the 1840s, a remarkable manuscript giving a unique insight into the life of a foundling who went to sea, which is preserved in the Coram Archive. As far as George King knew, he 'was born at Hemel Hempstead in the County of Herts on the 10th day of June 1787', and the woman who brought him up there was his mother. He goes on to record a few fleeting memories of the six years he spent with her. He was given a small wheelbarrow which he used 'to pick up Horse dung', thinking himself 'very superb'. In the village inn he was so terrified when he thought he saw on a carved wooden settle 'the lower part of a man's head apparently as if it had been sawn or split asunder', that he wept for an hour on his mother's knees before being taken home to bed. At the Hempstead Fair he had an orange stolen from him by a bigger boy, 'which caused me to cry incessantly for a length of time', until another boy rescued the orange and gave the culprit 'a sound drubbing'. He portrays himself as a rather fearful little boy, nicknamed 'the Jack of Clubs being nearly as thick as long'.[5] He can hardly have been ready for the abrupt end to his country childhood which occurred in 1793. Still in petticoats, George was returned to the Foundling Hospital to be trained in 'regular and early habits of order and attention'.[6]

> I was removed from my native place in a Stage Coach for a passage to London with my mother to a School in Holborn not without taking plenty of Ginger-bread where I had a regular surfeit on the passage.

No doubt the gingerbread helped to calm the child's turbulent feelings as he was separated for the second time from a mother's love.

* * *

Many foundlings pined for their nurses, and some even tried to run away to the villages where they had spent their infant years. Others, among them George King, adjusted to the highly regulated routine of the Foundling Hospital, where they were as isolated and as secure as Noah's animals on the Ark in the Bible story, which they were undoubtedly taught. George remembered that he was soon 'breeched' and clothed in the Coram boys' uniform, designed by William Hogarth, the artist who had been one of the hospital's first governors: loose breeches and a jacket of sturdy brown woollen cloth, both trimmed with red. He made no complaint about the hospital's plain but reasonably wholesome diet, with its regular helpings of meat, plentiful bread and absence of tea or beer. What he appreciated most, however, was the education he now received.

> I was put under the care of Mr Robert Atchison the Schoolmaster and a worthy Gentleman he was. ... I took a liking to learn my lessons for which I frequently got small presents from my Schoolmaster. In June 1794 I was put to Writing and in August 1798 I copied a Writing from my Schoolmaster addressed to the Treasurer of the School for which I received one shilling.

In teaching poor boys (but not girls) to write, the hospital was progressive, for at that time most labourers and servants could not even sign their names. Atchison was a former mechanic with failing eyesight and (by his own admission) 'no great literary attainments', who served as steward, chapel clerk and storekeeper as well as schoolmaster. According to his report of January 1800 he had ninety-five boys in his care, among whom eight (probably including George) were learning arithmetic in addition to being taught to 'write legibly and read the Bible'. He clearly favoured an intelligent boy who could help with his own clerical duties.[7]

When they were not attending their lessons boys and girls, who were kept entirely separate from each other, worked at useful chores. Boys were employed in knitting stockings and, as they got older, in cleaning the courtyard, working the pump and helping in the garden. They were even allowed to play with bats, balls and hoops in order to build up their muscular strength. Thus George spent time in the hospital's spacious grounds and saw a little of the outside world by observing the military manoeuvres which a local volunteer regiment was allowed to practise there. After they were over he kept 'an eagle eye' for spent cartridges, experimenting with them in pranks which suggest that the boys were not always strictly supervised:

> At one time I picked up as much as three Cartridges for which I was determined to make an experiment. So at even I got a lighted Candle and wrote my name in full on a large flat stone and placed the powder exactly over the letters to see whether it would leave a mark. My Companions looking on I took the Candle and set fire to the first letter my head then being over it. In an Instant the whole went off and I had the Satisfaction to have my eye brows completely shaved [and] for a minute I did not know whether I was dead or alive. I was always cautious afterwards so that I used to wet it with a little water.

George King also described an exciting occasion in June 1800 when King George III came to inspect the volunteers:

> His Majesty on that day with the principal parts of his family after reviewing the Corps was shewn into the Chapel where two Chairs was [*sic*] placed by the Aisle for him and her Majesty. When the

Organ commenced with the Coronation Anthem and after God
Save the King the Boys and Girls that sung were two Hundred.
After His Majesty had left at 5 o'clock we were regaled with plumb
Cake a great treat.

This gives us a glimpse of a distinctive feature of the Foundling Hospital,
as noted by one of its historians, an 'exposure to beauty such as most
poor children never experienced'.[8] George does not mention the works
of art collected by Hogarth, but he clearly enjoyed the fine chapel
music initiated by George Frederick Handel, another early patron and
governor, whose *Messiah* had been performed there annually until 1777.
The children's twice-weekly singing lessons included Handel's Anthem
for the Foundling Hospital, *Blessed Are They That Consider the Poor*, as
well as John Hawkesworth's Foundling Hymn for those 'In sin conceiv'd,
to sorrow born' who, but for God's mercy, would be, 'Alone amidst
surrounding strife, And naked to the storms of life.'[9]

For the occasion of the King's visit the children rehearsed Handel's
thrilling Coronation Anthem, *Zadok the Priest*, an experience George
always remembered. In later years he would try to recapture such times
in regular Sunday visits to the chapel when he would 'sing with the boys
… the hymns and psalms generally sung from each Sunday in the year'.
The foundlings were not, however, allowed any other musical education,
which would hardly contribute towards their training 'as plain but
essential members of the general community'.[10] But their chapel singing
helped to attract affluent visitors, as did the annual performance of charity
school children at St Paul's Cathedral described in William Blake's *Holy
Thursday*. The sight of their 'innocent faces', illuminated 'with radiance
all their own', and the sound of them raising 'to heaven the voice of
song', prompted generous contributions to the cathedral's collections.
The governors of the Foundling Hospital, 'the most fashionable charity
in the capital', which in 1796, for example, procured £1,845 5s 6d, also
knew how to 'cherish pity'.[11]

At the time of the chapel service for the monarch, George King was
approaching his departure from the hospital, though not for the sea
service which had once been the most common destination for foundlings.
'All things went on gaily', he reports, with no suggestion of the cruel

treatment or punishment which became commonplace under the later utilitarian dispensation, radically changing the character of Coram's Hospital.[12] In fact, for George, the greatest suffering came when he had to leave what had become his home over the previous seven years:

> The trying hour came when I was to be separated from my youthful Companions and especially one whom I loved to extreme.... On the twenty-fifth day of September 1800 I was bound Apprentice out of the school to Mr. John Browne, Grocer and Confectioner residing at No. 10 Fish Street Hill nearly opposite the Monument to learn the art of Confectionary and the day appointed for quitting the School arrived, and the thought of parting from my playfellows and especially from Rivington overcame me for a time.

The special friend referred to is Henry Rivington, number 18050, who had entered the hospital as a baby on the same day as George and was soon to be apprenticed in Clerkenwell. The boys were clearly very attached to each other and George was more upset with this parting than with those from his unremembered mother or unlamented nurse. Nearing his thirteenth birthday, he set out into a city of which he knew nothing more than he might have seen in one of the hospital's paintings, Hogarth's *March of the Guards to Finchley*, depicting scenes of drunken revelry in Tottenham Court Road. Discharged from the Coram ark, he now had to face the storms of life alone.

* * *

Yet foundlings were not cast entirely adrift when they left the hospital for the first time, clad in a new outfit still distinctively marking them out as Coram boys and girls – and as possible victims of mockery. Most served their apprenticeships within walking distance of the hospital, which they were always welcome to visit. And, like George, they were not alone as they set out for their new homes.

> I proceeded with my good friend the Schoolmaster to my new abode. On entering the Counting House I was handed over to Mr.

John Browne. I then shook hands with Mr. Atchison who gave me good advice respecting my future behaviour and conduct during my Apprenticeship towards my Master and the whole of his family as well as the rest of the Servants in his house.

The schoolmaster or matron visited all boys and girls during the seven years of their apprenticeship and the hospital intervened on receiving complaints from either side. It took legal action against masters who mistreated their apprentices and dealt with youngsters who misbehaved, either by sending them to sea or by administering its own punishment. In 1802, for example, George was taken back to the hospital and confined in its 'Dark Room' on a bread and water diet after throwing scalding water over another apprentice who had apparently been tormenting him. After a week, the treasurer records, he was returned to his master 'with every satisfactory expression of compunction and amendment'.[13]

As this story suggests, George's apprenticeship did not go entirely smoothly. He was thrilled, as any boy would be, on 'seeing so many Hogsheads of Sugar and boxes of Raisins', anticipating that he would soon have his fill of such delicacies. The temptation proved too much and he started to smuggle out raisins in his jacket pockets when he went on Sunday visits to Rivington, who had been apprenticed to a pocket-book maker. The boys would have fun together, 'occasionally calling at the school and at other times visiting Bagnigge Wells Tea Gardens as also Primrose Hill, Chalk Farm etc'. But George got a shock when two City Marshalls were called to the confectioners' shop after reports that 'a person belonging to his House was seen frequently on Sunday mornings to leave the side-door with a large bundle under his arm'. All the employees were searched apart from the apprentices, which was lucky since George had recently filled his pockets with raisins. He learned his lesson and thereafter 'shunned that practice'.

He had another narrow escape after breaking a bottle of rum he was taking to his master's house by travelling in a hackney coach rather than on foot. He seems to have settled down by 1804 and he had also begun to 'spring up in height'. But it was a blow when Rivington left London to join the army after his master went bankrupt. It was then that George consoled himself with weekly visits to the hospital, which he still regarded as his home, 'taking with me such fruit as were in season to distribute among the younger community'. In July, however, a train of events, not untypical for an adolescent boy, led to the end of his career in confectionery.

> Unluckily one morning I had overslept myself and did not arrive on Fish Street Hill until twenty minutes after eight. On my entering the shop I was accosted by the man who served behind the counter named James Elliott with these words 'Pray young gentleman what is the reason you were not here at seven?' I made a reply that I was not called as usual and had overslept myself when he jumped over the counter and began to beat me. The different porters looking on – one in the name of William Love – spurred me on to attack him and on finding I had one backer I immediately pitched into him and we had had a regular turn-to which lasted about twenty minutes.... On the arrival of Mr. Browne Senior at eleven o'clock I was ordered into the Counting House and after hearing the whole of the circumstance he ordered me immediately to go on my knees and beg Mr. Elliott's pardon for so he was styled. I refused to do any such thing he being a servant the same as myself but stated at the same time had I said anything injurious to any of his family I would willingly have done it. On the fourteenth of July I was ordered to clean myself and proceed to Guildhall with my Master who requested to see the City Chamberlain with a view of punishing me but on our arrival my Master was informed that the City Chamberlain would not be there until Friday morning following so we arrived home again this being Wednesday.

With the threat of Bridewell House of Correction hanging over him George went to the Foundling Hospital, perhaps to seek advice. Here he happened to meet another old schoolfellow. James Gardner, who had run away to sea from his apprenticeship as a bookbinder, had recently arrived in a merchant vessel from Archangel and seems to have been made welcome at the hospital despite having absconded. After hearing George's story James suggested that they should join another ship together at Chatham, a plan which George gladly accepted as a way out of his predicament. They 'paraded the streets' together for the rest of the day, ending up at James's lodging in the Lamb Public House where they took 'two pots of porter' and George smoked his first pipe of tobacco, which made him very sick. Then he spent his last night as a foundling apprentice before launching himself into a life at sea.

> About half past ten I took a candle and went up to my sleeping room when I commenced packing up my clothes in a large handkerchief and when done I went to bed sorrowful.

*   *   *

George's trepidation proved justified. Still only 16 and the product of a cloistered and highly controlled childhood, he was hardly prepared for an independent life. The journey to Chatham tested his wits at every turn. Near St Paul's Cathedral he sold the Foundling Hospital garments from his bundle to 'a Jew singing out "any old clothes"', who told him they were 'partly worn and only fit for boys'. He accepted sixteen shillings for them, knowing that they were worth over £2 and that he had been swindled. He was relieved after this to pick up his more experienced friend and together they proceeded to Seven Dials, a maze of poor streets and alleys near Covent Garden where they hoped to get George 'rigged out in the garb of a sailor'. Avoiding the street hawkers, they headed for a shop which sold cheap second-hand seamen's clothing, where they chose 'a Blue Jacket and a pair of common blue trousers so that you might shoot peas through them'. He exchanged this 'warfaring dress' for the clothes he was wearing and three shillings and sixpence, a better bargain than he had been able to strike on his own.

It was not long, however, before George lost his helpful companion. At Blackfriars Bridge, Gardner said that he had to collect wages owed him for his last voyage, promising to meet him at the Sun Tavern in Chatham. After walking on his own for two hours and getting drenched with rain three times, George was pleased to meet another 'seafaring man' on Shooters Hill, a stretch of road notorious for its highwaymen. They agreed to travel together into Kent.

Accordingly we kept company till we arrived at Gravesend but on our arrival at Dartford we halted and partook of bread and cheese with two pots of porter which I freely paid for and then we proceeded onwards. I was much delighted with his conversation respecting a Maritime life and I supposed at that time that I should have nothing to do but sit down and let the winds blow me along.

It sounds as though the naïve youth was so glad of companionship that he was happy to pay for this refreshment and for replenishment at Gravesend, where the sailor left to return to his ship. His loneliness is apparent in the poignant story he goes on to tell:

I had not proceeded above a mile on the road all along when a sudden impulse struck me respecting the disgraceful manner in which I left my good master in town. However, I persevered on my journey and when within four miles of Chatham the atmosphere became overset and very cloudy. On the road I met with no person when I became rather alarmed what with the rustling of the trees and the wind blowing a fresh breeze. I went along whistling as long as I could sometimes running and sometimes walking occasionally looking behind me and at this time rushed into my head the figures I had seen above the Settle at Hemel Hempstead and that caused me to perspire excessively.

Plucking up his courage George pressed on, arriving by midnight at the Sun Tavern where he had supper with the servants. Here he met with some kindness; he stayed on at the inn, meeting all the London coaches on which he hoped to find his schoolfellow, and was never pressed for payment by the landlord.

After four days Gardner had still not turned up, perhaps having found some better opportunity or been impressed into the Royal Navy, which always liked to get hold of merchant seamen. Not knowing what else to do, George set off to look for him on the London road, where he soon encountered a 'party of men' which he did not recognise as a press-gang. In his nautical attire he was accused of being a deserter, handcuffed and taken 'to the sign of the Cock at Chatham', which was clearly the 'rondy' (rendezvous) from which the gang operated. The only way George could undeceive his captors was to produce his Indentures and to confess that he had run away from his apprenticeship. This only got him into more trouble:

> They stated to me that they would put me in prison and write to my master which I begged and prayed that they would not do the like, saying that I wished to go to sea and that same time they asked me if I would drink a cup of grog which I assented to. In the meantime they destroyed my Indentures and in a few hours afterwards I found myself on board of His Majesty's Ship Polyphemus just fitting out in the Medway and commanded by Captain now Admiral Sir John Lawford.

George's memory served him well. HMS *Polyphemus* was indeed being repaired and manned in Chatham harbour in the summer of 1804 so as to be fighting fit for the renewed war with Napoleonic France. But it is clear that George was not actually pressed into naval service, for at the end of July he was paid over £12, the two months' advance wages due only to volunteers, a generous sum even after half had been deducted for 'necessaries, slops, stoppages and beds'. Another indication is that he was signed on not as a lowly landsman, but as 'one of the Marines borne as part of the complement'. These bare facts appear in the ship's pay book and muster,[14] but the part this mere foundling was to play in the impending contest for naval supremacy would be hidden from history were it not for the literacy imparted by Robert Atchison and George's urge to tell his story.

It was not long before *Polyphemus* was ready to sail and George soon experienced the swiftly changing pains and prizes of war at sea. Satisfaction at receiving his bounty turned to repentance at having left his master once the ship began to roll in a North Sea gale and he became seasick. This eased once he reached more southern waters, but now came the tedium of blockading the Spanish port of Cadiz which provided supplies and shelter for the French navy.[15] Three months of monotony were rewarded when *Polyphemus* was ordered to intercept

Spanish treasure ships from South America – even before Spain became an official ally of France.[16]

> We captured two Spanish ships from Buenos Ayres laden with hides and tallow ... [and] another laden with the same and about thirty or forty boxes of Doubloons on board. We manned them and sent them towards Gibraltar but sorry to relate that the last mentioned was accidentally run-down and eleven lives lost out of thirteen. On seventh of December following early in the morning we gave chase to a strange sail to Leeward and at three P.M. we came alongside of her and fired one musket which proved to be the Santa Gertruyda of thirty-six guns laden with spices amounting to 1,215,000 dollars with several chests of silver-plate and two large pigs of silver. She made no resistance. We immediately commenced taking out the prisoners and manning her with part of our ship's company – I being one of that crew.

George's elation at these events was dampened as the *Santa Gertruyda* sailed to an English port through gales and seas 'mountains high' in which she lost her rudder and mainmast, as well as all the hammocks. He describes the sailors' desperate efforts to keep the ship afloat and their unanswered distress signals before they were eventually towed into Plymouth harbour in January 1805. Then came the thrill of helping to unload from the hold tiers of boxes each filled with 3,000 blocks of silver 'and the crevices filled up with Cocoa'. But hopes of record prize money were to be dashed when the Admiralty ruled that only a quarter would be paid since war had not been declared on Spain when the ship was taken.[17] Not that George complained about this or about shipboard life in general. 'Dangerous, degrading and harsh' though it was, according to one authority, it provided him with living quarters, messmates, regular rations of food and generous supplies of drink.[18] It didn't take long for a Coram boy to make himself at home in Nelson's navy.

* * *

The volunteer militia which George had seen training in the Foundling
Hospital grounds was part of England's defence against a widely feared
French invasion. By 1805, when over 150,000 troops had assembled
at Boulogne, it seemed likely that Napoleon's threat would shortly be
fulfilled: 'Let us be masters of the Channel but for six hours, and we shall
be masters of the world.' Boney would soon pass by and tear naughty
babies limb from limb, if nursemaids' songs were to be believed. Thus
the Royal Navy had to intensify its blockade of the ports of France and
her allies, and *Polyphemus* (now commanded by Robert Redmill) soon
received the signal 'to resume our station off Cadiz'.

George recounts the ship's various manoeuvres over the next six
months, during which she captured another Spanish merchant vessel
and sailed the prize to Plymouth. Autumn found her in the English
Channel where she was 'joined by Lord Nelson with ten sail of the
line after his chase around the West Indies'. Of course George knew
nothing of Bonaparte's invasion plan, by which Admiral Villeneuve's
fleet decoyed his rival commander-in-chief across the Atlantic, hoping
to leave the Channel unprotected. The scheme failed because the French
squadron based in Brest could not get past the English blockade to join
the Emperor's invasion force in Boulogne. By this time Villeneuve had
managed to return safely to Cadiz. George is correct in remembering
that Nelson arrived back from the Caribbean at this point and that then
'his Lordship left for England' on shore leave. This was not a privilege
often granted to ordinary seamen or marine privates – but at least in the
Channel there was 'the chance of having a Torbay boat alongside of us
and we used to purchase potatoes and suchlike which was a great treat'.

Such homely fare was not at hand once *Polyphemus* had proceeded south
in a fleet of twenty-one battleships to strengthen Admiral Collingwood's
blockade of Cadiz. Even during this tedious vigil the crew managed to find
some comfort from one of the milking animals kept on board, as George
explains: 'The old goat used generally to take up her position among us
and sometimes I used to have a soft pillow by placing my head on her
loins and she used to be content if she had two or three heads on her and
never stirred.' He was aware also of more strategic matters, describing
Nelson's arrival in the *Victory* on 14 October, and the decision that there
should be no customary gun salute. Neither Nelson nor Collingwood

knew for sure that Napoleon had now abandoned his invasion plans and had ordered Villeneuve to take the Combined French and Spanish Fleet out of Cadiz through the Straits of Gibraltar into the Mediterranean. But they hoped to catch their foes unawares if they did venture out, by maintaining the quiet vigilance noted by George: 'The remainder part of the week we kept out of sight of land having the inshore squadron left to watch the motions of the enemy with the repeating frigates between us.'

It was not long before this watchfulness was rewarded for 'on the nineteenth the signal was made to our Commander in Chief that the enemy had put to sea.' Events moved quickly after this as the British Fleet, consisting of twenty-seven ships of the line, supported by other vessels, made all sail towards Gibraltar and stationed itself off Cape Trafalgar to await the enemy. Its readiness for action is indicated in a laconic exchange George witnessed between his captain and Lord Nelson just before midnight on 20 October:

We drifted alongside the Commander in Chief when we were hailed by his Lordship who accosted us thus, 'What ship'? The Captain answered 'Polyphemus', when his Lordship said 'Redmill, I suppose we shall have a warm day tomorrow', when the Captain answered 'I hope so my Lord.'

Captain Redmill did not log this conversation, but as the next day dawned with 'fresh breezes' he recorded the sight of 'the Enemy's Fleet consisting of thirty-three sail of the line ahead on the starboard tack'.[19] Meanwhile, marines and seamen alike prepared for action:

On the morning at 4 o'clock the 21st October the larboard [port] watch was called and we then retired to our hammocks. I had scarcely covered myself when the signal was made the French Fleet were in sight. The signal was answered and immediately the hammocks were piped up. We were then entirely fit for action as our tables, stools, clothing bags were continually in the cable tiers. .... At eight o'clock we piped the breakfast it being Monday Banyan [meatless] Day. The most part ate their dinner for breakfast and each man was served with half a pint of wine.

As well as fortifying himself in this way, George observed the prelude to what has gone down in history as the Battle of Trafalgar. He saw the British Fleet forming its famous two lines; he witnessed Nelson's signal 'that England expects every man will his duty'; he joined in when 'three hurrahs were given by the ship's company'; and he had a 'beautiful view of the combined fleets which had formed a crescent'.

Because *Polyphemus* was one of the smallest vessels in the fleet she was positioned towards the rear of the lee, or southernmost British column. Thus 'all hands were on deck to see the commencement of the Battle' as its leading ships sliced through the enemy line. Although accounts of Trafalgar differ in detail, George's narrative accords well with Redmill's log and with other eyewitness reports:

> About ten minutes to twelve the Royal Sovereign bearing the flag of Collingwood commenced action by running under the stern of a Spanish three decker and a French eighty [guns] by pouring in a few broadsides into the stern of one and the bow of the other. She then shot ahead and luff'd on the starboard tack close alongside the Spanish three decker and was hard at it. The remaining twelve ships in the lee line began to get within gunshots of the enemy which threw many a broadside away in waste, and shots falling short of our ships.

George points here to a decisive advantage the British Fleet had over an enemy which outnumbered it in ships and men. Its gun crews were better trained in rapid and accurate fire, and well fitted to act on the exhortation given on *Polyphemus* that morning 'not to throw their shots away in waste and to behave gallantly'. Even so, much of the fire levelled at *Royal Sovereign*, and the vessels which followed close on, did find its mark, inflicting carnage invisible to George. A nearer witness was another young marine, Paul Nicolas, a 16-year-old from a prominent Cornish naval family who had reached lieutenant rank on HMS *Belleisle*, the second ship in Collingwood's column: 'My eyes were horror-struck at the bloody corpses around me, and my ears rang with the shrieks of the wounded and the moans of the dying.' The frightened boy was naturally inclined to lie down as ordinary seamen were ordered to do, but he steeled himself to act as an officer by pacing the deck as an example of courage. Before the day was over, thirty-three of the *Belleisle*'s crew were dead and ninety-three wounded, while the vessel itself had been reduced to 'a mere hulk covered in wreck' – but Lieutenant Nicolas lived to tell his tale.[20]

It was another hour-and-a-half before *Polyphemus* drew near to the enemy, 'five places behind her prearranged position', and there was some suspicion that Captain Redmill had not sailed the ship with the speed of which she was capable.[21] In any case, 'all hands were piped to quarters' and she soon became engaged with two French ships, 'L'Achille on the starboard side and the Swiftsure on the larboard side'. George worked and fought alongside his fellow seamen rather than fulfilling the duties officially assigned to marines in battle: providing small-arms fire with muskets and acting as sentries to prevent sailors deserting their posts. As a marine lieutenant noticed during the battle, 'There was no distinguishing Marine from Seaman, all were working like horses.'[22] Manning one of the ship's sixty-four cannons, George was no longer in a position to observe the conflict:

> There not being sufficient wind to carry away the smoke, we could hardly see the ship we was engaging. At this time the Battle was general. It being a very warm sultry day we stripped ourselves to trousers only and blazed away for three hours. I being quartered at the second gun on the Forecastle, I alternately looked over the gangway to see the position of the two fleets but the smoke prevented me. ... To give any accurate description of the Battle is impossible but at the close of the firing I once more peeped over the Larboard Hammock netting and the smoke clearing away I could perceive a number of ships, both of us and the enemy totally dismasted and all appeared to be in confusion.

Firing ceased at about five in the afternoon. By this time the capture or destruction of eighteen French and Spanish ships had determined the outcome of the battle, the critical factor being, as historians confirm, 'the crushing superiority of British gunnery tactics'.[23] Thus George King had played his part in the famous victory – though it was the twelve leading ships which had inevitably borne the brunt of the fighting. They also suffered most of the casualties: 1,260 dead and wounded out a total of 1,690. *Polyphemus*'s log records 'two men killed and four wounded',[24] a low toll, which explains why George's account does not convey the visions of hell seen on the gun decks and in the cockpits of forward vessels. But as the day drew to an end, he witnessed rather more of the losses suffered by both sides:

> About six o'clock the L'Achille blew up with a tremendous explosion burying all the slain and wounded but previous to that the Entreprenante cutter and Pickle schooner had saved several hundred from a watery grave. Two hundred French prisoners were put on board the Polyphemus and placed down in the Cable Tiers with sentinels over them. The Commander in Chief being slain, Admiral Collingwood shifted his flag from the Royal Sovereign into the Euryalis frigate and at this time it commenced to blow a fresh breeze. The action having terminated the ship's company was employed in repairing damages and securing the ship.

The promptness and calm with which English sailors resumed normal duties as soon as the fighting was over amazed their opponents. A French captain, who saw another crew set to work just as George describes, wondered 'what the English seamen could be made of', and admitted that 'all our seamen were either drunk or disabled'.[25] With stray enemy vessels still firing and a storm brewing, George and his messmates received no respite or refreshment until after midnight, and even then his rest was not exactly undisturbed:

> Having nothing but water since eight o'clock in the morning we first jumped on the booms and pitched into the first bread bag we came athwart and began to eat bread and cheese, or meat if any. Then piped to supper with the lashings of the guns not secured. Every man on board was provided with a cutlass and brace of pistols ... and received his half pint of wine. ... We did not pipe the Hammocks down but plank'd it being exceptionally tired. I laid down in my mess berth and soon fell asleep first securing my brace of pistols but in turning about in my sleep, one of the pistols flashed

in the pan with the muzzle direct in my left arm pit which, I may thank Providence, did not go off otherwise it might have cost my life. At four o'clock we relieved the Larboard watch and commenced cleaning the quarters and main deck.

Over the next seven days a terrible storm raged, creating chaotic conditions in which many enemy vessels escaped their captors, only to be wrecked in the rocky approaches to Cadiz harbour. Meanwhile British ships suffered more damage than the battle had inflicted. In the midst of all this *Polyphemus* was given the honour of taking *Victory* in tow, so that Nelson's body (preserved in a cask of brandy) could be borne home as he had requested. George describes in more detail than the ship's log the difficult business of 'the stump of her foremast [being] made fast to our mainmast' with 'the gale still increasing'. After only a few days, however, he records that 'we were obliged to cast the Victory adrift or else she would have torn our stern post out', an account verified by the captain's log: 'At 6 cut the tow rope for the preservation of both ships.' George does not mention that a seaman 'fell overboard and was drowned', one of 2,000 Trafalgar survivors to die in the storm, despite valiant efforts to save the crews of sinking ships.[26]

Sailing in company with HMS *Neptune*, which had taken over the honourable encumbrance, *Polyphemus* proceeded to Gibraltar towing the French *Swiftsure*, one of the four remaining prizes, and holding her crew on board as prisoners.[27] On Sunday 3 November 'we anchor'd at the Rock where most of our Fleet had arrived to repair damages, and a beautiful sight it was.' Gibraltar's harbour must indeed have looked beautiful in comparison with the Bay of Cadiz, which an English observer described as 'covered with masts and yards, the wrecks of ships and here and there the bodies of the dead.'[28] But George's choice of words reflects also the general feeling of joy at the outcome of this battle. James Martin, one of the few other ordinary seamen to write an account of Trafalgar, described it as 'the Most Brilliant and Decisetive in the Annals of Naviel Glory'.[29] Though it certainly did not end the war, it removed any chance that Napoleon would cross the Channel and established Britain's dominance at sea for well over a century.

* * *

By the time George reached the safety of Gibraltar he was nearing the eighteenth anniversary of his Foundling Hospital baptism. His childhood was over and he was to spend the rest of his working life at sea. As Emidy had found, sailors were rarely allowed to set foot on shore for as long as the war lasted, lest they should be tempted to desert – though, in truth, there was little likelihood of that in George's case. With no home fires to draw him and no family or friends to rejoice at his safe arrival, he felt 'like a lost sheep' on land, especially after he learnt of the death of his 'dear friend Rivington'. He was happiest in the company of his shipmates.

After Trafalgar, Private King took part in all the activities the navy still had to conduct against France and her allies. Still aboard *Polyphemus*, he spent months watching the French fleet in the Channel and in the Mediterranean. This tedium would sometimes be broken by the signal for 'a general chase' if the enemy escaped, and by the capture of lucrative prizes. On his next ship, HMS *Melpomene*, he conveyed troops, equipment and provisions to South America and escorted merchant ships to the West Indies. And he helped to break the Continental System, by which all the European countries under Napoleon's control took part in a trade embargo against Britain. Thus in 1809, *Melpomene* was involved in two battles in the Baltic Sea where she was part of a squadron protecting British merchant ships against attack by Denmark and Russia. In the first engagement in May, later depicted in a dramatic painting,[30] she was attacked at midnight by twenty large Danish gunboats:

> They formed nearly a crescent on our larboard side when their Commodore hoisted a blue light in their centre. They commenced firing into us and kept up an incessant fire nearly to two o'clock. It being very dark, we could not discern how to point our guns except from the flash of their guns, their boats mounting two long thirty-two pounders and carrying eighty men in each. We expected that they would have boarded us. We suffered greatly from their grape and canister having cut away nearly all the larboard tower, shrouds and every topsail tye and nearly all the running rigging made us a complete riddle and having lost number killed and wounded about forty.

By morning the Danish ships had returned to shore and *Melpomene* had saved both herself and the merchant ships in her vicinity, but at the cost George so vividly depicts.

Two months later he was in even greater danger when he volunteered for a night raid on Russian gunboats anchored in Karlscrona harbour. 270 sailors set off in several cutters, all equipped with a case of rum, biscuits and small arms – or in the case of one 'desperate character' known as Bolt the Robber, a newly sharpened cook's axe which 'he intended to sink in the back of a bloody Russian'. In the fighting which ensued, six Russian gunboats were taken as well as merchant ships 'laden with pork and brandy', but at the expense of fifty British deaths. George does not shrink from describing the slaughter, which was worse than anything he had witnessed at Trafalgar:

> The Captain's coxswain was close along side of me. His head was blown clean off his shoulder, part of his head took my hat and his brain flew all over me. … On our boat arriving outside the harbour, we met with three gigs with the surgeons in them. They commenced using their tourniquets where it was required and dispatched us off to the Prometheus sloop of war which ship we reached about seven o'clock, but before we reached her, one of the Implacable's men having both his legs off close to his knee was laying down in the bottom of the boat being in such misery, had got his knife out of his pocket and opened it and was going to cut his belly right athwart but we took the knife from him. He then begged that we would heave him overboard. However before we reached the sloop he had drawn his last [breath].… About ten o'clock we regained our frigate and the Captain asked us if we could guess our loss. We said 'No'. He then ordered us a glass of grog each and the purser took us all down to his cabin and gave each of us a tumbler full of Hollands gin. I drank it off and went and laid down in my berth under the table and was soon fast asleep and never woke till the hammocks were piped up the following morning not having been disturbed or called upon to keep any watch the ensuing night.

Tots of rum and tumblers of gin were not the only rewards for the valour of ordinary sailors. To be sure, victory medals were normally presented only to admirals and captains, though after Trafalgar the engineer Matthew Boulton struck 15,000 commemorative decorations at his own expense to be awarded to surviving common seamen. If George received one of the tin medals he would have had to abide by the Admiralty's ban on its being worn on naval uniform. Many recipients were no doubt more interested in the large amounts of prize money paid after such battles. George's memoir carefully records the sums paid out by agents: 'six pounds and some odd shillings' for three Spanish ships; 'twenty-seven pounds six shillings each man for the capture of the Galleon Santa Gertruyda', and 'payment from another Agent amounting to seven pounds three shillings each'; 'four English Guineas for the capture of the frigates taken off Rochefort'; 'five pounds eighteen shillings and sixpence prize money for my former ship'; 'prize money for the galliot [flat-bottomed ship] taken that cruise amounting to ten pounds three shillings a foremast man and also eleven pounds eleven shillings for the gun boat and merchant ships'; 'no more than three pounds each man' for a few small prizes. After 1812, however, George mentions only his normal wages – the glory days were over.

Of course these were paltry sums compared to the fortunes gained by navy captains during the war, though some ordinary seamen were no doubt able to 'fulfil their dream of buying an inn and retiring on the proceeds'.[31] But most lacked the means and the worldly experience to save money and this was especially true of a foundling like George. He had no address to which he could send his cash, no experience of banks and no safe place in which to store his money on board ship. He also lacked the remarkable foresight and prudence possessed by the even more disadvantaged Joseph Emidy. During his very first period of shore leave the gullible George was robbed by 'ground sharks', after which he devised the scheme of 'ripping open the collar of my jacket and spreading the notes smoothly, always carrying a needle and a bit of thread inside my jacket as old saying is "once bit twice shy"'. Nevertheless, it was all too tempting simply to spend the money either on purchases from the 'Jews and other harpies' who thronged on board 'ready to swallow us up for the sake of easing us of our hard earnings', or by going on 'a regular spree' with his shipmates when allowed ashore. Sometimes he bought himself luxuries like 'a watch and two seals', or clothes 'which appeared very fine', until a more careful inspection might reveal that he had, for example, 'given eighteen shillings for a blue jacket with black sleeves in it'. Usually, though, rum, tobacco and 'doxies' swallowed up George's prize money and indeed led him into borrowing at an interest rate of 'five shillings extra for each pound', or selling some of his few possessions. At least he did not resort to the measures taken by one shipmate:

> He went with a petition round the lower deck stating that he had received a letter from his mother what had stated to him that she had lost her spotted cow, and he, being generally beloved, commenced making a subscription when in the course of the day after the grog being served out, accumulated about twenty pounds but whether he ever purchased another spotted cow for his mother I cannot tell.

As this story suggests, there was much genuine comradeship among crew members who often enjoyed less extravagant pleasures together: catching gurnards off Rochefort or mackerel off St Helena, 'singing some of Charly Dibdin's songs and dancing to the fife', 'going through the usual custom of shaving by Neptune and his Tritons' when crossing the equator, enjoying the 'beautiful sight of the comet' off Corvo Island, feasting off eggs, bread and wine on the island of Paros, or being applauded for the performance of three melodramas in honour of the governor of Malta. George remembered in particular his time on HMS *Orlando*, with an agreeable captain and an 'easy station', as 'the happiest days of my life'.

Orlando was George's last posting of the Napoleonic Wars but after the peace he was involved in one further operation against Britain's old enemy. In May 1816 he 'hoisted the flag of Rear Admiral Sir Pulteney Malcolm' aboard HMS *Newcastle* and made sail for St Helena. The vessel was part of a squadron 'sailing round the island in opposite directions' to prevent the Emperor's escape from his South Atlantic prison.[32] Between these patrols there was time for other activities. In the autumn of 1815 British sailors had been detailed to prepare Longwood House for occupation by Napoleon and his entourage. Now, as George records in his autobiography, Admiral Malcolm 'sent a party on shore to assist in the storehouses, each man receiving one shilling per day'. During the 1840s George gave more colour to this account when talking to Morris

Lievesley, Secretary of the Foundling Hospital, who recorded: 'Painters were wanted for Long Wood and to get on shore George designated himself a painter. He was sent on shore and Bonaparte took great notice of him and he frequently talked to him.'[33]

Was George spinning an ancient mariner's yarn, or was he adding authentic details which he omitted from his memoir? A reliable contemporary account confirms that Longwood remained 'in want of repair' during 1816 and that workmen were constantly employed in the house. Admiral Malcolm even dispatched one contingent of seamen to pitch a tent for Napoleon 'twenty paces from his house'.[34] It is not hard to believe that the bored Emperor, who was taking English lessons from his companion Las Cases, seized the opportunity to converse with a friendly and intelligent seaman who was painting his house. The experience on St Helena probably explains why George acted as a painter on some of his later ships and tried several times to find similar employment ashore. He also described himself as a painter (as well as a seaman and marine) when applying to enter Greenwich Hospital.[35] Such circumstantial evidence cannot prove the intriguing story of George's encounter with the exiled Emperor but, in view of the trustworthiness of his memoir, it is entirely plausible.

* * *

As well as the diminution of his income as the years went by, George suffered from the ailments common among seamen. He was struck down with yellow fever in Havana and with dysentery in Malta, from where he had to be 'invalided for a change of climate'. Several times after the war he was sent to hospital with typhus fever or with severe pains in his legs caused, he was told, by 'nodes on the shin bones'. Even so, he still relished shipboard life, which was just as well since his attempts to find employment in London as a confectioner failed, 'in consequence of being so many years from the business'. Occasionally he was able to put to use the skills he had been taught at the Foundling Hospital. On a voyage to South America in 1819 on board the *Owen Glendower*, for example, he had 'the means of gaining numbers of Spanish dollars being employed by several young gentlemen, midshipmen, to write their quarter watch and station bills for them and logs. Lord Edward Russell, Honble Mr. Ryder, Honble Mr. Anson and Honble Mr. Talbot … paid me well for my trouble.' Two of these idle but 'fortunate youths' were among those castigated by William Cobbett for the ease with which their aristocratic connections enabled them to be promoted 'in surprisingly quick time'.[36]

Lacking connections of any kind, Foundling 18053 was never able to progress from the lowest rank despite his skilled penmanship. But he did attempt to establish a family life for himself. He was afforded an example by his old school fellow, James Gardner, whom he met again in 1818, when they shared 'a glass or two together' in Bow Street. James had clearly left the sea and was married, but George does say how he was earning his living. He stayed with the couple in their Fetter Lane lodgings for three weeks, during which time he and James 'visited our old school', only to discover that 'our old schoolmaster had gone to sleep'. Since Atchison's memorial plaque in the old Foundling Hospital's chapel was dated 1818, this must mean that the 'diligent and affectionate master', the closest George had ever had to a father, had recently died.[37] The Gardners made George welcome several more times over the next few years when he was at a loose end between ships.

It may have been this experience of domesticity, impoverished though it probably was, that inspired George to get married himself on 4 March 1825. He was in the Cove of Cork at that time and in pretty good fettle, having been cured of his leg pains and paid prize-money for his part in successful anti-smuggling exercises. George does not name his wife or give their address, and the marriage does not appear in any surviving Cork registers, so that the rover's chance of coming 'home from the sea' remains a tantalising mirage.[38] It seems that he wanted to settle in Cork for, as he explains, he had served in the Royal Navy for nearly twenty-one years, after which he was entitled to an increase in the £10 annual sum he already received as a Greenwich out-pensioner on account of his ill health.[39] But a sailor's life rarely went according to plan. He remained in Cork for about three years, carrying out harbour duties and capturing smuggling vessels laden with tobacco, for which he received paltry prize money. In June 1828 he got the opportunity to complete his twenty-one years' service by joining HMS *Windsor Castle* dispatched 'to watch the Russian fleet' in the Mediterranean.[40] By the time he got back to Cork in

January 1831 his wife had died. Granted four days' compassionate leave, he visited his 'late wife's father and mother', and then spent 'two days carousing' with some shipmates: 'The whole of the Square being public houses, we were not at a loss for whisky punch [of] which we had our fill.' There is no mention of any surviving children so that his in-laws were the only family George had left. Whenever he sailed into the Cove of Cork he would seek them out and visit his 'old home', the only one he'd had since leaving his wet nurse at the age of 4.

The year 1831 was a particularly restless one for George. He was posted to one more assignment on the *Windsor Castle* 'to protect English property' during the Portuguese Civil War and was then paid off. After going ashore at Plymouth in a 'half fuddled' state, he and some shipmates treated themselves to 'an excellent dinner with plenty of grog', during which most of his friends departed, leaving him 'to pay the score'. The next few months were spent travelling (always with his 'bag of clothes') by coach and steamer between London, Bristol, Bath and Cork in search of naval or mercantile employment. November found him in Liverpool, so short of funds that he was living on 'one penny worth of potatoes every evening'. Eventually he was taken on as a steward on board the *Celia*, recently returned from transporting convicts to Australia and now bound for Charleston with six American passengers, all of whom tipped him handsomely on arrival. George's fortunes had taken a turn for the better – and indeed America was about to give him the chance of a new life.

Despite the captain warning him not to jump ship because 'a rolling stone gathers no moss', George did not return on the *Celia* but set off to explore South Carolina. In the course of his travels a new acquaintance asked if he would like to be a teacher in a school which had just been built in Walterborough: 'my heart lept at that proposal and I was very thankful.'[41] Thus, in February 1832, he was approved by the committee and took up the post at a salary of $200 a year. His job was to teach twenty-two children 'as well as grown persons', and he soon made himself at home in the small community – fishing and hunting with other inhabitants, attending the annual fair ('which consisted of one continual feast and excessive drinking and dancing day and night'), and being invited to a wedding (with 'an excellent supper, a profusion of every description and the room beautifully arranged with lights'). Yet, even though he was offered a salary rise if he stayed for a year, George was clearly unable to put down roots. He spent the summer vacation roaming around the state, encountering floods, alligators and 'firing from some of the Negroes from a rice plantation' – but also imbibing plenty of grog, whisky and porter. Back in Charleston he decided to take the first ship he could get for Liverpool. So, accompanied by his bag of clothes, he went on board the *Thule*. He really was a rolling stone which had not gathered much moss or, as the captain might more appropriately have put it, a piece of driftwood on the ocean of life.

George worked his passage across the Atlantic on this leaking brig in strong winds: 'we were continually two hours at the helm and two hours at the pumps ... [but] there was no stints of anything whatever, plenty of provisions and plenty of grog.' So he still had some dollars left when he arrived back in England in July 1832, and what is more, he was now entitled to £16 a year pension – which was roughly equal to a labourer's wage. This was not exactly generous, but it would have been just enough for a prudent and frugal 45-year-old bachelor to live on – especially if he had saved some of his prize money. Robert Atchison, by comparison, accrued over £350 to bequeath to his sisters, nephews and nieces, admittedly after receiving an annual salary of £50 a year from the Foundling Hospital.[42] George, however, was not one to garner his resources; after receiving a £12 pension instalment he cheerfully squandered the best part of it with his late wife's friends in Cork before working his passage to Liverpool to look for yet another ship.

*   *   *

A hard voyage lay ahead on the *William Mulvey*, a merchant brig bound for Italy. Unable to put in at Genoa, probably because the city was stricken with plague or cholera, she was ordered to the *lazaretto* port of La Spezia to spend three weeks in quarantine. There the crew landed their cargo of iron bars before proceeding to Terra Nova on the south coast of Sicily, described in a contemporary merchants' handbook as abounding in 'inexhaustible quantities' of yellow brimstone dug up from its volcanic mountains.[43] George and his shipmates stowed away 100 tons of this dangerous substance, which had many commercial uses apart from being administered with treacle to the boys of Dotheboys Hall. At Palermo half the brimstone had to be offloaded to another vessel and replaced with a more agreeable cargo of oranges, wine and sumac – an exotic spice still popular with modern cooks. At least the sailors were allowed shore leave during the two months spent in this port – though for George this pleasure was marred by his being robbed.

Boisterous weather and contrary winds made the homeward journey a 'tedious and wet passage of fifty three days' instead of the normal twenty, and worst of all, the crew 'received no grog from the captain [and] were now put upon allowance of pork having no more than two casks in the ship and not a piece of beef.' All their bunks and bedding were wet through by the time they docked but, in any case, George explains: 'I never turned into my bed again [for] a period of thirty-six days but used to get a nap as well as I could.' He had had enough. Back in Liverpool harbour at the end of March 1833, he threw his hammock overboard, gave away his blanket and rug and, after being paid for the voyage, took 'a parting glass' with his shipmates, telling them that his sea career of twenty-seven years was over. 'We got pretty groggy before we separated.'

Now George faced the prospect of surviving on his £16 pension. But a lifetime of having meals, accommodation, routine and companionship provided first by Captain Coram's foundation, and then by ships' captains, had not equipped him for managing on his own. Much of a further £12 pension payment was soon spent on a 'bowse out' in Cork and a working passage to London was followed by wandering about, taking lodgings in the Borough, and a fortnight's inactivity. After that George pulled himself together and tried to find an additional source of income. He made inquiries at Somerset House, but found that only a small sum of prize money was still due to him; he met by chance a former captain who tried to get him into the new Metropolitan Police, where he was found to be half an inch too short (though he was not sorry to be rejected by this unpopular force); he sought help from Neville Browne, a City Marshal and son of his old master, who barely recognised him and had nothing to offer. Not knowing how to last out until his pension became due, he felt 'completely lost for the want of a friend'.

It was late June by this time and George decided to 'have a trial at haymaking'. It was not a good year to be joining the ranks of seasonal day labourers. Declining real wages, enclosure, and the new threshing machines had exacerbated rural poverty, and in 1830 and 1831 'half-starved yokels' in many parts of the country 'rose at last against their hard masters and smashed the agricultural machines, and burnt ricks' in the so-called Swing riots. 'Oppression had made them mad' in the opinion of W.H. Hudson, who recorded memories of these years in Wiltshire.[44] George probably knew nothing of this, or of the harsh punitive measures which followed, and he was to find only good fellowship in the hay meadows of Middlesex. On his way there he fell in with two fellow seekers of work and 'gave each of them a pint of Porter', which cheered them all up. His generosity was repaid when, having nearly been dismissed for not being able to wield a pitchfork, he was instructed by one of his new friends. The three stayed together until early July when 'all the hay was carted', earning 'two shillings each night and one pint of strong beer each' at Stamford Hill, or a little more at Squire Gray's in Hornsey, and sleeping in the haycocks. Luckily for George, the remaining £4 of his pension was now due so that he was able both to reward his helpful friend with 'two or three pots of ale and half a crown', and to pay the rent at his lodgings.

For some months after that George would rise early and proceed to the West India Docks, but he always found 'above a hundred men on the same pursuit' and never got more than a few days' work. Reduced to one shilling in his pocket, he set out in September 1834 to try his luck in the hop gardens of Kent. Despite their reputation for drunkenness and 'cottage robbery', he soon struck up friendships among the gangs of 'miserable lean wretches' whom Charles Dickens saw every autumn, dragging themselves along the roads and sleeping under hedges near his house in Rochester.[45] With 'a farmering man ... looking for that same employ', George slept in barns, nervously stole windfall apples from the local parson's orchard, and shared a 'half of a two-pound loaf', until they found places on a hop farm. Here he buckled to under Mr Ellis, who arrived in his carriage and read out the rules from 'a platform erected for the purpose'.[46] Then he clubbed together with an old soldier's wife and her daughter, who made him coffee every morning and evening and cooked an improvised Irish stew on Saturdays. At night everyone 'slept in one hop house upon beds of straw – men, women and children all huddled together' – no wonder Cobbett on his 'Rural Rides' rarely encountered 'such an assemblage of rags' as he saw 'among the hoppers at Farnham'.[47] George himself had only the clothes he stood up in, but he washed his shirt in the river every Sunday, hanging it on the bushes – and taking care not to let it out of his sight until it was dry. With not even a blanket to his name, he could not afford to risk losing anything. Nor did the three weeks of picking help to restore his fortunes, for he had made 'only a bad harvest' and had only a balance of 4*s* 6*d* due to him at the end.

By the time he arrived back in London, having bought refreshment at the Black Bull and a new pair of shoes for his blistered feet, George had one shilling in his pocket. Getting 'trust for what I wanted', he managed to last out until Pension Day in early October, when he 'refitted' himself and moved to new lodgings on Ratcliffe Highway. This was the main thoroughfare which ran from Wapping to Limehouse through the area known in the 1830s as London's sailortown, 'charged and laden with the atmosphere of the ocean and a suggestion of things far off'. George must have felt at home among its constantly changing population of mariners, catered for by plenty of public houses and brothels.[48] He clearly spent money on some such low entertainment, for he was soon embarked on a renewed search for dockyard employment. Despite visiting Sir John Hall, the 'indefatigable Secretary of the St Katherine's Dock Company',[49] and producing 'certificates and characters received from the several captains of ships of war', he never got more than a few weeks' work. He attributed this to his not 'feeing the foreman who takes the person on for employment', but in truth he was probably overlooked in favour of younger, fitter men. For this ageing mariner there seemed to be no 'prospect of getting constant work'.

He had one final recourse. Greenwich Hospital, the Crown Charity established in 1694 for Royal Navy seamen 'who, by reason of age, wounds, or other disabilities, shall be incapable of further service at sea, and be unable to maintain themselves', provided not only out-pensions such as George had been receiving, but also a refuge in its elegant riverside buildings designed by Wren and Hawksmoor. As a veteran of Trafalgar, George stood a good chance of being taken in, especially during the governorship of Vice-Admiral Sir Thomas Hardy (1834–9), the former captain of the *Victory* who famously kissed Nelson on his deathbed. Even so, he had to apply several times among 'upwards of three hundred applicants waiting for admission', before the following addition was made to the record of Outpensioners Admitted in the dying days of 1834: 'Name George King; Reason Worn Out; Period Life; Number 1352'.[50] George himself records:

> I immediately set off accompanied by another man and arrived then at four o'clock and went to the Main Guard [at Greenwich Hospital], produced the note and was placed on the books upwards of seven years since, and thus ends the sequel of my story.[51]

He was to spend his old age as he had spent his childhood, housed, fed, clothed and disciplined in a charitable institution.

* * *

Since George ended his life story with his admission to Greenwich Hospital, it is hard to be sure of how he reacted to the routine shown in contemporary records, rulebooks and reports. Not being much used to home cooking, he probably did not object to monotonous dinners of boiled beef or mutton, even if they were 'ill adapted to the toothless mouths and feeble digestions of the great body of our veterans' – though his earlier comments on naval fare suggest that he would not have welcomed the Medical Officer's recommendation that pork should be served twice a week. Like other old sailors, George was at home with the hospital's system of serving food in 'messes' and no doubt, too, he approved of the daily allowance of four pints of small beer produced in its own brewery. And on Festival Days, he had the chance to relive his sprees of former years when this was replaced with strong ale, thus, in the words of the Medical Officer, 'legalising debauchery, the effects of which are well known and to none better than the nurses in the infirmary who are always prepared for a number of "festival fits"'.[52]

There were, of course, penalties for such behaviour – though pensioners were not flogged as they would have been on board His Majesty's ships. Until the 1830s miscreants had to wear special yellow coats and do menial duties, but by George's time this system had been abolished on the recommendation of William IV, the 'sailor-king', who thought it unworthy of 'Greenwich heroes'. If George got drunk, he would have been deprived of his beer allowance, fined or restricted to the hospital. As these punishments suggest, Greenwich inmates had an allowance of money – though one shilling a week did not go as far as it had when it was introduced in 1704. They could also leave the premises, as long as they were 'clean in their persons' and decently dressed in their uniforms of blue coats and waistcoats, trousers (replacing the breeches which in King William's opinion were not 'Navy clothes') and round black hats (the old cocked hats being reserved for Sundays).[53] Thus George would no doubt repair with his 'tobacco money' to the riverside Trafalgar Tavern, built by the hospital in 1837.

Inside the hospital premises there was not a great deal for the 2,000 or so pensioners to do. They had few duties beyond mounting guard at the gates once a fortnight though some acted as 'boatswains' and 'mates', receiving extra pocket money in return for supervising the men's halls and bed-cabins. Pensioners could spend time and even eat meals in their own cabins, which were often 'filled with small prints' and other mementoes from far-off lands.[54] Or, boasted a visitor's guidebook, they could mingle and smoke their pipes in 'a commodious piazza', or spend time in the library 'containing about 1,500 well selected volumes [and] supplied with daily and weekly newspapers'.[55] The visitors using this guide flocked (as they still do) to view Wren's splendid buildings and especially the Painted Hall, which contained at that time many Nelson relics and paintings donated to the hospital. But was this grand palace suitable accommodation for the rough-and-ready old salts who thronged its long galleries and spacious colonnades?

In 1857 a Royal Commission was set up to answer this question. It was prompted by a sharp decline in the number of inmates during the 1850s as more ancient mariners chose to live on their out-pensions rather than enter its precincts. It concluded that the hospital offered pensioners 'a dull and dreary monastic existence', lacking 'everything that enlivens and endears a home', so that 'debauchery is their only resource against ennui'. The First Lord of the Admiralty added his opinion that pensioners found the place 'intolerably wearisome', and passed 'their days in a state of listless idleness and mental vacuity [and] resort to the ale-house or to worse places'. All agreed that it should be abolished and the charity's funds devoted to increasing out-pensions.[56] And this is what happened; the institution which had provided George King with a refuge closed its doors in 1865, eight years after his death.

Yet there is no indication that he shared in the dissatisfaction noted by the commissioners. After an institutional childhood and a long shipboard career, George was used to a plain diet, strict regulation and the absence of loved ones. The years between his retirement from the sea and his entry into Greenwich had been lonely and anxious. Once there, he no longer had to worry about where the next meal was coming from, he could step out freely with a little money in his pocket, and he had constant companionship. From the Foundling Hospital he brought not only the resilience to cope with a cheerless routine, but also an education which could help him to rise above it. We can picture him spending time in the library, musing over memories (and quite possibly diaries) of his many voyages in times of war and peace. Presiding over the room was a statue of Charles Dibdin, which may have inspired the title George wrote at the head of the memoir he completed in 1842, seven years after entering the hospital: Ben Block. This name appears in several Dibdin songs, as well as in contemporary plays and prints, to personify the veteran British sailor: a 'staunch' and 'sturdy' character, 'as honest as e'er biscuit broke', fond of beef and a 'jorum of grog', a brave gunner's mate who has fought for his king amid the 'cannon's loud roar' before reaching his 'Greenwich snug dock' among true messmates.[57] And these are just the characteristics which George reveals about himself in his autobiography – his life at sea had enabled the erstwhile foundling to reinvent himself.

Of George's physical appearance there is no record but he must be one of the 350 or so pensioners depicted in the *Illustrated London News* on 12 April 1845. The print shows 'an impressive ceremony' in the Painted Hall, where the veterans were presented (in the presence of the boys from Greenwich Royal Hospital School) with a medal commemorating the erection of Nelson's Column in Trafalgar Square in 1844: 'In addition to the Medal, each man received a sum of ten shillings.'[58] A couple of years later George heard that the Admiralty was to issue an official Naval General Service medal to all ranks of seamen who had participated in naval battles between 1793 and 1840. Over a thousand names were submitted by Greenwich Hospital, but few qualified for the two clasps on their medal which George received: one for Trafalgar and one for the capture of Russian boats on *Melpomene* in 1809.[59] It was the first time that the government had given recognition to the role of ordinary seamen.

George's unusual degree of literacy led to his being appointed as a governor's clerk, which no doubt brought payment and privileges.[60] It may have been this more elevated status which gave him the security to get married for a second time, necessitating his moving out of the hospital. The place and date of this marriage are as elusive as those for his Cork wedding, but the 1851 Census reveals that George King was living with his 45-year-old wife, Caroline, at 42 Thames Street, very close to the Greenwich Hospital. He is described as aged 63, born in Hemel Hempstead (the birthplace George believed to be his) and employed as Clerk of Greenwich Hospital chapel, details exact enough to identify him without any doubt. It is even possible that the couple had been together for over ten years, because the Census of 1841 lists George, a 50-year-old confectioner and his wife Caroline, 35, living at Aykman's Buildings Greenwich.[61] This offers a tantalising vision of George having a longer marriage and an independent trade, but the match is not close enough to be taken as reliable evidence. Even so, it is heartening to think that George spent some of his later years in a home of his own.

This domestic existence did not, however, last to the end of his days. Records disagree on the exact date, but testify that George King's death occurred in Greenwich Hospital in late July 1857.[62] Infirmity, widowerhood, or poverty may have driven him to repair to this sheltered abode just as his birth mother had sought refuge for him in another. But his precious manuscript survived whatever troubles afflicted him, so that he bequeathed to future generations an autobiography as illuminating and stirring as any admiral's memoir or novelist's tale of adventure.

Chapter 4

Othnel Mawdesley 1790–1812:
An Adventure in Spain

As part of his training as a naval officer, a midshipman had the chore of writing a daily log, recording navigational, geographical and climatic details of the voyage – often illustrated by alluring sketches of exotic coastlines. But it was seldom that he got the chance to tell an adventure story similar to those he had read as a child. This was the task that fell to a 17-year-old midshipman on HMS *Theseus*, Othnel Mawdesley, after he was made a prisoner of war by the Spanish in 1807 along with Acting Lieutenant Andrew Mitchell, twelve seamen and two marines. On paper hastily purchased in Spain and in clear handwriting remarkably similar to George King's, he recorded the circumstances of their capture, their treatment in enemy hands, their marches through Galicia, their attempts to escape and their eventual achievement of freedom. At some point this 14,000-word journal of 'Private Remarks during the time of being prisoner in Spain' was handed over to Mitchell, whose descendants treasured it for over 200 years. In 2016 its most recent owner, Bridget Somekh, asked my advice about what to do with this increasingly fragile manuscript. I transcribed it with mounting interest in the vivid account of a youth abruptly flung on to a hostile land after only eighteen months at sea. Eventually I suggested that the document should be passed into the safe hands of the National Maritime Museum, where it is now being expertly conserved and preserved. Othnel's story has never before seen the light of day.

There was nothing exciting or even naval about his origins – although he was born in Chester's Watergate, part of the old sailors' quarter. His father, the Rev. Thomas Mawdesley, was curate of Holy Trinity church, adjoining the Customs House which had once served a flourishing maritime trade. By the time of Othnel's birth on 29 April 1790, the River Dee had become less navigable so that many of the wharves and shipbuilding yards had fallen into disuse. In contrast to neighbouring ports and industrial towns like Liverpool and Manchester, Georgian Chester was a respectable social and administrative centre with a 'well established winter season'. The 'large resident gentry' and local landed families enjoyed frequenting its cathedral services, music festivals, shopping galleries, markets, fairs, Freemasons' lodges, May races, coffee houses and inns.[1] One of the city's main attractions was (and remains) a promenade around its Roman ramparts, which Othnel was to remember fondly when captive in Lugo, a Spanish town 'wall'd entirely around in the same manner as Chester'.[2]

When Othnel was 4 years old the Rev. Mawdesley was appointed Assistant Chaplain at St Peter's in the centre of Chester, a poor church like Holy Trinity, which could not provide an adequate living for its incumbent, let alone for a lowly curate or chaplain. Even St Oswald's, the parish where Mawdesley became vicar in 1803, had a benefice of only about £30 a year although there was a vicarage to accommodate the Mawdesley family, which by that time included three sons and two daughters. Such paltry clerical incomes would not have been enough to launch the boys on careers or enable the girls to enter Chester's fashionable society. Yet we know that the oldest son, Thomas, attended Brasenose, his father's old Oxford college, and entered the church in his turn, while Othnel and his younger brother Robert gained commissions in the Royal Navy and the King's Own Light Infantry respectively. Meanwhile the *Chester Chronicle* noted the attendance of the Misses Mary Ann and Frances Mawdesley at such events as the Chester Races, the Festival of Music and Ladies' Bazaars.[3] It seems that the family, which had owned Mawdesley Hall in Lancashire until 1737, still possessed some property, which is described (but not specified or valued) in Rev. Mawdesley's will as 'my real and personal estates'. These had become a fortune by 1891 when Frances, the last surviving member of a family which left no heirs, died as a spinster leaving about £10,000 to various friends and charities.[4] The family also had a coat of arms, featuring a chevron between three pickaxes, and forebears who bore Othnel's unusual name. Certainly there is no hint of deprivation in the midshipman's career or writing. Indeed, when he ran out of cash during his captivity and was forced to borrow from Lieutenant Mitchell, he 'felt this want most severely, having never been put to such a shift before'.

The confident style of the journal indicates a sound education but there is no record of where Othnel went to school. If the family adopted the common custom of the time, he and his brothers followed in their father's educational path. In that case, they attended the Tudor foundation described as Nowell School in Rev. Mawdesley's matriculation document.[5] More commonly known as Middleton Grammar School, it was generously endowed by former pupil and Brasenose graduate Robert Nowell, to provide 'for the free instruction of 200 scholars and for the maintenance of thirteen exhibitions from that school to Brasenose College'.[6] Thomas Mawdesley junior was probably one of the scholars who took up such an exhibition and it is likely that Othnel and Robert also made the 38-mile coach journey to Middleton and spent their school days as boarders in this silk-weaving market town to the north of Manchester.

What is not in doubt is that Rev. Mawdesley used his strong ecclesiastical connections to launch his middle son on a naval career at the rather late age of 16. His 'good friend', the Registrar of Chester Diocese, wrote to the 'venerable' Archbishop of York, William Markham, whose son John was both an admiral and an MP. In the event, Mawdesley was able to inform the admiral that he need take 'no farther trouble' since another 'worthy friend', Dean Hugh Cholmondeley, had procured Othnel's appointment as a midshipman with Captain George Hope on the 74-gun HMS *Theseus*.[7] In the ship's pay book the date of his arrival is recorded as 7 July 1806, his age (wrongly) as 17 and his first wages as £14 15s.[8]

It was a weathered and war-torn vessel that he joined. In 1797 she had been Nelson's flag-ship during the Battle of Santa Cruz, a costly defeat at which the admiral lost his right arm. A year later *Theseus* contributed to Nelson's decisive victory at the Nile, but in 1799 she caught fire and exploded during the Siege of Acre. The accident, caused apparently by a midshipman's tomfoolery, led to the death of the captain and many crew and the ship needed a complete refit. Further damage resulting from a hurricane in the Bahamas meant that *Theseus* was not present along with George King's *Polyphemus* at Trafalgar and was still under repair when Othnel went on board at Chatham. Once seaworthy she would be part of the Channel Fleet engaged in the vital task of blockading the windswept coasts of western France and northern Spain, both in the grip of Napoleon Bonaparte. It was a far cry from the comfortable solidity of Chester.

*   *   *

Othnel's movements over the coming months can be tracked through the daily log kept by the captain of *Theseus*. It recorded the ship's exact position, weather conditions, the state of supplies and any unusual incidents – but never any details about the crew, who were only mentioned by name if they received punishment or died. At the end of each voyage these log books were placed with the Admiralty so that they were (and still are) carefully preserved – unlike the rather more personal reports which the 'dutiful and affectionate' Othnel doubtless sent back to the Chester vicarage.[9] My exhaustive search of local records and attempts to trace the legatees of his last surviving sibling revealed no boxes of salt-stained letters.

By October he had certainly been put on his mettle. *Theseus* gave chase to several 'strange sail', captured and boarded one French frigate and took in prisoners from another. Nine sailors caught attempting to desert received twenty-four lashes each and two men died, their bodies being committed to the deep.[10] Even a raw midshipman like Othnel had to play his part in rigging sails, relaying messages, keeping watch, commanding small boats, supervising gun batteries and disciplining the men. With no previous experience of navigation or nautical astronomy, he had to learn quickly, aided when there was time by lessons from the captain. After three months at sea *Theseus* rounded the Lizard and put in at Plymouth where she sent off her prisoners, underwent further repairs and took on supplies before plying for Falmouth to set off on her next expedition.

It is unlikely that Midshipman Mawdesley or even Captain Hope understood what lay behind orders issued by the ironically nicknamed Ministry of All the Talents, which had come to power in February 1806 after the death of Pitt the Younger. It had no clear strategy for the defeat of Napoleon, who now controlled most of Europe, and distant naval officers 'were left to fend for themselves'.[11] *Theseus* was one of four naval warships despatched in November to accompany 4,000 troops under Sir Robert Crauford, who was issued with what has been described as 'one of the most extraordinary sets of instructions ever given to a British commander'. He was to sail around the Cape of Good Hope to Botany Bay and collect some of the marines guarding transported prisoners. Thus reinforced, he was to travel across the Pacific Ocean to attack Spanish seaports and fortresses on the west coast of South America. It seems that 'nobody in London was bothering about geography'.[12] Captain Hope's logbook demonstrates a quite different turn of events. *Theseus* reached the Cape Verde Islands in the mid-Atlantic on 14 December and was unaccountably moored there for a month, during which the crew was employed in painting the ship, before being ordered to sail southwards. By the time the squadron reached Cape Town on 26 February 1807, *Theseus* (and no doubt other ships) had been reduced to short bread rations. New dispatches now ordered Crauford to head straight across the Atlantic to South America but *Theseus*, it seems, was no longer needed as an escort. She departed from the Cape on 29 March for an uneventful homeward voyage of three months. This muddled expedition was not only futile, it had cost the lives of several seamen who had fallen overboard – a common accident on sailing vessels.

Othnel Mawdesley, however, was hale and hearty and also had full pockets after receiving two sums of around £20 in the course of 1807. These compared well with the normal wages of £2 8s a month for a midshipman on a third-rate ship such as *Theseus* and they suggest that the Rev. Mawdesley made his son an allowance. Such monies were normally paid to the captain's agent and issued in instalments, a sensible practice designed to 'check extravagance among the boys'.[13] It is unlikely that Othnel saw his family in the few weeks that passed before his ship embarked on another voyage now under the command of Captain Sir John Poo Beresford. *Theseus* was busily engaged over the next few months in enforcing the government's new Orders in Council, which outlawed trade with France or her allies. On 18 July, just two days out of Spithead, Beresford recorded actions against ships bound for French-controlled ports, which certainly involved Othnel and his fellow junior officers (who now included Midshipman Peter Richardson, a 16-year-old who also hailed from Chester).

At 1 Boarded a Danish Galiot from Marseilles bound to Copenhagen, detained ditto, sent one Petty Officer to take her to Portsmouth.

At 2 Boarded an American ship from Baltimore bound for Rotterdam.[14]

This was to be the pattern of events for the rest of that year.

By mid-August *Theseus* was stationed with a squadron off Cape Finisterre on the north-west coast of Spain. She was so near to the shore that her midshipmen would have been able to sketch Corunna's ancient lighthouse, known as the Tower of Hercules, Vigo's Castro fortress and Ferrol's mighty arsenal. These impressive defences guarded fine natural harbours in which floated Spanish and French battleships – for Britain's decisive victory at Trafalgar had not totally annihilated her enemies' fleets. It was currently Napoleon's aim to gain control of Britain's old ally, Portugal, whose navy and long coastline could contribute much to his aim of starving Britain into submission with a trade embargo. *Theseus* and her sister ships were strategically placed to thwart this strategy.

The logbook for the next four months records the boarding of fifteen merchant ships, often after a chase and exchange of shots. Such a long period at sea necessitated the risky task of watering the ship by sending small boats to enemy shores to collect supplies from local rivers and lakes. In December, British transport ships arrived off Finisterre with provisions such as flour, sugar, oatmeal, beer, lime juice, meat, butter and cheese, all of which had to be brought on board in launches. It was a busy time for young officers like Othnel, who directed all this activity, often amid Atlantic squalls and gales. Sometimes too they had to dish out punishment to recalcitrant seamen such as one Richard Warn, who received 'three dozen lashes for drunkenness, quarrelling and disobedience of orders' in August, and a further eighteen in November for 'insolence'.[15]

Theseus also had orders to destroy enemy ships if she got the chance, for Napoleon was already replacing some of those lost at Trafalgar. Two of the captain's terse entries describe an attempt to carry out such a mission in Vigo Bay:

1 November At 7.30 sent 2 cutters man'd & arm'd under the command of Lieuts Smith & Ready up to Vigo to destroy a French line of battleships lying there.

2 November At 1.30 the Boats got close to the ships but imagining the enemy were prepared to receive them, and being fired upon with small arms and great gun, they retreated & returned on board at 6 without receiving any damage.[16]

If, as is almost certain, Othnel was on one of these cutters he had a foretaste of the misadventure which was to befall him at the end of the following month.

* * *

Back in Vigo Bay on 28 December, Captain Beresford wrote an even less informative entry in his log book, recording simply that boats went out 'for watering' with 'the large cutter on Duty'. Overnight 'strong gales with heavy squalls of rain' aroused fears, when the cutter had not returned by morning, that 'she had been driven on shore'. It is only in Midshipman Mawdesley's 'Private Remarks' that the true purpose of the exercise and the fate of the cutter's crew are made clear:

Monday December 29th 1807
It being thought practicable by Captn Beresford to destroy a French line of battle ship laying above Vigo, preparations were accordingly made for that purpose, and at about 6.20 PM the following boats mann'd and arm'd left the ship. 1st Cutter Lieut Smith. 2nd Cutter Lieut Ready. 3 Mr Mitchell (Acting Lieut) in which boat I was myself. As it was our intention to set fire to the Frenchman [battleship] the one I was in had a great quantity of combustibles, also 2 chains which were intended to fasten the boat to the ships cable and leave her there....

The night was uncommonly dark and it now blew a gale with rain.... The tremendous sea then running and breaking on the rocks, added to the darkness of the night and the expectation of the boat going down every moment, render'd our situation most awful, and caus'd sensations, which those who have been in the like situation can alone conceive. ... By hard work we at last clear'd these dreadful rocks but had not a Good Providence aided us, I may well say our labour would have been in vain....

Daylight show'd us a prospect little better that the night.... We were now close to the town and had reason to expect the batteries would fire on us as soon as they made us out. It was the ardent wish of all the men to run her at once on the beach, heave all the arms etc overboard first, and to say we had been watering and driven on shore by the weather. This was soon done. Mr M. and myself tore our orders we had receiv'd from Captn Beresford but kept our swords. On our approaching the shore the alarm bell was rung and the beach was soon lined with soldiers, but such soldiers I never before saw. The boat was soon taken possession of and the whole of us (the men, Mr M & myself) marched by the soldiers with fix'd bayonets to a guardhouse.[17]

In contrast to the ship's official log, Othnel's story of the boat's capture enables us to hear a boy's voice – to understand his fear, to admire his sense of duty and to share in his excitement. The ensuing narrative is equally illuminating as we follow the adventures of two young officers, 17-year-old Othnel and the 20-year-old son of an admiral, Andrew Mitchell from Scotland, a Master's Mate who had been appointed acting lieutenant.[18]

Their experiences in Vigo also throw light on the situation of Spain at this time. They were 'strictly and separately examin'd' through an Irish interpreter about their reasons for being in the harbour but insisted that they had come in only to collect water for the ship. Whether or not the Spanish officers believed this fiction, they treated the two men honourably, recognising them as officers and gentlemen despite their youth and non-commissioned status – one even gave up his bed 'in a very polite manner'. The next day Lieutenant Smith was allowed to come ashore from the *Theseus* under a flag of truce to meet the two captives in the governor's house. He brought them cheering news of their shipmates' safety as well as some clothes and money, including a letter for Othnel 'from Messrs Hall and Blandford with 9½ guineas'. Over 'an elegant dessert of all kinds of drinks and wines' the governor explained with seeming reluctance that he could not release the prisoners as he had to defer to the captain general of Galicia, who was 'in Portugal with the Spanish army at present'. He did not mention (and probably did not even know about) the secret Treaty of Fontainebleau that Spain had recently signed with Napoleon authorising the passage of French troops into Portugal and dividing that country between them.

Since there are few other first-hand accounts of Britons captured by Spain during its 'parasitic alliance' with France, it is difficult to judge whether the generosity with which Othnel and his companions were treated in Vigo was typical. It is, at least, borne out by an episode in James Silk Buckingham's autobiography. About ten years earlier the young sailor had been taken prisoner by a French privateer and released along with his fifty shipmates after a few months of confinement in Corunna, when their 'maintenance became too burdensome'. During their march through Galicia to Portugal they were courteously treated, especially in Vigo where a group of Spanish sailors recently released from imprisonment in England insisted on treating them to a banquet, 'alleging that seamen were brothers all the world over'. The fraternal occasion was marred only by the behaviour of the English seamen who added brandy to their wine and became 'helplessly drunk', embarrassing their young shipmate by his 'countrymen's weakness'.[19]

During the few days which the two officers spent in this hospitable town they had the 'liberty to walk in the square' and in its 'narrow and dirty' streets. Thus they were able to visit several coffee houses, to have supper with the captain of an American schooner and to change their English money. It seems that Othnel used some of this to purchase the paper on which his journal is written for the watermarks indicate that it was made in the Spanish town of Alcoy by a manufacturer with the Catalan name Abat.[20] The ink and quills could well have been transferred from the ship with his other possessions, perhaps in a small writing bureau such as gentlemen carried in those days. The amount of detail in the journal and its diary format indicate that Othnel wrote it up as they went along rather than after his eventual release. He would have had to do this discreetly knowing, like the nineteenth-century travel writer Richard Ford, that 'a stranger making drawings or writing notes in a book creates great suspicion and is thought to be a spy'.[21] The need for caution must explain why Othnel was not able to draw 'the numberless beautiful scenes' through which he was later to pass.

On New Year's Day 1808 the prisoners set off under armed escort for Corunna, the capital of Galicia, where the captain general or his deputy would decide their fate. Mitchell and Mawdesley were pleased to discover that the twelve seamen and two marines captured with them had also been 'extremely well treated' in Vigo – though they were not accorded the privileges they themselves had received. These distinctions, normal for prisoners of war at this time, persisted on the journey. The officers and their trunks were mounted on mules (which performed in Spain 'the functions of the camel in the East'),[22] whereas the men marched on foot and carried their own bags. By the time they reached the pilgrimage city of Santiago after four days of 10-mile marches and nights spent in poor lodgings, one man had badly swollen legs and most of them were so lame that the Spanish officer decided on a day's rest. The officers had not been idle on the journey. Othnel recorded the number of enemy ships at anchor in Vigo harbour (including a Russian frigate), the sight of 'a large train of ammunition destin'd for the Spanish army in Portugal', the 'extremely good' state of the roads and an encounter with two Lancashire velvet manufacturers who had settled in Ponte Vedra, 'not a bad town & has some good buildings in it'.

The day's respite gave the officers the chance to explore Santiago. The clergyman's son reacted like many other English Protestants to flamboyant Catholic display. He attributed the magnificence of the cathedral to the 'bigotry of superstition' which claimed that the city's patron saint was buried there – and would doubtless have agreed with Ford that this was 'a self-evident' trick'. He wondered at 'the number of ropes, torches and people' attending a funeral procession, and at streets 'crowded with priests, monks & friars' (whom the Duke of Wellington described as 'the real power in Spain').[23] On the whole, however, the young men were pleased with what they saw before resuming the march to Corunna. It was then that they began to have 'trouble with Warn', the sailor who had been punished several times on board *Theseus*. Othnel relates that during the night the seaman 'hir'd a mule from one of the peasants in order (as he said) to fetch some wine from a distance', but was discovered by the Spanish officers, brought back and put in the stocks for attempting to escape. The fact that the men were lodged 'in a miserable hovel with only a little straw to keep them from the cold frosty ground' may help to explain Warn's seeking either his freedom or some alcoholic cheer.

The whole party was cheered a couple of days later as they neared the coast again. In his formal schoolboy prose, Othnel struggles to express the captives' emotions:

> We soon got sight of the sea, which was very pleasant indeed to us, as we had all along entertain'd most sanguine hopes of being sent on board on our arrival at Corunna. As the steeples and lighthouse rose gradually to our view I know not how to say how I felt, what between hope and fear of our exchange. On our nearer approach we plainly made out one of our frigates close in with the town. Then was the cry of 'What would I give to be on board etc?'

These hopes were soon dashed. After marching through the busy streets of Corunna, with everyone 'staring and gaping' at them, they were taken straight to the main guard house. The two young officers were 'plac'd in a small room, with one small window grated with iron, having neither bed, table, or anything in it but an old chair'. The men, whom they were allowed to visit the next day, 'far'd far worse than ourselves, having been lock'd up in a <u>black hole</u> all night & slept on the bare stones without even a little straw to stretch themselves on.' Othnel's account indignantly sums up their 'truly unpleasant situation', which persisted despite Mitchell's complaints that they were not receiving the allowances of money and food due to them as prisoners of war:

> We found ourselves very uncomfortable now, instead of being order'd releas'd as we hoped on our arrival here, we were strictly confin'd in a guard room, without anything given us to eat or drink, subject to the intrusion of every person, two men much in want of a surgeon and the rest half starv'd. It will appear almost incredible that for six days and a half in a barracks full of soldiers sixteen prisoners of war should be confin'd without a morsel to eat or drink, and had it not

been for the money sent from the ship we might all literally have starv'd. ... I was driven back by the sentinel for only looking out at the door. One day a very young officer was on guard, & seemed very fearful of our escaping, so much so that he accompanied us to the ne-c-y [lavatory].

Eventually they learned the reason for their close confinement – two masters of merchant ships had recently escaped from Corunna. Now, since no exchange was likely, the prisoners were to be taken sixty miles inland to Lugo so that they could not easily follow suit. As the party set off from Corunna on 17 January they had the 'tantalizing sight' of *Theseus* in the bay below them: 'Little did they think on board that on the hills they so plainly saw many of their shipmates are trudging to prison.' Faced with the possibility of spending the rest of the war in captivity, Othnel no doubt shared the feelings of another midshipman, Donat O'Brien, who was imprisoned in France at the same time: 'I was losing the prime of my youth in captivity ... deprived of being able to afford my country, my friends or myself the least assistance ... unless I could release myself from bondage.'[24] But Othnel was a resilient lad and he used the march to Lugo as an opportunity to view and comment on his captors' country.

It was at this point that he felt frustrated not to be able to draw a landscape 'of hill and dale and numerous streams', described by the young Buckingham as 'romantically varied'.[25] He did not hesitate, however, to write pen portraits of the rather less picturesque towns and villages at which they lodged: 'ill-built and dirty' Betanzos, 'miserable and straggling' Carvallont, and Barnondi, 'a similar place to the last'. He was clearly shocked by poverty more wretched than anything he had witnessed in and around Chester:

The dirty horrid cottages of the poorer sort of the Spanish peasants beggars all description. Cows, pigs, fowls etc are the inmates of the house. They have no grates or chimnies, a few stoves and a hole in the roof supply these wants. Straw in their bed, and the whole furniture consists of a large chest, a few wooden spoons and trenchers, and an earthen pot or two. Fingers are more in fashion that knives and forks. It is not uncommon to see the little children naked crawling about the fire, cover'd with dirt. In short savages cannot be worse off.

Thus the midshipman used this journey to produce a travelogue as informative as that of Richard Ford, who was to record forty years later that 'people sup without chimneys and sleep without beds'.[26]

Meanwhile the footsore ordinary seamen tramped on and must have been relieved to arrive at Lugo, even though they were put into a 'small & abominably filthy' jail. They were at first allowed some freedom to walk about the town but soon this liberty was withdrawn on the pretext that the men were disorderly. It is true that the incorrigible Warn had disgraced the party with further 'infamous drunken behaviour', but Othnel soon discovered the real explanation for the sailors' close confinement and drew his own conclusions:

> Some thousands of French troops were expected to march through this place and the Spaniards were afraid the French officers would take umbrage at the liberty allowed the English prisoners. This plainly shews how much Spain is under the influence of France and whose government is the most prevalent.

It was not long, however, before the officers' treatment improved. The commandant allowed them to find their own lodgings, hire a Portuguese servant, keep their swords and discipline their own men. All in all, they 'managed to spend the time pretty well', getting to know some local families, admiring 'the Spanish beauties' and attending the *tertulia*, a gathering of friends for conversation, cards and occasional dances. One particular young gentleman, the 'immensely rich' Don Antonio Gil, visited them frequently to practise his English and to share his best wines. The smartly uniformed Englishmen were clearly quite a draw. Othnel even began to feel at home in Lugo, a riverside city of about the same size as Chester, with Roman walls, a fine cathedral, numerous churches and impressive municipal buildings. Overriding any pleasure he and Mitchell derived from their pastimes, however, was the feeling they shared with Midshipman O'Brien in the French fortress of Verdun: a 'relentless will to be free'.[27]

*   *   *

There was some talk in Lugo of a possible exchange of prisoners with the crew of a large French ship recently captured by the British squadron off Corunna. In the meantime, the two young men planned to take matters into their own hands. While they were still in Corunna the Irish interpreter they had met in Vigo, Michael McEgan, had visited them to discuss the 'means of escaping from Lugo, should we not be put on parole of honour on our arrival there'. The gentleman's word of honour remained sacrosanct during the Napoleonic wars and fugitives who broke it faced a cold reception at home, with the risk of being expelled from the army or navy.[28] Thus it was a great relief to both officers that they were not put on parole in Lugo despite the privileges they were granted, so that 'there now remain'd no bar to our attempt to escape'.

To their astonishment, McEgan took the 'great risque' of coming to their house in Lugo, where they plotted a getaway. This involved misleading another captive midshipman who now shared their lodgings, Mr Baillie from HMS *Solebay*, as well as the men in their charge and their friends in Lugo. 'It was painful to practice such deceit on them', Othnel lamented, 'but what depended upon it? Our hopes of Liberty.' They exploited the liberty already allowed them by hiding some clothes in a tavern outside the town, telling Baillie that they were going to stay for a few nights with a gentleman they knew on the road to Madrid and making arrangements to accompany Don Antonio to a *tertulia* the following night. So, on 12 February 1808, after cutting off the buttons on his greatcoat 'to appear more like a Spaniard', and leaving behind his precious sword, Othnel walked quietly out of Lugo with Mitchell and McEgan to make his bid for freedom.

There followed two months of 'anxiety, misery & fatigue', during which the resolute pair managed to keep their 'spirits up very well'. The plan they had worked out with McEgan was to reach the coast where he would procure them a boat in which they could rejoin their squadron in Corunna Bay. Despite the Irishman's provision of mules, sustenance and 'a country man to shew us the way' named Santiago, the first part of the venture proved fraught with danger. After seeing 'numberless tracks of bears and wolves', which put him in mind of Robinson Crusoe's footprint in the sand, Othnel was alarmed when a 'tremendous large wolf' crossed the road and eyed them before going on its way. He knew that the region was also 'much infested with robbers', but they had the 'good fortune to see none'. Their greatest problem on this forced march to the Galician shore was exceptionally severe weather with constant rain or snow, which slowed them down and made nightly shelter imperative. Wayside huts provided this until they reached a village twenty miles from Corunna, where they lodged in Santiago's cramped and flea-ridden home. They had, of course, to keep 'very close to prevent our being seen by anybody', a challenging task since the house served as the local tavern. On market day, when their host was selling Indian corn and beans from the room in which they were concealed, they had to be hidden in the bed behind a makeshift curtain, 'with strict instructions from the old man not to speak or breathe but lie quite still'.

In these precarious circumstances the officers stayed for ten days while McEgan tried to make arrangements in Corunna. They did not, perhaps, appreciate the risks run by Santiago as the 'fear of suspicion' mounted, leading the peasant first to demand more money and then to threaten them with eviction.

> Judge what we felt at this, what a wretch'd situation we were in. Prisoners run away to be turn'd out of doors in the middle of the night without knowing which way to turn our heads.

Only a severe reprimand from the local curate, who had been let into the secret, put a stop to Santiago's demands. Meanwhile the Irishman had had trouble in procuring a boat, since local fishermen were under orders to name and number their boats, guard them at night and only to put to sea 'at stated times & then at the leave of the Commisary of the place'. Clearly the authorities were trying to prevent the theft of vessels by English fugitives, but McEgan managed to bribe one of the officials 'to allow one to go out at night'.

It was with great relief that they left 'this curs'd house' with McEgan and Santiago on the night of 25 February to make for a cottage within a mile of the sea. But this was a 12-mile journey and the travellers were thwarted by quite unexpected hazards:

After having gone two miles our guide was so drunk that he fell off the mule, and although remounted several times by us, he as often roll'd off. At this unfortunate time McEgan's mule stumbled, and fell with his rider into a deep hole. The scene was truly laughable; old Santiago crawling drunk in the grass about the mule's feet and McEgan in the ditch calling out in his Irish accent for assistance. At last he got out with the loss of his bridle, which he found after half an hour's search. By this accident & our guide's drunkenness we were prevented from proceeding and oblig'd to return to the house and wait for the next night.

It was a good job that Othnel was young and optimistic enough to see the funny side of things and to make a fresh start. But his troubles were not over. Recalcitrant fishermen, poor weather, protracted 'close confinement' in various 'filthy cottages', and the 'tantalizing sight' of English ships offshore sapped both young men's health and spirits. The journal becomes more incoherent at this point and seems to have been written up at intervals when its author had sufficient light, space and peace of mind. His dates are no longer precise, but it was at least three weeks before McEgan found an amenable fisherman – as well as 'a boy called Ignacio who entered into our service' – and another three days before the boisterous weather moderated enough for them to make a bid to reach the *Naiad* frigate off the coast.

This nocturnal venture was beset by as many perils as the one which had brought them into captivity three months earlier. The fisherman refused to act as a guide; Ignacio was seasick from the start; McEgan was 'no more able to pull than a cow'; there was a 'nasty swell on the sea' and they could not get their improvised sail to function.

Finding that we were losing instead of gaining ground, not being able to keep the boat's head the right way and seeing no hope of the frigate, we thought our best plan was to return from whence we came and endeavour to get somebody to assist us the next night. ... Our situation was critical now: a fog was rising and we were about 4 miles from the shore. We set to work to work with a will and (although greatly fatigued with pulling all night, and with our hands

badly blister'd) we managed to get into the port just at daylight. ...
It the evening it came on to blow very hard, and most probably had
we staid out at sea we should have been lost; we found most things
happen'd for the best.

Othnel spoke too soon. Fearing that people who spotted them on their
way back to the fisherman's cottage would inform on them, the runaways
moved to the 'hospitable house' of McEgan's friend, Don Juan Failde,
and started to make new plans, determined 'to leave nothing untried'.
But on the night of 7 April, Ignacio wakened them with the news that
the justice and a party of soldiers were searching for them. He rushed
them off to a large house, 'almost like a castle', the owner of which had
promised them protection. Othnel's breathless account of the final stages
of their flight contains elements of the classic escape story: a pair of shoes
dropped by Mitchell with tell-tale English 'written inside'; concealment
in a wine press behind a secret old door; 'soldiers searching everywhere';
news that McEgan had been arrested 'with a letter in his pocket', and that
Don Juan's house had been ransacked. The officers realised that the game
was up – they must make their own way back to Lugo as fast as possible
to avoid being taken there under guard.

It was a forlorn return journey in which they managed to pass themselves
off as Frenchmen. After encountering smugglers on the run, dodging
parties of Spanish soldiers armed with 'musquets' and spending their
last supplies of money on hiring horses, they arrived back in Lugo. The
fugitives were again fortunate in their treatment in this town. The friendly
governor paid more attention to 'the intercession of several ladies', who
argued that there was 'no place fit to put us in', than to orders from the
captain general at Corunna. Thus he allowed them to go back to their old
lodgings in return for a written guarantee that they would not leave the
city. Soon the arrival of more captive officers provided pleasant company
in which they could pass their time 'more agreeably than ever'. Mitchell
and Mawdesley seem also to have interceded to gain more comfortable
conditions for the seamen, who had become 'enraged' at the 'shameful
reductions made from their pay' during their officers' absence and tried
to make their own escape. But none of this would have compensated for

sharing the fate of most British captives in this war, who 'stayed to the end, with the Allies in Paris and Napoleon himself in prison'.[29]

*　*　*

Othnel and his fellows did not have to wait until 1814 for their release, which came not by way of Galicia's stormy coastline, but as a result of Spain's tumultuous politics. While still in the fisherman's cottage near Corunna in March he and Mitchell had heard of King Charles IV's abdication in favour of his son, Ferdinand VII. They also learnt that 'the Prince of Peace was robb'd of all his honours and imprisoned', but may not have realised that this was the title bestowed on Prime Minister Godoy, the queen's lover, for making peace with France in 1795 and fostering the disastrous alliance which now caused his downfall. Back in Lugo in early May 1808, reports reached the two officers that King Ferdinand had been summoned to Bayonne by Napoleon, who forced him to vacate the throne in favour of the Emperor's brother, Joseph Bonaparte. Couriers also brought alarming accounts from Madrid of the *Dos de Mayo* uprising against French domination being crushed with the ferocity so memorably portrayed by Francisco Goya.[30] The prisoners also heard that a French general they had seen pass through Lugo with 'a star on his breast and the riband of the Legion of Honour' was hissed and booed on his way to Corunna by Spaniards, 'who seem'd to show the greatest animosity to the very name of French'.

Othnel's journal goes on to give a first-hand account of Lugo's participation in the countrywide popular revolt which now erupted:

> Every Spaniard wore the national cockade (red) in his hat, and seem'd zealous to defend his king and country. A deputy from every town in the province was summon'd to the Council at Corunna; Don Josef Maria Prado set off immediately being elected for this city. ... On Sunday the 5th [June] the Commandant at the head of a party of fine grenadiers march'd through the streets with a flag in his hand, having Viva Ferdinando 7th written on it, and in a speech called upon all to stand in defence of their king, which was answer'd by repeated shouts of Viva Ferdinando. ... Two field pieces arriv'd

from Corunna with a party of soldiers. Up the country men were call'd in to be made soldiers of; in short there was every appearance of war.

In fact, Othnel was witnessing the beginning of the long, bloody Peninsular War in which the Spanish helped British and Portuguese armies drive the French out of the Iberian Peninsula. By 10 June 'there were 8,000 troops in Lugo and 20,000 on their way from Portugal with a French General prisoner'. As a result of this unexpected diplomatic revolution, all English prisoners in Spain were immediately released so that they could play their own part in the defeat of Napoleon. Thus, on 11 June, Mawdesley, Mitchell and Baillie heard that they were to 'march on the morrow for Corunna, to be sent on board an English ship':

Sunday 12th We waited on the Captn Gen who gave us our passport and liberty to proceed to Theseus before the men. At 2 we mounted our horses and left our old habitation. In galloping through the streets, Mr Baillie rode over a Spanish grenadier, which caus'd some disturbance. We call'd on the Spanish ladies to take our leave and then rode out of Lugo; at the outside we gave three cheers and took a last look at the walls.

* * *

So expeditious was their departure that the muster roll of *Theseus* for 1 July 1808 includes both Midshipman Mawdesley and Masters Mate Andrew Mitchell, who were still on board in January 1809, by which time Mitchell had been made a lieutenant.[31] The journal of their adventures in Spain was also on board, safely stored in Mitchell's sea chest, remaining with him after the pair were parted later in 1809, and thereafter preserved for posterity. Letters which no doubt reached St Oswald's Vicarage, Chester, to inform the Mawdesleys of their sailor son's safety have not survived the intervening 200 years.[32] It is not likely that Othnel, or any of the released prisoners, got home leave, for the Royal Navy still needed all the men it could marshal. Midshipman Baillie's *Solebay* departed for West Africa as one of the first ships sent to suppress the

British slave trade, which had been made illegal in 1807. Another new role for the navy was acknowledged by Major-General Arthur Wellesley (later Duke of Wellington), British commander in the Peninsular War: 'If anyone wishes to know the history of this war, I will tell him that it is our maritime superiority which gives me the power of maintaining my army while the French are unable to do so.'[33] Sometimes, however, the navy had the less glorious task of evacuating troops. In January 1809, just a few months after Mawdesley's deliverance and in the same Bay of Corunna, naval vessels protected transport ships as they rescued some 19,000 survivors of Sir John Moore's army after it had been defeated by the French. As the year proceeded Admiral James Gambier's Channel Fleet, of which *Theseus* was a part, was instrumental both in protecting British supply ships and in preventing the French from using the sea to convey equipment and food for the sustenance of their armies in Spain and Portugal.

It was in pursuit of these tasks that the ship took part in the Battle of the Basque Roads in April 1809, when the Admiralty ordered a fireship attack on eleven French battleships at anchor in this sea channel in the Bay of Biscay. Gambier considered this 'a horrible and anti-Christian mode of warfare' and left the operation to be carried out by the 'bloody-minded radical', Captain Lord Cochrane, whom Napoleon nicknamed the Sea-Wolf. He employed not only twenty-one fireships, but also explosion ships of his own invention.[34] Now that there are no more of Othnel's 'Private Remarks', only the ship's terse unpunctuated logbook can help to illuminate his own part in this battle. He may have been one of the volunteers included on 10 April when Captain Beresford 'sent Lieut Smith & a petty officer & men to the Apollo Fire Ship'. The next day he was almost certainly aboard one of 'the Boats manned and armed to the Caesar, the fire ships [and] explosion vessels'. He could not help but observe 'a vessel explode & the Fire Vessels on fire driving towards the Enemy's Fleet between the Isle d'Aix & Olleron'. It was, in Cochrane's more dramatic words, 'one of the grandest artificial spectacles imaginable ... [when] the air seemed alive with shells, grenades, rockets, and masses of timber, the wreck of the shattered vessel.' On 12 April, Othnel was on hand at dawn when the captain 'unmoored ship & cleared for Action'; he was on deck in the afternoon when *Theseus* 'received the Fire of the

Battery on Isle d'Aix'; and he was ready in the evening to man one of 'the boats to take prisoners from the Aquilon & Varsovie'. Finally, the captain records that at 6.30 on 13 April his ship was 'anchor'd near the Admiral', fourteen miles offshore, which confirms the judgement of contemporaries and historians that the cautious Gambier (known in the navy as 'Dismal Jimmy') failed to follow up Cochrane's initial success, with the result that the French lost only four battle ships. Nevertheless, this was a devastating battle 'which had a very bad effect on French morale'.[35]

Unrevealing as the captain's log is, it is clear that Othnel distinguished himself at the Basque Roads and also managed at some point to demonstrate his knowledge of seamanship and navigation before a board of three captains. For soon after this, on 13 June, he received his commission as a lieutenant aged just 19, and after less than three years of naval service. As announced in the *Naval Chronicle*, which unaccountably named him as Hon A.F. Berkely Othnel Mawdesley, he was posted to HMS *Ajax*, a new 74-gun battleship with a very fine figurehead at its prow, signing his name on the muster as fifth lieutenant.[36] After the ship had been prepared and provisioned at Spithead, she sailed south in convoy to Cape Trafalgar, Gibraltar and Minorca. For reasons best known to the Admiralty, Othnel was soon transferred to another new ship, HMS *Milford*, under the distinguished captaincy of Sir Henry Bayntun, who had fought at Trafalgar and acted as a bearer at Nelson's funeral. *Milford* joined the hard-pressed Mediterranean fleet commanded by 60-year-old Admiral Collingwood.

A particularly testing part of this area of operations was the Adriatic Sea between Italy and the Dalmatian coast, both of which were under French control. It was only occupation of the hotly contested island of Lissa (now Vis) which allowed Britain to trade with that part of Europe and to hamper French supply routes. In 1812 *Milford* was to be found in this region, now captained by Sir John Duff Markland and with Othnel Mawdesley still on board, promoted to second lieutenant. The master's log for that summer and autumn records her cruising along the Dalmatian coast, returning to the base at Lissa for repairs and provisions and frequently sending out small boats with the perilous task of investigating and engaging with French vessels:

Sunday 8th November Sent away the blue cutter armed with two gun boats.

Monday 9th Nov The blue cutter and gun boats returned. Lieut Mawdesley severely wounded. … departed this life Lieut Mawdesley.

Thus Othnel died, aged only 22, carrying out a dangerous mission very similar to the one which had led to his captivity in 1807. This time, it seems, enemy gun batteries had opened fire and found their mark. The log simply records that three days later he was buried on Lissa 'with the usual ceremony and honours', and that his effects were sold on board, fetching £106 6s, an unusually large sum for such a young man.[37] Some of this may have been collected as prize money, though the Adriatic was hardly the 'prize turkey shoot' described by a modern historian who blithely concluded that 'the occasional casualty apart, these were halcyon days'.[38]

Identical death notices were published three months later in the *Chester Chronicle* and the *Gentleman's Magazine,* confirming that Second Lieutenant Mawdesley was fatally wounded 'while reconnoitring a strange vessel', and that he was 'interred in the Church-yard at Lissa', adding that 'the funeral was attended by Admiral Freemantle [commander of the Adriatic campaign], Captain Markland, and his brother officers, all anxious to pay every mark of respect to the memory of one they so highly esteemed and loved'. It is unlikely that Othnel's island grave survives, but his death 'on service in the Adriatic' is commemorated in a family window in St Mary-on-the-Hill, Chester, his father's final parish.

Of Othnel's life in general, the obituaries record:

He was dutiful and affectionate to his parents, correct beyond example in the discharge of the duties of his profession, and upright and honorable in all his dealings. The virtuous and religious principles which had supported him through life, did not fail him at his death. He died, as an eye-witness observed, 'a hero and a Christian.' It is difficult in bearing testimony to departed worth, to avoid the appearance of partiality; yet one well acquainted with him even from his birth, unwilling to allow merit uncommon as his to pass unnoticed, makes the above statement from a conviction of its truth.[39]

Neither the childhood friend nor the deathbed witness can be identified today. All we have is the evidence of Othnel's own writing which bears out some, but not all, of these valedictory tributes. We certainly see him behaving correctly, honourably, and even heroically during his captivity, fully deserving his subsequent promotion and the esteem of his fellow officers. No doubt, the clergyman's son remained a Christian, but his journal contains no pious sentiments – nor even any mention of religious observance. The only ceremony he mentions is wearing an oak sprig in his hat on 29 May, a royalist tradition with pagan tree-worshipping associations. The merits he demonstrates are those of a good schoolboy: a respect for truth except in the most extreme circumstances, the prudent use of money, a proper concern for subordinates and an ability to record his experiences accurately. Othnel was not the paragon of virtue eulogised after his untimely death, but a brave young sailor with a boyish zest for adventure, gentlemanly manners and an eye for the 'Spanish beauties'. A more apt tribute would be the one paid by old Admiral Collingwood to the gallant youths under his command, as they scaled towers and stormed redoubts around the Mediterranean, thinking nothing 'beyond their enterprise'.[40] Their 'activity and zeal' kept up his spirits during this long and arduous war – in which Othnel Mawdesley could no longer play his part.

Chapter 5

William Barlow 1792–1811:
Child of the Raj and Sailor

In the early months of 1800, 8-year-old William Barlow left his parents and four younger siblings to board a sailing ship for the six-month journey from Calcutta to London. With him were his 11-year-old sister, Eliza, and his brother George, a year older than himself. The three young Barlows were dispatched on their own, as was common for the children of East India Company employees on the way to England for their education. At the very same time the *Porcher*, for example, left the Hooghly River carrying three Bawn brothers aged between 9 and 5 as well as John, William and Charles Marshall who were all under 8; no parent, relation or 'native servant' was listed among the six adult passengers.[1]

It is true that William's brother and sister were considered mature enough to look after their young brother, for they were older than most Raj children sent 'home' before they could suffer the supposed ill effects of an Indian upbringing. As chief secretary to the governor general of India, George Barlow understood all too well the terrible hazards of the journey around the Cape of Good Hope to Britain and no doubt delayed their departure for this reason. His colleague, Chief Justice Sir Robert Chambers, had never ceased to mourn his 7-year-old son Thomas, lost off the coast of Africa in 1782, when storms sank the *Grosvenor*, on which he was travelling. Ever since the outbreak of war with France in 1793, added perils were posed by French warships and privateers operating from Isle de France in the Indian Ocean. Even more worrying was the French conquest of the Netherlands in 1795, bringing with it the risk that the Dutch colonies of Ceylon and the Cape would threaten British ships en route to and from India. But recent news that the Royal Navy had managed to establish control in both these areas gave George and his wife Elizabeth the confidence to dispatch their three oldest children.

It was, after all, time for Eliza to acquire the 'useful and virtuous' accomplishments she would need to make a good marriage. The serious, delicate George, his father's favourite, was already rather old to be embarking on the public-school education he would need if he were to make, as the family hoped, a 'noise in the world'.[2] Of greatest concern was William, a high-spirited boy not much given to study. As George was a bookworm and often ailing, William may well have sought the company of the servants' children. There was glorious fun to be had roasting corn cobs and cashew nuts on an open fire, making brightly-coloured kites with which to bring down those of other flyers, hunting for snakes in the garden, squatting on the floor of Indian houses tasting curries and hot sweet tea, buying forbidden sweets in the bazaar or hearing rude stories about a host of Hindu gods. His father's long hours in Government House and his mother's many social engagements provided William with the chance to engage in such larks. Any consequent Bengali speech and lack of progress in Latin no doubt worried his parents, but they hoped that the attentions of Mr Barlow's brother William, who had agreed to take care of the boys' education, would soon eradicate such shortcomings.

Like most Raj children about to be uprooted from the only world they knew, William was bound to suffer pangs of dismay at his impending departure from India. How would he like to live with an Uncle William he had never met? How would he adjust to a country which, he had heard, was always cold and grey? How could he bear to be sent away to school to learn more Latin and be beaten when he forgot it, as he always did? How would he tell his Indian playmates that he was going over the black water, never to see them again? But as a young lad familiar with the daring deeds of Elizabethan mariners and the fictional adventures of Robinson Crusoe, he probably looked forward to the voyage itself. Current rumours about the French corsair Robert Surcouf roaming the Indian Ocean were likely to arouse as much boyish excitement as trepidation. Meanwhile, his sister and brother were no doubt more apprehensive about separation from their parents. Eliza would miss the dear Mama with whom she played the piano and sang of nymphs and shepherds. And George would lack the guidance of a father he admired.

It is difficult to know how far the children's regrets were reciprocated. Would the Barlow parents suffer the pain endured by Dr William Dick and his wife Charlotte, who had already sent off their first three sons, lamenting that they would no longer 'have the pleasure of superintending their education, of rejoicing at their improvements, of watching over their health, or of securing their affection'?[3] George Barlow was not a man to express such feelings. Hard work and integrity had won him promotion in the East India Company, but many found that 'his manner in society was cold, distant and formal'. Although the memoirist William Hickey thought this denoted a man with no 'friend in the world nor one individual person about whom he cared', Barlow clearly had private passions. When he married Elizabeth Smith in Calcutta in 1789 she was already pregnant and they went on to have thirteen more children in the next twenty years. The fact that Barlow kept all their letters after they were sent to England suggests more fatherly concern than he was able to express – as well as providing a store of evidence about how they fared. Hickey's malicious judgement is typical of the snobbery which characterised Anglo-Indian society: Barlow, he said, was but 'the son of a silk mercer', more at home behind a shop counter in Covent Garden than a desk in Calcutta's Government House.[4] Mrs Barlow was less likely than her husband to repine for her three absent offspring, for she had plenty of distractions: daily rides in the maidan, her famous tiffin parties and the nightly balls of Calcutta's cold season. There were also four children left at home to entertain any idle moments with songs and puppet plays. Elizabeth did not see the trio again for six years and there is no evidence that she ever wrote to them.

*   *   *

As they parted from their parents, siblings and native land, Eliza, George, and even William, would have behaved with the decorum expected in their day. After being taken by river boat through the Hooghly's treacherous sandbanks to Diamond Harbour they embarked on an East Indiaman, a lightly armed merchant ship, in one of the fleets which left Bengal every year. They were always protected by one or two Royal Navy frigates and loaded with goods such as silks, spices and large quantities of saltpetre, a vital ingredient in the gunpowder demanded by the French wars. Their captains also found room for a score or so of passengers, whose fares boosted their profits. Since it is unlikely that Mr Barlow had paid over £200 apiece for the comparative luxury of a cabin in the roundhouse, the three youngsters were probably lodged in the cramped and stuffy steerage area, where they would have been nauseated by noxious fumes and attacked by cockroaches, bugs and red ants.

All ships' captains kept careful logbooks and passenger lists, many of which have survived the salty battering to which they were subjected. My search for a record of the Barlows' voyage proved fruitless, but I have built up a picture of their months at sea by using the logs of sister ships making the same voyage. The three children sailed in the fleet which left Diamond Harbour in January 1800 in time to take advantage of the North-East monsoon in the Indian Ocean.[5] Much as William may have craved adventure, these captains reported no encounters with enemy frigates or pirate-ships. Even so, there was plenty of danger on hand. The *Caledonia*'s captain, for example, tells of rigging, sail and provisions lost in squally weather and records the death of many *lascars*, Indian sailors who had fallen prey to the cold. By the time she reached the Cape in March, *Caledonia* was 'in great distress, having lost her masts, and being rendered a complete wreck in several furious storms'. She sailed from the Cape in May after extensive repairs, but was taking in 12in of water an hour by the time she arrived at St Helena a month later. During the last leg of the voyage home this increased to 30in, 'so that the ship was only kept afloat by continual pumping' until she limped into London docks in September. Meanwhile *Exeter* (a chartered ship with the same name as one of the regular East Indiamen) was 'rolling very deep' in heavy swells and, when poultry and other livestock were swept from the decks, some of her adult passengers complained about the short supplies of fresh food.[6]

They were lucky not to have had more to endure. In August of the same year the Company's own ship, *Exeter*, was sailing off the Brazilian coast en route to China when her convoy was mistaken for a fleet of warships by a French squadron led by Commodore Jean-François Landolphe. As Landolphe turned to escape, the East Indiamen were ordered to give chase, preserving the illusion that they were the superior force. As night was falling after an hour and a half's pursuit, *Exeter* came alongside the French frigate *Médée* and arranged lights behind all her gunports so that she resembled 'a fearsome, leering jack-o'-lantern'.[7] Rather than do battle with what he believed to be a heavily armed warship, the French captain surrendered, only to realise his mistake once he came on board *Exeter*. An engagement involving no loss of life or limb had inflicted a serious defeat on a French naval force and *Exeter*'s captain was subsequently commended for his feat – the only instance in this long conflict when a merchant vessel captured a French warship. However, not all those travelling in this fleet lived to tell the tale. As the *Kent* navigated the Bay of Bengal a gang of Surcouf's hatchet-bearing sailors rushed on board. Male passengers were armed with cutlasses but they could not prevent the *Kent*'s capture. Five lost their lives along with sixteen of the crew, though Surcouf allowed the remainder, some of whom were wounded, to be taken on to Calcutta aboard another ship.

Even without such adventures to alarm or excite them, the young Barlows were certainly at risk, Eliza from the advances of lascivious seamen, the boys from corruption by hard-drinking fellow-passengers, and all of them from the infections which regularly swept through these ships. Yet there were diversions to allay the disquiet and break the tedium of months on the high seas. They could watch the albatrosses, sheer-waters and pintado birds which accompanied vessels around the Cape, and see whales spouting and surfacing in the South Atlantic. They might participate in the sailors' sport of catching sharks, sea-snakes and turtles. They certainly paid court to King Neptune in the wild pagan ceremonies which accompanied the crossing of the equator and took part in more sedate deck-games and amateur theatricals. At ports of call such as Cape Town and St Helena they were free to disembark with any willing adult escorts. If he was lucky, William would have palled up with other lads to race around the decks, lord it over younger children and create 'noises and distractions' such as those which 'tried the presence of mind' of Sir James Mackintosh on board the *Caroline*.[8] Sometimes lone children were taken in hand to be hushed and spruced up by the ship's officers or motherly fellow-passengers – though it seems unlikely that the wilful young William welcomed such attentions.

Meanwhile, owners of the ships and their cargo, as well as passengers' friends and relations, awaited news that the fleet had reached the shores of Britain. Their anxiety is reflected in regular reports which appeared in the *London Chronicle*. In April readers were reassured that a rumour of the *Princess Charlotte* being captured by French frigates in the Bay of Bengal received 'very little credit in the City'. And in September the newspaper was pleased to announce 'the late arrival in the Downs of the East India Company extra ship, the Exeter, Capt. Anthony Dunlop, from Bengal. This ship sailed from the island of St Helena on the 21st of June last, in company of the Thames and other ships, which arrived at Falmouth on 1st September. The Exeter lost company some days before and fears were entertained of her safety.'[9] No doubt the Barlows' new guardians studied such reports closely, but we do not know whether they were at Deptford to greet their charges as they disembarked. Still, it is easy to imagine the children's apprehension as they took up residence in London, Eliza in Marylebone with a great-aunt Butcher and the boys with Uncle William in Blackfriars.

* * *

As for William Barlow senior, it was not easy for him to receive the boys. A London merchant, he was clearly quite prosperous and he and his ailing wife had no children of their own. He willingly took on his younger brother's children out of family duty and to render himself 'more useful in this world', but he often found it a daunting task. It is clear that he always favoured George who had 'more thought and reflection than is usual for a boy of his age', confessing that he 'draws all my attention when he is at home'. It was more difficult for him to deal with William, 'a strong fellow ... but extremely idle, obstinate and bad-tempered', in sore need of a 'very serious lecture' from his father.[10]

The Rev. Roberts, to whose boarding-school in Mitcham the brothers were soon sent, also judged William lazy. George Barlow had selected this establishment on the recommendation of the governor general, Lord Wellesley, whose sons, Richard and Gerald, attended it. These boys had not been born and brought up in India and were just the sort of pupils Roberts welcomed to his exclusive seminary which charged £200 a year to prepare boys for Eton. And William Barlow was happy to send his nephews there, having established that Roberts would give them personal attention and that his wife, 'a most pleasing sensible woman' who had no children of her own, would be able 'to devote her whole time to the care of the boys'.[11]

It did not feel quite like that to the pupils themselves. Thomas Acland who was sent to the Mitcham school all the way from Devon, no doubt because of its reputation for securing public school places, felt crushed there. He described the 'system of arrears of work which none but a very few clever boys could avoid', and quoted Rev. Roberts's menacing words: 'If I can't wipe off the arrears I must whip them off'. Nor does the domestic regime sound very motherly: the last one down in the morning would be flogged, so the boys resorted to such devices as soaping the water overnight. Another young scholar, who liked the school and included Latin verses in twice-weekly letters to his Yorkshire home, tells of a 'desperate scuffle' in which 'Nash got a bloody nose and other boys were hurt'.[12] Such fights among boys frequently arose from ragging and name-calling to which children recently arrived from India were often subjected. Lady Wellesley herself said that the Barlow boys resembled monkeys compared with her sons, which suggests that taunts of this kind were commonplace at Roberts's school.[13] William, at least, is unlikely to have submitted to insults without a fight.

One consolation for George and William was that they were close enough to Uncle William's home to be able to return there if they were ill or injured. 'My brother William has been at home with a sore neck', reported Eliza in March 1801. It is difficult to tell precisely how they fared when at school. The weekly letters George apparently sent his uncle have not survived and there is no record of William's writing to him at this time – perhaps he was always too busy catching up with his 'arrears'. The first letter to his parents from their 'dutiful son' William was penned in a large childish hand at Blackfriars in June 1801: 'I am to return to school tomorrow, my lesson is in the Latin Grammar from Dativus post verbum to Verba Passiva.' Anxious though he was to impress his father, poor William evidently failed to master his Latin verbs and almost certainly fell victim to the stick or rod. George was later to report to his father that Roberts had a 'deficiency of patience' and used these punitive instruments too freely in his attempt to drum the classical curriculum into his pupils. He himself managed by great industry to master 'the first rudiments of the dead languages' well enough to gain a place at Eton, but

William admitted ruefully that after four years at the school he still did not 'know much about them'.[14]

In 1804 William's poor academic progress prompted an exchange of letters about his future among the senior Barlow brothers. Uncle William was rather overwhelmed by his responsibilities, which now included two younger nephews, Henry and Robert. He had remarried after the death of his first wife and now employed a man and his wife to help with the children. It is clear that he was a 'very attentive' uncle who took his meals with the children, and in young William's judgement he was 'always so kind to us that I think it impossible any one could be more so'.[15] Problems arose, however, from the inattention of George Barlow senior and from the boys' troublesome behaviour: letters and financial remittances from India arrived infrequently while the children sometimes gave way 'to the most violent passion'. The worst culprit was young William who was 'averse to learning anything', and 'unwilling to 'encounter the least difficulty'.[16] William Barlow did his best to improve the boy's behaviour and disposition but was glad to hand him over to the oldest brother, Sir Robert Barlow, captain of HMS *Triumph*, who promised to launch him into the Royal Navy. But for all William's errant ways, there is no evidence for the recent claim that Sir Robert 'took charge of Sir George's son upon William's expulsion from school'.[17] The boy was approaching his twelfth birthday, when his 'time of service must commence' if he was to have a successful naval career. It was a natural time for him to leave a preparatory school.

*   *   *

Although William would not have been consulted, he was probably quite happy with this move. After all, many a boy in his day ran away to seek a life on the ocean wave – as did George King in this same year. And Sir Robert certainly intended to do his best on his nephew's behalf. He was, however, a busy man nearing 50, with six children of his own, with whom he had spent so little time that 'were we to meet on the street at Bath we should not know each other'. What is more, he was unexpectedly appointed to home waters and could not therefore supervise William's training on board the *Triumph* in the Mediterranean as he had hoped.

Nevertheless, he promised to do by him 'as I should by my own son'. He placed the boy instead with his friend Captain Blackwood, 'a perfect Gentleman and an excellent officer' who commanded HMS *Euryalis*, one of the finest frigates in the navy. He had 'a good schoolmaster and several very genteel boys about him of whom he takes great care', and he would even be prepared to take William into his own cabin 'for a short time till he gets his sea legs and begins to feel himself at home'.[18]

Uncle and nephew met for the first time in Portsmouth during 'very severe weather', just after William's birthday in December 1804. Sir Robert found him 'tall and stout for his age', and was amused by his free-spoken manner, an example of which he related to the boy's father: 'I just now observed that my letter was written in such haste that I feared you would have difficulty in reading it, yes says William and you know he is a great criticiser'. When challenged, William resolutely defended his own word as more appropriate than the more normal 'critic'. After this brief encounter Sir Robert departed to spend Christmas with his own family in Bath, leaving William alone in Portsmouth to wait until the *Euryalis* had 'a fair wind to go out of harbour'. As he explained to his brother, there was no harm in letting the boy fend for himself, since 'nursing is not a good initiation to a life of enterprise and hard work.'[19]

It seems that William was not yet ready to stand on his own feet and nor did he meet Captain Blackwood's expectations of his genteel boys. At any rate, by the New Year Sir Robert had decided that his nephew was 'too young to begin his [naval] career'. Had he remained on board *Euryalis* he would have become one of the youngest participants in the Battle of Trafalgar, with the added honour of being part of the crew when the frigate became Admiral Collingwood's flagship and bore the captured Admiral Villeneuve to England. Instead, it was arranged that the boy should attend Mr Burney's private academy at Gosport, on the shore opposite Portsmouth harbour, reporting occasionally to the master of another ship. He was to be prepared for entry to the Royal Naval Academy at Portsmouth unless, in the meantime, Sir Robert was given a new command in which case, he promised, 'I shall probably take him with me.'[20]

* * *

William's studies appeared to go well enough for a time. In April 1805 he wrote to his father dutifully, if somewhat inaccurately, describing his work under Mr Burney: 'I am going through a regular system of mathematical education together with fencing, dancing, drawing and French. I write Latin exercises daily, say Grammar and a lesson in Caesar's Comentaries [*sic*] so that you will see I have my time fully filled up at school.' Sir Robert was pleased with both boy and school when William came to stay with his family in Bath during the summer holiday: 'He gives very favourable accounts of the Gosport Academy and indeed I believe they have done him every justice. ... I think him a clever boy and we agree very well thus far.'[21]

Meanwhile, however, the nephew sent begging letters to Uncle William, despite the fact that Sir Robert was supposed to 'supply his wants'. The lad could hardly confess to the distinguished naval officer that his money was 'all expended by going over the water to see my friends', since this probably meant illicit expeditions from Gosport to some of the many taverns which flourished in wartime Portsmouth, charging high prices for their wares. To his more indulgent uncle, William reiterated his urgent need for 'a fresh supply of money', giving assurances that he had made progress in his lessons and protesting that he had not acted in a play as had been reported in a newspaper. Clearly Uncle William had his suspicions – and it is not certain that he acceded to nephew's financial demands.[22] After William had spent (or misspent) a year at Mr Burney's, Sir Robert was offered a vacancy for him at the Royal Naval Academy through the influence of his friend, Admiral Lord Keith. In February 1806 he decided to send him there 'in preference to having him at sea with a stranger'. 'William did not much relish the change' reported Sir Robert, 'but I hope he is now reconciled to it.'[23]

If William had reservations about seamanship being learned behind a desk rather than aboard a man-of-war, he was not alone. The Royal Naval Academy had been established by the Admiralty in 1729 as an alternative to the rather haphazard system of ship-board training, but it was not popular with naval officers, who feared that it would interfere with their patronage, even though it educated only a tiny percentage of aspiring midshipmen. Among the latter were Jane Austen's brothers, Francis and Charles, who voiced no complaints and went on to successful careers, both eventually reaching admiral status and winning the admiration of their sisters. Other young gentlemen nursed a sense of grievance, finding a life of study dull compared with 'the excitements of life at sea aboard a man-of-war'.[24] To judge from family correspondence William Barlow was one of them. Sir Robert soon had to confess that the boy had disliked his 'return to the restraints of a school', and was 'not over given to application'. In an effort to induce more diligence, he wrote to the headmaster asking for 'a proper person to attend him out of school hours to keep him at his Latin'.[25] We can imagine how much William welcomed that.

It seems that he was not the only wayward student at the Academy. Shortly before William's entry it had received a visit from the First Lord of the Admiralty, Lord Barham, who described it as 'a nursery of vice and immorality'. He echoed the words of an earlier First Lord, the Earl of St Vincent: 'The Royal Academy at Portsmouth is a sink of vice and abomination.' There were certainly recorded instances of students escaping into the town in 1797, being found 'dead drunk' or 'behaving shamefully ill at Church', emulating perhaps the sailors of nearby Spithead anchorage who mutinied in that same year.[26] William's slapdash attitude was itself a form of disaffection, but there is no evidence that he indulged in the 'vice' deplored by their Lordships. Meanwhile his worthier brother George resisted the 'Idleness, Luxury and Vice of every description', which he encountered at Eton.[27]

It is difficult to establish what happened next because, as George found, William was 'not a good correspondent and when he does write he is in general very concise and laconic'.[28] In May 1806 the Admiralty closed the ill-famed Academy for an extensive overhaul and reorganisation. This was not completed until 1808 when the renamed Royal Naval College was inaugurated in the same building to receive seventy fresh pupils.[29] Yet letters of William's siblings and uncles refer to his being at the Portsmouth Academy throughout 1806. As late as September 1807, Uncle William insisted that 'William must be directed in all things by his Uncle Robert, he may pass his holidays with me for the purpose of being with his brothers but to his Uncle he must look up to get forward in the service.' It sounds as though Uncle William was anxious to wash his hands of his troublesome namesake, which is hardly surprising in

1. Charles Royer Davis (extreme right) with three of his seafaring brothers in the 1870s.

2. The clipper ship *Macduff* making the perilous entry into Melbourne harbour.

3. The weathered gravestone of Charles Royer Davis in Williamstown Cemetery, Melbourne.

4. Surgeon Bowes Smyth's list of 'Children, brought out or born on Board' the *Lady Penrhyn*.

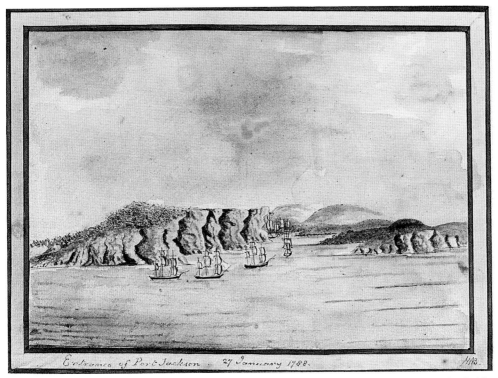

5. The First Fleet's arrival in Port Jackson depicted by William Bradley, an officer on the lead ship, HMS *Sirius*.

6. Young convicts in New South Wales, 1793.

7. Slaves, including several children, are auctioned in Brazil.

8. Tile panel depicting the potteries and close-packed houses of Lisbon's Mocambo district where Joseph Emidy probably lived.

9. Joseph Emidy leading other Truro musicians on his violin.

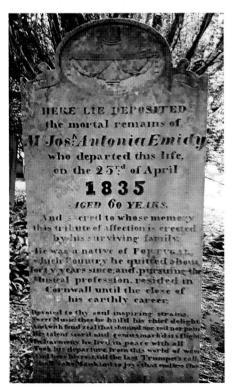

10. Joseph Emidy's grave in Kenwyn Church cemetery, Truro.

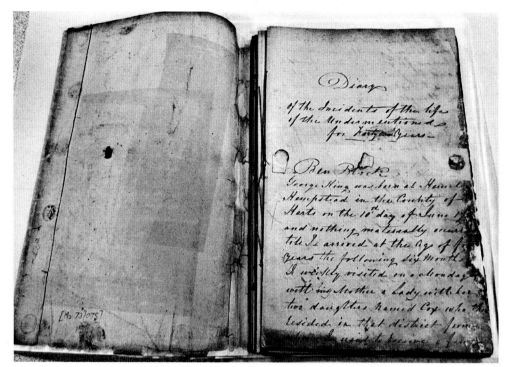

11. George King's autobiography addressed to Ben Block, a name like Jack Tar often given to the British sailor.

12. Boys playing at the Foundling Hospital, supervised by their schoolmaster.

13. George King's first ship, HMS *Polyphemus*, depicted in a Bahamas postage stamp commemorating the bicentenary of Trafalgar.

14. Figurehead of HMS *Polyphemus*, representing the head of the mythological giant Cyclops.

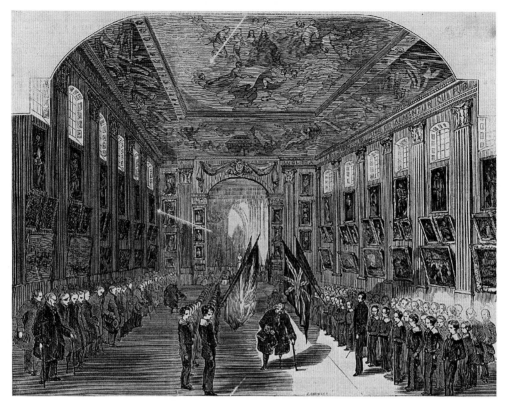

15. George King is somewhere in this picture of the ceremony in the Painted Hall. of Greenwich Hospital at which veteran sailors were presented with Nelson medals.

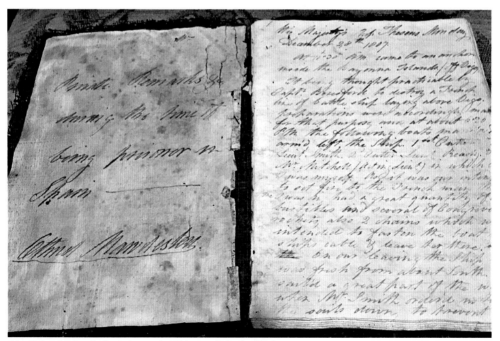

16. Othnel Mawdesley's journal of his captivity in Spain.

17. Mawdesley family memorial window in St Mary-on-the-Hill, Chester which commemorates the death of Othnel 'on active service in the Adriatic, 9th Novr 1812, aged 22'.

18. Midshipmen between decks caricatured by George Cruikshank.

PORTSMOUTH POINT.

19. Thomas Rowlandson portrays the pleasures of Portsmouth in William Barlow's time.

PLAYER'S CIGARETTES.

MIDSHIPMAN EASY.
"MR. MIDSHIPMAN EASY."

20. A midshipman at ease on a masthead like the one from which William Barlow fell to his death.

21. A young midshipman directs action on the *Queen Charlotte* during the bombardment of Algiers.

22. Portrait of Commander Charles Anstruther Barlow in his full-dress uniform.

23. One of Charles Barlow's oil paintings of the frigates on which he spent much of his life.

24. Two-year-old Sydney Dickens, known as the Ocean Spectre, painted by his father's friend, Frank Stone, 1849.

25. A diminutive thirteen-year-old Sydney Dickens, 'all eyes and gold buttons'.

26. Ada Southwell (centre) photographed with two of her siblings before disaster struck the family.

27. Barnardo child Ada Southwell.

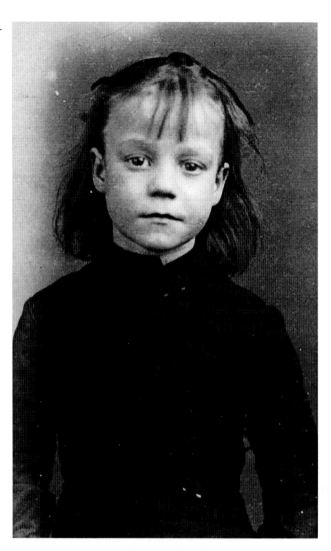

28. Barnardo girls (including Ada Southwell, unidentified) put on a brave face for the camera as they await emigration.

29. The SS *Polynesian* (or 'Rolling Poly') on which Ada Southwell travelled from Liverpool to Quebec in 1884.

30. Captain John Stedman (centre) bids farewell to his slave-wife, Joanna, and the baby son, Johnny (held by the woman on the right) who would later follow him over the sea to Holland.

31. Evacuees en route to Canada, rescued after the *City of Benares* was torpedoed in 1940.

32. A refugee child reaches European shores after a cold voyage.

view of his additional responsibilities. Elizabeth Barlow had been in England since April but was already planning to return to India, leaving her brother-in-law with the 'great and arduous task' of caring for nine of her eleven children.[30]

Even if William remained in Portsmouth, he does not seem to have completed the Academy course as there is no record of his passing any examinations. In October 1807. Sir Robert was still anxious to do anything in his power towards his nephew's 'advancement and well-doing', especially as George Barlow had eased his own son's entry into the East India Company's service. William should, at this point, have joined a ship to train as a midshipman. But had he absorbed enough of the demanding, strongly mathematical syllabus? Or had he been all too easily distracted from such dull fare by the temptations of the rowdy harbour life depicted in Thomas Rowlandson's engraving *Portsmouth Point*? Was his free-spoken manner considered too disrespectful by the Royal Navy which, as Charles Austen was told, expected obedience from midshipmen 'learning their Duty'.[31] On the answers to such questions William's future depended – and it seems that he did not come up to scratch. Sir Robert clearly felt let down by his nephew, who is not mentioned in his letters for the next two years.

* * *

The time had come for the prestige of Sir George Barlow's name to be put to full use. After being made a baronet he had served as acting governor general of India from 1805 to 1807. Disappointed not to secure this as a permanent post, he was given the governorship of Madras as a consolation prize. It would be difficult in the circumstances for the East India Company to turn down a nomination on behalf of his son for the college it had just established at Hertford Castle to train boys for its service in India. Luckily for William, there was no entrance test in the early years of the college before it moved to new premises at Haileybury in 1809. His father's connections were enough to give him another chance to make good. 'I like my situation here at present very much and I think it much better than the Navy ... because this holds out much better prospects for me', he explained to his father towards the end o

1807. The 'dutiful and obedient son' ended his letter with an attempt at reassurance: 'I hope whatever I may be deficient in Latin I shall make up to your satisfaction in the Oriental Languages.'[32]

His hope was not realised. Many of the students were daunted by the Sanskrit, Persian, Arabic, Bengali and Hindustani taught by professors with high academic distinction, but no idea how to convey their arcane knowledge to unruly young men of 15 to 20. A later pupil, George Yule, described long lectures 'in three languages we know scarcely anything of', after which 'we have to work more than five hours by ourselves to get the lessons for the next day, that is those that wish to get a good character.' Less diligent students preferred to spend their afternoons in sport rather than swotting. Alternatively the 'fast men' might repair to the conveniently close tavern, the East India College Arms, and perhaps take the speedy dog-cart it provided into Hertford or Ware. All students had to be back by 5.30 to dress for formal dinner in Hall followed by Evening Chapel. After that they were free again for private study, revelry in their rooms or expeditions to local public houses. The 'beaks' who patrolled the Quad to control rowdy behaviour had little success in breaking up 'lushes' before 2 am, or in preventing intoxicated youths from screaming and fighting as they were discharged from the dog-carts. 'Last night', recounted Yule, 'plenty of windows were broken and more doors kicked through.'[33]

Neither William's previous record, nor his correspondence with his Uncle William, suggests that he was one of the quiet and scholarly students. One letter poured scorn on a new idea that monitors should be elected to report wrongdoing by their fellows: 'How they will manage ˻ get them I know not for not one of us will be a monitor unless we are ˻mpelled.' Later he reported the rumour that a new officer was so strict ˻he intended to impose a ban on speaking at dinner: 'However I do ˻ink he will be able to carry that plan into execution.' Promises of ˻ine fish' in return for repairs to his rod and requests for further ˻ons of money suggest that his afternoons were not spent in

˻was right in judging that rules stood little chance of being ˻the first principal of the college, Samuel Henley, who was ˻ble 'to grasp any nettle'. When students were occasionally disciplined for being outside lock-up at night, absenting themselves during term or insulting the professors, the response was a general riot, in which professors were stoned, coal-scuttles hurled, windows and lamps smashed and fireworks exploded. During William's time at the college, there were two such disturbances in which the hot-tempered lad was clearly involved. His name appears in the college records on a petition signed in 1808 by many students, expressing 'their every sincere contrition for the great impropriety' of their behaviour. When his younger brother Henry made similar apologies two years later for taking part in another 'unhappy disturbance', he managed to 'wipe off the stains' on his character. But William received no such absolution; in 1809 the East India Company's Directors expelled him from the College and debarred his 'being appointed to their service in India'.[35]

It is not clear from the Barlow archive whether William entirely deserved expulsion. The loyal Uncle William was quick to defend him, telling Sir George that the Directors of the East India Company had 'formed a most erronious [*sic*] opinion that William wished to leave the college and return to the Navy', whereas the boy had actually 'flattered himself that he should have been one of the number ordered to proceed to India this season.'[36] William clearly felt that he had to apologise to his father for what he referred to as a slip, but received a milder response than he had expected: 'I am very much rejoiced that my quitting Hertford has not excited your anger so much as I had reason to conclude my behaviour would have done. I will endeavour [to follow] as correctly as possible the line which you laid down in your letter.' Neither father nor uncles gave up on William or treated him as a black sheep. It is true that Uncle William never expressed 'utmost affection' for him as he did for his 'gentlemanly' brother George, but he continued to welcome him to his house. And even the sterner Sir Robert hoped that his reprobate nephew would now 'do all in his power to redeem the past time'.[37]

*   *   *

How was this to be accomplished? Public school, the Indian Civil Service and the Royal Navy had rejected William and he seems not to have considered enlisting in the army as his older brother had done that very year. In a series of earnest letters George had persuaded his reluctant father that 'a good soldier can be a good man,' rendering 'humble service to [his] country,' and Uncle William had succeeded in getting him a commission in a good regiment. George was soon to depart to fight Napoleon in Portugal 'with the love and admiration of all who know him'.[38] It was lucky for William that the navy too had a vital role in defeating Napoleon, so that even a recruit with as dubious a record as his was welcome. It was also fortunate that Sir Robert Barlow carried even more influence with the Admiralty now that he was a commissioner at Chatham Dockyard. Thus it was not long before William had an interview with Sir Roger Curtis, commander-in-chief of Portsmouth, and was told that 'Captain Cottrell of the *Nyaden* will take me with him', presumably as a midshipman. By December 1809 he was on board in Spithead harbour preparing to sail for the West Indies in the company of other frigates and hoping 'to get into action'.[39]

From his voyage of 1800, William knew something of the perils ahead of him. Now the 'very tempestuous weather' which prevented HMS *Nyaden* from sailing endangered those stationed, as he often was, high up on the foremast. Still at Spithead as the year turned, William witnessed serious ship-board accidents resulting perhaps from New Year high jinks. He had to hold down a man while his hand was amputated after an incorrectly cleaned 6-pounder exploded as he was loading it. Another young man 'fell down the hatchway out of his hammock and entirely cut up one nostril as clean as it had been done with a knife'. Such mishaps were all too common and often resulted from skylarking in the evenings under the effect of the alcohol to which young cadets were entitled. One 11-year-old midshipman told his father that wine was no luxury for him: 'I have two glasses at dinner every day and two at supper.'[40]

Once the fleet went to sea, sailors faced further risks, and not only from France and her many allies. In fact, *Nyaden* captured three enemy ships without loss en route over the Atlantic, bringing the prospect of prize money to officers and men. She encountered none of the hurricanes which often rage in the Caribbean, but while she lay at anchor off the Leeward Islands an epidemic of yellow fever swept through the ship, killing forty-seven of the crew. William was lucky, suffering 'not the least symptom of disease during the time I was in the West Indies.' He found that he 'liked being abroad much better than being on a home station.'

Moreover, the lad seemed to be trying to turn over a new leaf. Letters to his father became longer and more detailed – though they did not match George's exhaustive accounts of the Peninsular War. Obviously following paternal guidance, William resolved to 'keep a journal of whatever may be worth mentioning so as to have a letter to hand at a short opportunity and I shall always put the date of the circumstance at the top'. Producing such a journal was in any case expected of a midshipman and might help him to get rated as a lieutenant. This was now William's ambition – though there is no record of his pursuing any further studies. While still in the West Indies in May 1810, William changed ship to HMS *Sceptre* under Captain Ballard, a friend of both the uncles who were helping to forward his career. He hastened to assure them and Sir George that this move had not been caused by any disagreement with Captain Cottrell and that his conduct on *Nyaden* had been 'such as you approve of'. He hoped apparently for 'a higher rating and better accommodation' on this new vessel.[41]

By the end of the year William had moved again, to be taken on by a powerful patron with ties of family as well as friendship. After travelling back to India with her mother, his sister Eliza had married Captain Pownoll Pellew, one of the sons of Sir Edward Pellew. Sir Edward had always been eager to use his influence on behalf of friends and relations and had taken his own sons on both *Indefatigable* and *Impetueux* at a very young age – though it's unlikely that they had much to do with Joseph Emidy who served on both ships. Now he agreed to be 'a second father' to his new nephew, promising Sir George that William would be 'as safe in my hands as your own'. To 'dear Lady Barlow' he wrote: 'I shall ... take him under my wing until he can fly alone as a Post Captain and I entreat you to be at rest that I will take the utmost care of him and teach him to love me if I can win him by kindness.'[42] Pellew obviously knew about William's poor reputation, but his own past encouraged him to indulge youthful misdemeanours. He had run away to sea to escape a flogging at Truro Grammar School and risen to the rank of midshipman before being sent ashore in disgrace for drawing a caricature of the captain's mistress. Since then he had proved his courage and ability on many

occasions, most notably in the destruction of *Droits de l'Homme*. Now he
was an admiral and commander-in-chief of the North Sea aboard HMS
Christian, on which William joined him in December 1810.

The Barlows remained optimistic that 18-year-old William would
progress in similar fashion and were encouraged when Pellew sent
word that the boy was going on to his 'entire satisfaction', despite the
misfortune of 'his having lost so much time'. 'He is extremely liked on
board', he went on, 'and bids as fair to be an honor to the Service as any
young man I know.'[43] When he spent a few days at home in February
1811, Uncle William found that 'his understanding seems enlarged and
his mind more refined' and trusted that 'he will now do very well'. Eliza
and Pownoll Pellew, now back in England, heard 'very good reports
of William from many quarters' and agreed that he looked set 'to do
extremely well'.[44]

In April 1811 Midshipman Barlow wrote to his father with the
exciting news that he would soon be heading for the Mediterranean
'with Sir Edward Pellew who hoists his flag on board HMS *Caledonia,* as
Commander-in-Chief of that station.' He was confident that service on
this fine ship (which happened to bear the same name as one of the East
Indiamen in the convoy which first brought him to British shores) would
give him 'the best opportunity of seeing some action'. He would take part
in the blockade of the French fleet anchored in Toulon harbour: 'If they
should ever fairly get out to sea I have little doubt but what they will return
in a very maimed condition from the known skill and gallantry of our
Admiral.' He also hoped 'with the Admiral's interest to have a lieutenant's
commission' within three years.[45] Pellew's letter to Sir George a few days
earlier did not express quite so much confidence. He professed still to be
satisfied with William, but had to admit that he had been 'unruly' and
'wants a little polish'. Nevertheless, Sir Edward was confident that he
had seen the folly of his ways and would now be able to hone his skills in
the Mediterranean. And, he added glumly, 'as we are to have eternal war
or rather are threatened with subjugation in these campaigns after Boney
gets 100 sail of the line, he will be in time to command a ship.'[46] The
admiral sent a rather more triumphal message, of course, to his fleet of
seventy ships as it sailed into the Mediterranean in early June: 'He looks
forward to that glorious day when in the presence of an inveterate enemy

he may unite his efforts with Companions of approved bravery, zeal and loyalty in the noble cause for which Nelson bled and from which, under Providence, he anticipates the surest victory.'[47]

*   *   *

Midshipman Barlow was to enjoy neither the chance to further his career, nor the sight of a glorious victory. HMS *Caledonia*'s logbook for 26 June when she lay at anchor in Cadiz Bay records: 'Moderate and fine Weather. At 12 Departed this Life Mr William Barlow (Mid)'.[48] Admiral Pellew did not witness the accident which led to William's death but arrived on the scene shortly afterwards. He was told that the lad had gone up the foretop mast with two young messmates, seeking a cool place to sleep, 'the weather being very hot'. They awoke in the early hours and made their descent in the dark. Two came down safely but William missed the stay for which he grasped 'and fell down head foremost on the forecastle on a tiny bolt', dying hours later 'from the bursting of a broken blood vessel in the head'. The anguished admiral wrote Sir George a hasty letter which has been preserved by the Barlow family. It related this painful story and assured them that their 'poor dear boy who was beloved by all on board' had been buried with military honours in Cadiz, 'amidst numerous British officers who have fallen in this country'. He ended with words which express both the stoicism of his time and the grief in his heart: 'May God give you and dear Lady Barlow fortitude to bear this shock as one of the events of life directed by Providence for the chastening of our minds and may the God of Mercies make it useful to us all.'

As was only natural in the circumstances, Pellew comforted William's parents with the assurance that boy had won his affection 'by his regular conduct and very good sense'. He made no suggestion of any misbehaviour leading to this 'dreadful catastrophe', even though it was somewhat irregular to mount the masthead for no good nautical reason. There may, in addition, have been some post-prandial skylarking up on the tops. It is significant that the next day the captain punished one of the other midshipmen 'with twelve lashes for being drunk on guard'.[49]

In August, Sir George's third brother, the Rev. Thomas Barlow, offered 'the united condolence of Mrs Barlow and myself on this melancholy occasion.' Sir Robert Barlow followed suit, offering his 'earnest prayers that you may be endowed by the Almighty with those resources which alone can administer consolation to the affliction with which he has been pleased to visit you.' The uncle who had received William and brought him up seems never to have referred to his premature death. The only sibling to write of it was the loyal George who was on active service in Spain. On 12 March 1812 he replied to a letter his father had written on 27 June 1811: 'Alas, my good father, how little must you have been aware, at the moment of writing, that your kind solicitude was then of no avail: two days previous my poor Brother had left this for a better world.' George did his earnest best to console both himself and his father with the thought that 'he is gone to those realms of joy and bliss, where tears are no more, nor pain and unhappiness can disturb his soul: but enough.'[50]

William Barlow's woeful maritime career, so different from that of his near contemporary Othnel Mawdesley, closely resembles that of Dick Musgrove in Jane Austen's *Persuasion*. Dick is depicted as 'a very troublesome, hopeless son ... sent to sea because he was stupid and unmanageable on shore', becoming one of those midshipmen whom 'every captain wishes to get rid of', and meeting his end before reaching his twentieth year. The novelist penned a cutting epitaph for the boy: 'He had been very little cared for at any time by his family, though quite as much as he deserved; seldom heard of, and scarcely at all regretted when the intelligence of his death abroad had worked its way to Uppercross'.[51]

I think it quite possible that this unusually malicious portrait is based on William's story. For Frank Austen had been the captain of HMS *Caledonia* until May 1811 when Pellew took over and turned her into a 'family ship', putting his inexperienced son-in-law, Richard Harward, in charge, and appointing his brother Israel captain of the fleet. It must have been galling for Captain F.W. Austen to record a 'launch employ'd getting on board Admiral Sir Edward Pellew's stock' and to answer and sign for a new midshipman (who might well have been William). The Austen family received prior knowledge of Frank's displacement through a contact in the Navy Office and their dismay is reflected in a letter from Jane to her sister Cassandra: 'Frank is superseded in the Caledonia. ... Sir Edwd Pellew succeeds Lord Gambier in his command, & some captain of his succeeds Frank. ... This is something to think of. ... What will he do ? & where will he live?'[52] Jane could well have heard some weeks later, while Frank was still high and dry in England, about the tragic death of the youngest, least qualified member of Pellew's seafaring clan. If so she would have stored it up, as she did other naval episodes, and brought it to mind when writing *Persuasion* in 1816. In reality, William's story was not quite as unhappy as Dick's. As his uncles' untiring efforts, his father's 'kind solicitude', his older brother's deep sorrow and the affection of his shipmates suggest, it is not the case that nobody cared for William. He may have been troublesome, but he was not unloved.

Of the three youngsters who set out over the seas in 1800 the only one to achieve 'consequence' was George – at the expense of very great effort. In Uncle William's judgement, his strength was 'not equal to his spirits and exertions', so that he often came home at the end of school terms 'with a cough, much fatigued and very thin', and his speech (as well as his letters) had 'an unpleasant monotony'. After enlisting in the army he was twice invalided home to be nursed back to health by his devoted family. But he went on to serve with courage, wounded both in the Peninsular War and at Waterloo, the battle medal for which is proudly displayed in a portrait of him as a tall, dark and very handsome war hero. In 1817 he married his cousin Hilaire, daughter of Sir Robert Barlow, and was sent on service to India. But there in the land of his birth he died, probably of malaria, at the age of 33.[53]

Eliza's history is more akin to William's. After a gloomy year or so with the ailing and inattentive Mrs Butcher she was, like him, kindly treated by three uncles, often knowing that she was a 'great inconvenience' to them. Like William, she disliked school and could not, reported the Rev. Thomas with whose family she spent holidays, 'patiently submit to restraint and the constant but proper attention that is paid to her manners and disposition by the ladies who have the care of her education'. And, like William, she got into serious trouble. Seven years after her hasty marriage in Madras to Pownoll Pellew, she had incurred both debts, which she concealed from her husband, and disgrace, caused by her 'revolting and insupportable behaviour', and 'dreadful language'. She apparently had a passionate affair with a young army lieutenant in Brighton (the scene of Lydia's elopement in *Pride and Prejudice*) and ran off with him to Ireland, where she was later discovered 'far advanced in pregnancy'. In the legal separation which followed in 1818, Eliza lost the custody of the three small children born during her marriage, as well as the support of a family which had treated William's misconduct with some degree of tolerance. She had 'in any way not criminal' to establish her future accordingly – and it is not known what became of her.[54]

In defence of both Eliza and William it can be argued that theirs had not been an easy childhood, as Pellew recognised when he referred to his late midshipman as 'a hard used boy'. They had been torn from the land of their birth at a sensitive age, shunted from one benign but overburdened relation to another, and sent to harsh boarding establishments for an education to which they were ill-suited. Above all, they lacked, as Eliza lamented, 'the happiness of being under maternal care' for many years. Even the inarticulate William expressed the relief with which he would behold his mother 'after our long absence'. It was George who most eloquently voiced his sense of deprivation, but only after 1815 when Lady Barlow was banished from the family home in England on the discovery of her long liaison with Captain George Pratt Barlow, her husband's young cousin and aide-de-camp. He poured out his feelings in a letter to his father: 'Alas I never knew the sound of maternal fondness, no not even the slightest whisperings from my earliest period of being able to be acquainted with them.' This clumsy emotional tirade suggests that even in India, Elizabeth Barlow's 'love of wine and dancing' had outstripped her devotion to her children. Once back in England after Sir George's retirement, she apparently 'behaved with great unkindness towards all her children' and did not 'know one more than another'.[55]

For whatever reason, William Barlow had lacked the tenacity, self-control and deference he needed to make his way in the tough world of the early nineteenth century. But there is no evidence that he was a bully or a cad in the manner of George Macdonald Fraser's Flashman, and he always got on well with contemporaries and equals – his brother-in-law, for example, found him 'the best-tempered amiable lad' he had ever known.[56] Had he survived beyond the age of 19 he might well have gained greater command over his turbulent passions and lived, after all, a seafaring 'life of enterprise'.

Chapter 6

Charles Barlow 1800–1805:
A Life Lived Through Letters

E ighth child and fifth son though he was, Charles Anstruther Barlow could not have been more prized in his early years. Born in Calcutta on 5 February 1800 (soon after the departure of his siblings George, Eliza and William), he was given his middle name in honour of Sir John Anstruther of Fife, Chief Justice of Bengal. The choice of a name (and probably of a godfather) associated with the Scottish aristocracy suggests that his father, George Barlow, a man of humble origins who had risen to be chief secretary to the Indian government, had high hopes for Charles. Anglo-Indian society was acutely class-conscious – as is suggested by the combative relationship between Charles's mother, Elizabeth, and Lady Anstruther. In the 'malicious Billingsgate dialogue' in which they often engaged when their husbands were absent, each was apt to accuse the other of having been born in an Irish hovel.[1]

When Charles was 5 years old George Barlow, now a baronet himself, was appointed acting governor general of India and the family moved into the magnificent new Government House, to the delight of the sociable Lady Barlow. By this time three more of the couple's children, Charlotte, Henry and Robert, had been sent to England, leaving Charles to take on the role of senior resident son, whose constant companions were his sisters Louisa and Frances (Fanny), a year older and younger respectively. One of Sir George's first duties was to tour the domain over which he now ruled, a journey involving several months away from home and resulting in a regular correspondence with his wife. Lady Barlow's incoherent and colloquial letters give every sign of being hastily written between the receptions, levées, balls and masquerades she so much enjoyed. Even so, they give vivid glimpses of the infant Charles whose very words are often quoted by his mother.

Lady Elizabeth Barlow to her husband, 27 October 1805:

> The pianoforte came home yesterday – only think of Louisa and
> Charles requesting me to sing to them, which I did. When I had
> done Charles said 'Little time to go Mama, then again you sing' and
> this I did this morning. When I had done their suppers they each
> took a chair and sat down by me begging I would sing to them.

As above, 1 December 1805:

> You would be surprised and delighted to hear Charles talk. He said
> to me the other day 'Pray Mama to come to the Hall and explain
> (what a word for him) some of the pictures to Louisa and me. Play
> about with us a little, you are always working.' I hope if God pleases
> Charles will make a great man; he has, dear child, every virtue at
> present that will make him as good a man as his father. ... Charles
> I think will in addition to his justifiable pride feel affection for you.

As above, 16 December 1805:

> When I wrote yesterday I could not bring myself to tell you what
> notice Charles took of 'my Lady [Anstruther]'s' conversation
> relative to your return. When I made her comprehend how soon it
> was likely you will be back the little fellow's eyes glistened and off
> he set to Louisa. ... Charles does so follow me about that I told him
> the other day I would put a ribbon around his neck and fasten him
> around my waist.[2]

Sir George was due to return on Charles's sixth birthday and the child
grew so excited in the new year that his mother felt the need to curb his
high spirits.

Lady Elizabeth Barlow to her husband, 16 January 1806:

> Charles says 'Now nobody comes [and] there is no noise in the
> house, Mama, when Papa comes then [he] will make bash bash bash

every minute.' What an odd little creature he is! Such a mixture of innocence and observation, spirit and mildness; he is a thousand times more like my dearest B in disposition than any one of the family. Did your Mama whip you as I have done Charles?

A few days later, however, Lady Barlow felt proud of her son's precocity. She recounted to Sir George a conversation held as she and the children took the evening air on the banks of the Hooghly River with a group of imperial dignitaries. Charles explained to the East India Company's chaplain, Claudius Buchanan, that 'Papa's name is Governor-General ... because he governs all India, and all the people in India.' Rev. Buchanan was apparently 'astonished' by the child's definition.[3]

Thus we can picture a serious, good-looking little boy, 'a handsome creature' with the dark hair and eyes shown in a later portrait. We feel his yearning for the company and approval of his elusive, unpredictable mother and the pride he took in his father's exalted position. We witness the curiosity aroused by his new abode – the domed and colonnaded Calcutta palace chock-full with paintings of British victories, portraits of empire-builders and busts of the Caesars. We can imagine him in one of its banqueting halls enjoying the celebrations for his sixth birthday, dressed perhaps as a harlequin or a soldier (for fancy-dress costumes were popular with Raj children), encircled by his proud parents, sisters and baby brother, Richard, as well as by the children of other high-ranking British officials and many Indian servants. We can hear music and song, applause and toasts to the 'great man' Charles was expected to become.

We shall also be able to follow the child's development by means of the rich (and rare) collection of Barlow family letters in the India Office Library. Since Charles became a much more diligent correspondent than his unruly brother William, we can trace through them which of the conflicting sides of Charles's character identified by his mother would predominate as he matured. Would he have sufficient spirit to stamp his mark on the turbulent world into which he was born? Or would his mildness and virtue equip him better for domestic life in more settled times?

*   *   *

Only a week or so after the birthday party, Charles, Louisa and Fanny kissed and embraced their parents, siblings, friends and servants before setting out on the Hooghly River. They were embarked not on a pleasant boating trip in the cool of the evening, but on a 50-mile journey, piloted through sandbars and mudflats, to the East India Company's anchorage at Saugor. Here a fleet of ships had already been loaded with cargo and awaited only their passengers before setting out for England. Among them was the *Surrey*, the logbook of which has survived. Its fragile pages reveal that the ship received fifteen male passengers, four 'ladies' including the captain's wife, Mrs Cumberlege, accompanied by two children, and Mrs Fraser, who had six offspring with her. The Barlows were among the ten remaining youngsters (aged between 7 and 4) who were travelling without guardians – though some of the seven listed 'native servants' may have been deputed to look after them.

With war against Napoleonic France and her allies still raging at sea as much as on land, *Surrey*'s passengers faced a perilous voyage. The captain was always careful to note the proximity of her sister ships in convoy and was reassured by the sight of the 74-gun *Culloden*, flagship of Admiral Sir Edward Pellew, commander-in-chief of the East Indies, which was stationed at Point-de-Galle, Ceylon. With such protection *Surrey* escaped attacks from the French privateers which prowled the Indian Ocean on the track of richly-laden East Indiamen. The log does, however, record many of the normal hazards of this six-month passage: 'hard squalls', 'strong gales', 'confused seas', 'sailmakers repairing sails', 'pumps used on thirteen inches of water', and 'fumigation of the gun deck'. Captain Cumberlege held several courts of inquiry: at one a sailor was found guilty of 'striking one of the invalids' and was punished with 'two dozen lashes at the Gang Way'. A joiner and a private soldier died and their bodies were 'committed to the deep with usual ceremony'. An incident which no doubt made an impression on the Barlow youngsters occurred on 22 April, when a young midshipman was knocked overboard and drowned, even though 'every exertion was made to save him'.[4]

The emotional turbulence through which the Barlow children passed on leaving home can only be imagined. They clearly had plenty of playmates to distract them from the pangs of separation, but would have lacked motherly care had it not been for the kindness of an already overburdened Mrs Fraser. Sir George's brothers William and Robert obviously felt that no proper arrangements had been made for the voyage, or indeed for their arrival in England.

William Barlow to his brother, George, 1 August 1806:

> I have the satisfaction to inform you of the safe arrival of your three dear children Louisa, Charles and Fanny all in the best of health. They were delivered to me as clean and nice looking as if they had come out of their Mama's nursery. I find the persons whose care you had committed them to were dismissed from that service by Captain Cumberlege. ... I learn also that you are much indebted to Mrs Fraser as well as to the Captain for this good management. ... As all your children have come home in time of war you are very fortunate in their safe arrival.

Sir Robert Barlow to his brother, George, 1 August 1806:

> Somerset Place [his official residence as Deputy Controller of the Navy] is fortunately a large house as your dear children Louisa, Charles and Fanny arrived at the door about three days after we had taken possession of it. Six of them were with us last week but they are to be disposed of in the following manner –
>
> Eliza: during her holidays to divide her time between us & Mrs Robert Barlow
>
> Charlotte and Fanny: To go on the 5th Aug to Halberton [the Devon village where George's brother, Thomas, was Vicar]
>
> Louisa: To remain with us until her Mama comes home
>
> William: Gone to Portsmouth Academy
>
> Charles: With his Uncle William who left London yesterday for Brighton, taking with him George, Robert & Henry.[5]

It is clear that the disposal of Sir George's exiled offspring presented a mounting burden to his brothers and that this often overrode the 'familial form of patriotism' noted in a recent study.[6] As 17-year-old Eliza realised, it was a 'great inconvenience' to Sir Robert to receive so many children into his official London residence, spacious though it was. But she and 15-year-old George were genuinely pleased to meet three more siblings, two of whom had been born after their departure from India. They could well understand how much the trio missed their parents, as well as the sights and sounds of their native land. Both noticed in particular the sweet temperament of 'dear little Charles'.

George to his father, Brighton, 1 August 1806:

> I must not omit to inform you that I first beheld the three little travellers at my Aunt's house in Hanover Square. Charles ... is a sweet little boy, so innocent, so mild, so engaging, so free and open and so meek and placid in his temper. I really think he has the fewest imperfections I ever beheld in a little boy. He is in very good health and often talks about Papa and the tiger at Barrackpore. He is in memory of several circumstances of his voyage. He is free from deceit and is in short a sweet little boy. Forgive this long digression; it is the natural affection of a brother's tenderness in expatiating on the qualities of one whom he so tenderly loves. I do not think that there is a Boy who will ever be so good if he is well taken care of and educated. ... Whilst in London we visited Col & Mrs Fraser in order to thank her for her many kind attentions to my sisters and brother during their voyage home and waits.[7]

All the young Barlows were longing at that time for the arrival of Lady Barlow, who planned to travel to England later in the year with Anne, Richard and the new baby, Harriet. They all wrote regularly to their parents, despite knowing that their letters might find 'a watery grave', and looked out for replies whenever ships came in from India.[8] Having made the journey themselves, they were all too conscious of the great expanse of stormy waters separating the family.

*   *   *

Once in the care of Uncle William at Clapham, Charles undoubtedly pined for his adored parents and also for his early companions, Louisa and Fanny. But at least he did not have to suffer the 'low living and half starving' to which his four older brothers were subjected at Rev. Roberts's school in Mitcham. Instead he boarded at Mr Sketchley's nearby academy in Clapham Rise, where his uncle thought him so happy he liked it more than being at home and George was able to assure his father that Charles's acquirements were 'extremely creditable': 'He can write and spell perfectly well.'[9]

The school was also within easy reach of Wood Lodge, the comfortable Streatham residence where William Barlow installed the pregnant Lady Barlow and all twelve of her existing children after she arrived in the spring of 1807. The house was large enough also to accommodate 'two footmen, a coachman and a helper in the stable, a gardener and how many woman servants I know not'. Eliza told her father that they were 'very agreeably settled at Streatham', and several of the children described their family life in glowing detail. Henry delighted in the large garden with a 'nice lawn' on which they could all play as well as 'two fields, a shady walk and a shrubbery in which Mama sometimes walks with us'. Fanny and Louisa wrote of their expeditions with Mama to the pantomime and the Harlequin, by which they were much amused. Charles does not seem to have written to his father at this time but Lady Barlow proudly reported that he had received a prize for 'being at the top in Latin always', and that an artist who came to the house had found his 'countenance one of the finest he has ever seen, a face that would be equally handsome and animated and intelligent.' His 'handsome likeness' was the only one she decided to purchase – but sadly it does not survive.[10]

Delightful though this ménage sounds, it did not last long. By August, Lady Barlow was already planning her return to India. There are several possible reasons for this sudden change of plan. William Barlow thought that his sister-in-law found it difficult to manage so large a family, especially with the older boys 'at their riotous age'. He also got the impression that her return was necessary for the comfort of his disappointed brother, who had been ousted from the governor generalship and sent to be governor of Madras. What no one yet knew was that Captain Pratt Barlow, Sir George's cousin and aide-de-camp who had escorted her to England, was

Lady Barlow's secret lover. He visited Streatham to ride with her almost every day and often took her on pleasurable excursions into London. But now he had to return to his duties in India, leaving her to decide between him and her children. And so it was that after less than a year of active motherhood, Elizabeth sailed for Madras early in 1808, taking her two oldest daughters with her and leaving her brother-in-law with the 'great and arduous task' of caring for the rest of her offspring.

William Barlow to his brother, Clapham, 17 September 1807:

> We cannot be supposed in the short period since the receipt of your letters to have finally settled a plan for the disposal of your children, except that Eliza and Charlotte are to accompany their mother. ... I see no alternative but for me to return to my old Duty ... [and] my present plan is to reside in the house fitted up for Lady Barlow at Streatham. ... The proposed undertaking of helping to keep the greater part of your family together is with the view and anxious hope of rendering your mind easy, and that you may have the consolation to think your children are under the eye of those who have almost the same feelings for them and desire to promote their welfare as yourself.[11]

William Barlow was as good as his word. He moved into Wood Lodge with all his remaining nieces and nephews apart from the two babies, who went to Lady Barlow's mother in Bath. For the next five years he and his wife looked after the children, treating them with kindness and affection as well as giving them 'proper direction' when their high spirits got out of hand. The girls were taught at home by a governess and the boys attended boarding schools, joining the household for the holidays – when passionate quarrels often erupted. For another year or so Charles remained at Mr Sketchley's school endeavouring, as he assured his father, 'to improve myself as much as possible because I think it will give you great pleasure'. In 1809 he and his brother Robert were sent on the day-long journey by stage coach to Woodford School in Linton, Cambridgeshire, run by the Rev. Holt Okes. Okes was a donnish man who had close links with Cambridge University and was engaged in the superhuman task of calculating the exact date of Christ's crucifixion. Also a scholar, his brother had recently written *A Compendium of Chronology, intended as a Short Introduction to History from the Creation of the World to the Year 1806*, especially for the use of the young gentlemen at Linton School, from which the boys no doubt benefited. Charles's dutiful letters, occasionally written in Latin to his 'caro pater', give further particulars of his studies.

Charles to his father, Linton, 5 February 1811:

> We came from Streatham on the 30th of January and arrived in Linton on the same day. I saw in the papers that George's regiment had been engaged and very few men killed and wounded, but I am happy to say that he escaped without any injury. I am now reading Caesar, Selecto e Profano, Ovid's Metamorphosis & Evangelia. I have also begun to read Numa Pompilius in French and in Arithmetic I have proceeded to the middle of fractions.[12]

All the surviving letters by or about Charles during his schooldays reveal a stoical child. He did not pour out his feelings as did his contemporary Thomas Babington Macaulay when he was packed off to his Cambridgeshire school: 'I do not remember being ever more gloomy in my life than when I first left Clapham [and] got into the Cambridge Stage.' Nor did Charles beg for letters which would comfort him amid 'the vexations which absence from home and the plagues of school' might well have caused him.[13] In fact he plainly gave his uncle less trouble than his brothers. He did not, like William and Henry, get involved in disturbances at school; he was more industrious than the 'idle and careless' Robert, and there is no mention of his suffering the poor health which afflicted George and Edward. He clearly got on well with Rev. Okes, who pronounced him 'a good boy', and may well have been imbued by him with religious sentiments, as well as being invited into his study for readings from books such as *The Rival Roses* or renderings of *Songs Moral, Sentimental, Instructive and Amusing*.[14] Above all, Charles aimed to please the father from whom he was separated for eight years and to impress him by his industry if not by any special distinction. He was, reported Uncle William, 'growing a noble fine boy and has declared his inclination to be a sailor.'[15]

*   *   *

The choice of a naval career was by no means unusual for a boy born and brought up during the Napoleonic Wars. On his voyage from India, Charles had witnessed the protective presence of Royal Navy vessels and in England during the years after Trafalgar he no doubt observed regular celebrations of famous naval victories, attended plays which re-enacted them or sung some of Dibdin's *Songs Naval and National*.[16] Apart from its patriotic allure, the navy promised social status and excellent chances of promotion as long as the war lasted, especially for a boy with patrons like Admiral Sir Robert and Sir George Barlow. In February 1811, when Charles declared his inclination, the navy was fully occupied in defending British trade against Napoleon's Continental System and blockading the ports of France and her allies. Young hopefuls were still flocking to join and among them was the older brother who had just been taken on by his uncle-in-law, Admiral Pellew. William was on leave in Streatham at that time, boasting, no doubt, of the action in which he hoped soon to take part. Only time would tell whether such a hazardous life would suit his dutiful young brother.

If he still remembered the fatal accident which befell a midshipman on his voyage from India, Charles was already aware of some of the dangers of shipboard life, especially for young and inexperienced sailors. Then, soon after he had decided on his calling, he heard of William's fatal fall from the topmast of HMS *Caledonia* in June 1811. Surviving letters give no clue as to when or how the news of this dreadful event was received in the Streatham household – but it clearly did not shake Charles's resolve. On 14 November the following year the 12-year-old boy boarded HMS *Victorious* as a first-class volunteer, a new rank for 'young gentlemen intended for the sea'. He joined the ship at Portsmouth, where she was being repaired after living up to her name in a five-hour battle in the Adriatic to capture a newly built French warship. *Victorious* had suffered heavy casualties, including her captain, John Talbot, who had been badly wounded by a splinter in his head. But on 22 November, a week after

Charles had boarded, captain, ship and crew were fit enough to sail with a convoy for North American waters to engage with Britain's new enemy, the United States.

With its strong, modern warships, the Republic had already captured several British vessels and was causing serious damage to Britain's trade with the West Indies. Over the next months, as Charles explained to his father and uncle, *Victorious* first helped to protect British cargo ships bound for Barbados and then participated in the navy's blockade of the North American coast, sometimes conducting punitive raids inland. In October 1813 he told his father that he was 'amply satisfied' with his choice of a 'station in life',[17] and at the end of that year he was officially rated as a midshipman. It is only in a rather confused letter to Sir Robert that he reveals the dangers and hardships of the North America posting – as well as his own youthful woes and fears.

Charles to Admiral Sir Robert Barlow, HMS *Victorious*, off New London, April 1814:

> I hope in my next to inform you of an attack on the Americans which will astonish them. We have not begun the war with them yet although it has been declared nearly two years. ... You have most probably heard several accounts of our being lost but I can assure you that it was generally supposed it would have been the case. We were ashore on the enemy's coast for six and thirty hours during which it was blowing very hard off the land and so cold that even the bread froze in the oven and turned to lead. Several of our men had their fingers frost bit. ... We must have been lost inevitably, we were not twenty yards from the shore. I have undergone a severe illness since I wrote last, for when we went to Bermuda from Halifax, I had the jaundice very severely. During my illness Captain Talbot was so kind as to let me [have] whatever I wanted.[18]

The ship's log reveals that *Victorious* was herself the victim of climate and geography. In October 1813 she had 'struck against a rock and in staying killed John Lannon, Seaman, and broke the after part of the wheel'. A month later the ship suffered serious injury in a hurricane while in Halifax harbour. After another encounter with a sunken rock in 'very thick foggy weather' in July 1814 she sustained so much damage that she had to return home for repair. As part of a successful campaign to thwart American naval activity, *Victorious* had chased and captured many ships from America's navy or from countries trading with her. Charles makes no mention of these thrilling events, even though he was surely entitled to a small share in the prize money. Nor does he reveal that Captain Talbot several times took on board runaway slaves who thus gained their freedom.[19] After the captain had steered the leaky vessel back into Portsmouth harbour on 10 August 1814, he sent a report on his new recruit to the admiral who had recommended his nephew to his care. There is a hint in the wording that 'very fine' though he was, the boy was not exactly cut out for a naval career, a feeling echoed a few weeks later by Charles himself.[20]

Charles to his father, Woolwich, 13 September 1814:

> I am sorry to relate to you what has been my thought the whole of the night almost which I hope will meet with your approbation, that is my intention of leaving the service by your permission. My dear father I beg you will consent to anything but going to sea. You shall have a good reason for it when we are together. I am not too old to choose another profession. Let me go to school and you shall see me prosper in my studies. This short letter I have written will I hope convince you that I have good reason for so doing.[21]

Sir George had by this time been recalled from Madras after failing to deal satisfactorily with an army mutiny, so Charles was able to meet his father soon after this *cri de coeur*. How did he explain his startling change of heart? In the aftermath of arduous action and dangerous illness, it would not have been surprising if he felt daunted by the sheer physical demands of naval life. Although such a tough existence fostered Hornblowers and Aubreys, by no means all midshipmen thrived on the crowded conditions, harsh punishments, inadequate food and sleep, unpredictable perils and relentless labour. In Charles's case there were probably emotional factors at work too. As a serious youth, who resembled his shy and aloof father and rather priggish oldest brother, George, he was likely to have been the butt of ragging from more raucous shipmates, for no captain could protect his new recruits from 'the nefarious forces [which] were free to operate unseen in the nether regions of a ship'.[22] Subsequent letters show that Charles was worried about the examinations in seamanship and navigation, which he would have to pass in order to win promotion, and about how he would be able to study in the dingy, noisy midshipmen's mess. And he was no doubt suffering too from the homesickness which he was increasingly prone to express in years to come.

Evidently, though, Sir George stiffened his son's sinews to such an extent that he was willing to embark on a new ship when another family connection, Captain John Bastard, agreed 'to find room' for him.[23] Bastard had distinguished himself in East Indian waters soon after the *Surrey* and her juvenile passengers had passed through them in 1806; as captain of HMS *Rattlesnake*, he captured the mighty *Bellone*, one of the French frigates which had long preyed on British merchant vessels. During the last year of the wars he commanded HMS *Meander,* mostly in home waters, and did his best to support the shaky midshipman revealed in Charles's letters home.

Charles to his father, HMS *Meander*, Woolwich, 26 September 1814:

> I received your letter today which has so encouraged me that I could undergo the greatest hardships imaginable. I am pretty well versed in Navigation for the short time I have been at sea for there are several young men who have told me all that they have been questioned and there are a few more rules which I am certain I shall know by when I have served my time. I am in a great hurry you must excuse my bad letter which I hope will show you what encouragement your last letter has afforded me.

After suffering two further illnesses, a 'severe cold in the face' and an 'attack of lumbago', Charles eventually began to find shipboard life more congenial.

Charles to his father, HMS *Meander,* off Dungeness, 9 November 1814:

> I am very much pleased with the ship as I am confident there is not
> a better ship in the Navy, judging by what I have seen of her as yet.
> She sails very well, not only the ship but the Captain and officers
> all; the former allows us to go into his cabin whenever we like and
> take any books that we wish to read and there is always a fire and it
> is very comfortable as you may suppose. We go in the morning and
> learn one or two problems of Euclid, which one of the midshipmen
> is so good as to teach us. I can assure you that there is not a more
> comfortable ship in the Navy both for officers and men.

As above, 14 November 1814:

> I shall do my best endeavour whilst I have such a fine opportunity
> of learning but I am sorry to add that the Midshipman who was so
> good as to teach us, is at present very ill and not able to attend, for
> which I am very sorry indeed, as there is not a more good-natured,
> attentive messmate in the ship. When we do not understand anything
> he would stand over us for an hour or until we did understand it; as
> for me I feel myself under great obligations to him, I cannot answer
> exactly for my messmates as I am not thoroughly acquainted with
> them.

These are not, however, the kind of letters one might expect of an eager
young sailor in a navy inspired by the example of Horatio Nelson. Rather,
they dwell on Charles's frequent ailments (which did not apparently
include seasickness), his anxiety about mastering nautical astronomy
and trigonometry, his dependence on the support of his father and of
his fatherly captain, his detachment from most of his shipmates and
his appreciation of a little home comfort. His last letter from *Meander*
was addressed to his mother from Marseilles in August 1815. He
sends sympathy to his brothers as the 'poor fellows' went off to school,
suggesting that he too was longing for home.[24] The thought of children
leaving home clearly brought back memories of his own separations,
just as the sight of people parting from their children always did for his

contemporary and fellow Indian exile, William Makepeace Thackeray, who had departed for boarding-school at the age of 6: 'Twang goes the horn: up goes the trunk; down come the steps. Bah! I see the autumn evening: I hear the wheels now: I smart the cruel smart again.'[25] At 15 years old Charles may have found his sea-legs, but he was still finding his feet in the Royal Navy.

Meander had spent the first six months of 1815 in the Mediterranean, which had proved 'a very bad cruising ground', with few prizes to be taken. This was the time of Napoleon's last European campaign after his escape from exile on Elba, in which the navy 'had little to do except re-establish the blockade'.[26] Once Napoleon had been escorted to a more distant banishment on St Helena in August, Captain Bastard told Charles that 'all the ships on the Mediterranean would be ordered home in a very short time to be paid off.' By the end of the year *Meander* had docked in Northfleet and Charles was worried about his career prospects, despite bearing a satisfactory testimonial from his benign captain.

Captain Bastard to George Barlow, HMS *Meander*, 5 December 1815 & 5 July 1816:

> Your son has uniformly conducted himself to my satisfaction, his disposition is good, as well as his Principles. He is attentive to his professional duties and promises fair with his abilities added to the experience which only time can give him.
>
> I give testimony to his uniform good conduct whilst with me and my assurance that if he continues the same path, I have little doubt of his turning out well and being both a comfort to his family and useful in his profession.[27]

On the other hand, as Charles told his father, midshipmen were leaving the service very fast now that the war was over and he had still not passed his examinations. In his desperation to master the essential principles of navigation, listed by one midshipman as 'logarithms, sines, tangents, cosines, secants, cosecants, horizontal parallax, semidiameter, meridian altitude [and] all the heavenly bodies',[28] he turned for assistance to his old school. Fortunately, the learned Okes (as well as two Barlow brothers) was still in residence.

Charles to his father, Woodford House, Linton, 25 March 1816:

Mr Okes received me very kindly and recommended to me the best book which I could learn viz The System of Mathematical Education at the Royal Naval College by the Revd J. Inman. Mr Okes is so kind as to have me in the Study every evening for an hour or two extra which I find a great help to me as he is the only person that can give me any information about mathematics, not even the Usher. Richard and Edward send their love to all at home.[29]

*   *   *

Neither the 'comfortable ship' *Meander* nor the attentive Captain Bastard put to sea again. The former was soon broken up and the latter retired to Sharpham, his fine estate near the Devon shore, adjacent to that of Admiral Pellew, now Lord Exmouth. Through the influence of both these officers Charles was posted, in July 1816, to HMS *Queen Charlotte*, the flagship of a punitive expedition the admiral was about to conduct against the Dey of Algiers. Twice that year Exmouth had sailed to North Africa to impose treaties on Barbary rulers which would end their old custom of capturing Christian slaves from foreign shores, including those of Devon and Cornwall. In May that year the Dey had not only refused to sign such a treaty, but had massacred about 200 European fishermen. It was to avenge this action and to rescue captive slaves that Exmouth raised his flag on the *Queen Charlotte* and mustered a crew. Charles Barlow was to serve as his aide-de-camp – but the poor fellow had only a vague idea of the issues at stake in the conflict. His mind was set on the ordeal of his impending examination, in which he would have to answer questions put to him by three captains on such matters as splicing ropes, reefing a sail, the use of Mercator projection maps and the observation of the stars to determine the course and position of a ship.

Charles to his father, HMS *Queen Charlotte*, Portsmouth, 11 July 1816:

You need not alarm yourself concerning me as I shall adopt the same line of conduct I have heretofore pursued, though I am sure not very long on the Queen Charlotte, as it is certain we shall not be here more than four months, unless we begin to negotiate with these barbarians, which I hope we shall not. ... When the fleet were at Algiers the Dey ... was at his quarters with his troops examining every place and encouraging his men and he said he would not fire the first gun but that directly we began he would retaliate.

As above, en route to Algiers, 17 July 1816:

You will be no less astonished than disappointed when I tell you I made an attempt to pass my examination but could not succeed. ... I am in hopes that there will be sufficiently weighty reasons ... to convince you that it was not for want of attention or will that I did not succeed but I hope the next opportunity I have of making an attempt that I shall succeed. I should not speak falsely if I said that partiality [was] carried on in this case, ... for my answer was the same with one of this ship's midshipmen but as I did not work at the same way [they] would not grant me the certificate. That self same person was asked to dinner by the Commissioner.[30]

It is difficult not to sympathise with Charles's disappointment at his failure after all the hard work he had put in – and indeed his father did not cast any blame. The accusation of 'partiality' on the part of his examining captains might sound peevish, but favouritism was common practice in his day. What is surprising is that Charles sent no detailed account of this dangerous and exciting two-month expedition, culminating in a decisive victory in Algiers harbour on 27 August. In the words of Abraham Salamé, Lord Exmouth's interpreter, this 'released slaves, restored money, abolished Christian slavery, made treaties, concluded peace and settled everything.'[31] Midshipman Barlow would have been on the quarterdeck of the 100-gun flagship alongside Lord Exmouth throughout the action. Sharing his experiences was a fellow midshipman who described them anonymously in a spirited letter to his local Devon newspaper, making light of the day's bloody action.

Letter to *Trewman's Exeter Flying Post*, 19 September 1816:

> Our old Queen Charlotte was the Madame Saqui [a French tightrope walker] of the piece and danced beautifully on the tight rope by which she was made fast to the Mole. I dare say the Dey thinks we must be all near-sighted, for we seemed to think we never could get close enough. … The pirates began firing just about two o'clock, as I have since heard, for I forgot to look at my watch. The position of the Queen Charlotte was exactly at the entrance of the Mole, where we had a complete prospect of what they used to call the marine. They must now find a new name for it, for they have no marine left. This enabled us to have a beautiful view of the commencement of the action; I cannot describe to you the immense crowd of men that covered the Mole and all parts of the marine; they were as thick as hops. … At last, Fire! Fire! Fire – and bang. I think I saw 500 or 1000 of them bang down in an instant. After that I did not see much, until our boats, taking pity on our darkness, set fire to a frigate close to us, just by way of light to see what we were doing. … Now the grief of the story is, that we had no officer killed, so no promotion; the Dey's balls seemed to have the navy list to heart, and took care to avoid every body who would have made a vacancy. The Admiral had a sore dowse in the chops, which did not I believe draw blood; if it did he swabb'd it up directly without saying a word about it, though he must have had a good deal of jaw of his own, to be able to stand such a thump.[32]

The ship's log records 'ruined rigging' and 'the foremast much wounded', as well as 'the loss of 8 killed and 127 wounded' by the time firing ceased towards midnight.[33] The detailed casualty lists which appeared later show that five of those wounded on the *Queen Charlotte* were midshipmen, three of them 'severely'.[34] On the ten other ships of the fleet, eight midshipmen were killed, one was dangerously wounded, seventeen had severe injuries including an arm amputation, and twelve were slightly hurt. It may well be that Charles was reticent because he did not want to worry his anxious family about the perils to which he had been exposed, or he may simply have shrunk from the task of describing the gory details of battle.

A few days later he no doubt joined the remaining able-bodied midshipmen in taking command of small boats sent to embark over a thousand Christian slaves as well as large sums of compensation money from Algiers. On 3 September, its mission successfully completed, the fleet made sail for the homeward journey, during which the Exeter newspaper's account of the *Queen Charlotte*'s casualties was rendered inaccurate when Lieutenant J.T. Johnstone, 'departed this life of his wounds received at Algiers on 27th August'.[35] Even so, no vacancy was created for the hungry midshipmen since the ship never again left Britain's shores after docking in Portsmouth harbour in early October. Charles Barlow and his disrespectful messmate would have to seek another billet.

* * *

Lord Exmouth must have been sufficiently satisfied with Charles to recommend him to a new ship, HMS *Rochfort*, which was sent to guard against smuggling along the Kent coast, where his duties proved somewhat testing, as the letters relate.

Charles to his father, HMS Cutter *Cameleon* (a small 10-gun vessel used to combat smugglers), Lydd, Kent, 16 April 1817:

> I am left in one of the batteries on the coast with a boats crew of six men and eight days provisions to look out for smugglers. It is a most wretched place as I have no companion at all and it is three miles from any house whatsoever. My Duty is always to launch my boat during the night if the weather will permit and if not possible to do that, to tramp the beach all night so that you may imagine what sort of a life a person leads sleeping the whole day and looking out all night.

As above, HMS *Rochfort*, 4 August 1817:

> I hear that it is in contemplation to give us £130,000 for Algiers. I hope it is true [as] that sum will give me about £20. My cold has not left me entirely and I must nurse for a night or two and not go out.

As above, 28 August 1817:

> We are to get a small prize, small indeed for the smugglers were
> too strong for me, four of us against about a hundred or so of them
> [and] I began to wish myself somewhere or other away from them.
> It would be a very unpleasant thing to shoot a fellow ashore for the
> sake of a few casks of spirits, therefore one knows not what to do,
> for when we first made our appearance among them and fired over
> them, they gave up the goods and when they saw we were so weak
> they took them from us again and gave one of my men a good beating.
> … Fortunately I had a pistol and that kept them at bay or perhaps
> I should have suffered the same. The Captain of the Gang (as he is
> called) had the audacity to offer my men a bribe before I came up,
> but they were proof against that. The Lords of the Treasury will
> offer a reward to detect the offenders.

As above, 6 October 1817:

> I have received your letter … the contents of which must be highly
> satisfactory to the feelings of so young a Servant as myself and is
> of course an incitement to continue in the same line of conduct. I
> shall soon take my examination in Seamanship. [Another Mid] is
> in a serious scrape because his men have been caught stealing and
> threatened to shoot the Mayor, for which he is held responsible. If
> they are in fault he will probably be turned out of the Service.

As above, 1 November 1817:

> I am sorry to tell you that we have had a very serious quarrel (our
> mess) with the rest of the shipmates in consequence of a boat we
> engaged to attend the ship, although I except myself from it. Still it
> is a very disagreeable thing to see dissension among any mess, but
> particularly aboard a ship.[36]

This unusually honest account of lonely smuggler patrols and of turbulent
shipboard life suggests more mildness than mettle in Charles's nature;
although not lacking courage he was easily cast down by conflict.

The letters contain no reference to the discord in his own family. In 1816 his mother's adultery had been exposed in a widely publicised divorce case leading to the dissolution of her marriage to Sir George and the loss of contact with any of her children except the last-born, Frederick, who was the son of Captain Pratt Barlow. In these sad circumstances, only the prospect of prize money and cheering letters from his loyal father had kept Charles's spirits up. He probably did not yet know about the collapse of another marriage, that of his sister Eliza to Lord Exmouth's oldest son, Pownoll Pellew. Their bitter separation may partly explain the dashing of hopes he expressed of joining the mighty 98-gun HMS *Impregnable* which was captained by Pownoll. In any case, Charles had to content himself with the much smaller *Revolutionnaire* under the command of Lord Exmouth's second son, Fleetwood. He was an 'ill-tempered profligate', who had been disgraced in 1813 when seven seamen he'd had sentenced for mutiny on his ship *Resistance* were pardoned after an appeal from his own father.[37]

Revolutionnaire spent the next four years with a fleet in the Mediterranean, surveying harbours and coastlines, transporting dignitaries between ports and generally asserting Britain's naval supremacy. It sounds a pleasant enough operation apart from the normal hardships of shipboard life: two men fell overboard, the captain sometimes put the ship's company on short rations, seamen were frequently flogged for drunkenness or insolence and the surgeon had to remove one of a man's testicles after he fell across the gunwale. Nor was the expedition without its special dangers: a violent collision with another British ship in Naples Bay, plague epidemics on various Greek islands and the continuing presence of the 'piratical gun-vessels'.[38] These exploits feature in the beautifully illustrated journal kept by Henry James, one of *Revolutionnaire*'s midshipmen, and it is also through his pen that we view Charles in action against the pirates of the Mediterranean.

Logbook of Midshipman Henry James, HMS *Revolutionaire* [*sic*], Zante, 18 May 1821:

Two fishing boats arrived and complained to the Governor of having been robbed of their nets, arms and ammunition and severely beaten by two piratical boats on the Indrea shore. Sent 2nd and 3rd barges with Lt Morrell and Mssrs Pim, Leven, Barlow and Groves Mids, Mr Coleman Ass Surgeon and 37 seamen and marines with 3 days provisions to look for them.

As above, 19 May 1821:

Lt Morrell and the barges returned with the two pirate boats and 2 small trading vessels found with them (one under Ionian colours) and 11 prisoners which they succeeded in taking after a desperate resistance of twenty minutes. Our loss was one marine killed and 4 blue jackets slightly wounded. Interred the body of the deceased and of a Greek who died of his wounds coming over. Sent the suspects and prisoners to the Lazaretto.

For this daring capture bounty money was due – though it was 1834 before payment was made. In the midst of such adventures and his many other duties, Midshipman James found time to pass his examination in seamanship at the Old Hospital in Valetta. He also records that there was 'an examination on two candidates for Lieutenants' on board the ship.[39] Clearly Charles, too, availed himself of these opportunities to qualify for promotion. After the voyage ended in July 1822 he was appointed a lieutenant under Captain William Clarke Jervoise on HMS *Dispatch*. But, as he ended his nautical apprenticeship, he could not escape the effects of his motherless childhood. Subsequent correspondence with his remaining family reveals that depression, loneliness and self-doubt were to haunt Charles Barlow for the rest of his naval career. He was all at sea because his heart was at home.

* * *

A month after his promotion the raw lieutenant found himself embroiled in an embarrassing incident. In the Italian Mediterranean port of Leghorn he was challenged to a duel by the headstrong Edward Trelawny, captain of Lord Byron's schooner, *Bolivar*.

Edward Trelawny to the lieutenant of HMS *Dispatch*, Royal Oak Hotel, Leghorn, 12 August 1822:

> Not having succeeded in finding you on shore I am under the necessity of writing to say that your conduct in hauling down the pendant of my friend Lord Byron's boat (under my charge) without apprising your Captain was both officious, ungentlemanly and insulting, and that your representation to Captain Jervoise of the words which took place between us under your stern was maliciously exaggerated, which cannot be sheltered under the plea of duty, and for which I demand satisfaction.

Charles's immediate instinct was to write a hasty note admitting that he had been in the wrong: 'I have officiously (and therefore insultingly) done more than I ought, if which is the case nothing remains to be done but to make the most ample apology'. But this document is marked 'letter not sent' in Charles's handwriting. Instead, he acted on the advice of Captain Jervoise and wrote to defend his action, denying ungentlemanly conduct and putting the affair in the hands of the Admiralty, which took over a year to resolve the matter in his favour.[40] In the meantime Charles was tactfully posted to HMS *Prince Regent*, the flag-ship of Admiral Sir Benjamin Hallowell based at Chatham. A shipmate on *Dispatch* wrote to Charles, assuring him of the general opinion that he had done his duty 'in an honourable and most officer like way', congratulating him on his 'early appointment to so large a ship', and hoping that he would soon be restored 'to perfect health'.[41] His career seemed set fair, but his self-confidence was at such a low ebb and his state of mind so turbulent that he came close to wrecking it. The whole affair had upset him so much that he felt compelled to return to the bosom of his family.

Charles to his father, Chichester, 12 January 1823:

> I am sorry to inform you that I am afraid it will be necessary for me to resign my appointment in consequence of ill health, as the dancing at Chatham together with the following day's journey quite knocked me up, insomuch that … I must undergo a course of medicine to

re-establish me. The above will be very unwelcome to you I am sure but I am of the opinion that you have overvalued the advantage of my present situation. Certainly an acquaintance with such an officer as Sir Benjamin Hallowell is a great object, but you must remember that he has relations of his own to bring forward independent of other followers. My advancement will not be retarded were I to remain ever so long onshore as it is all the same whether I were to remain on half pay for ten years. As to professional knowledge, that is out of the question in toto. Besides my inclinations and spirits are not equal to it at present. I have maturely weighed the whole and I think it best to write to my Uncle for his sanction and then apply to be superseded on the plea of ill health.

It was three years before Charles put to sea again. He devoted them to looking after his health 'by care in diet and guarding against taking cold', and making himself useful to his family. He spent time in Hastings with his invalid brother Edward, making arrangements for his tuition and lodging; he procured for his father a house in Bristol 'with every modern convenience ... and a pew in the church belonging to it';[42] and he spent time with his unmarried sisters, Fanny, Anne and Harriet, mourning the death of their childhood companion, Louisa.

In February 1826, with restored courage and through the good offices of his father and uncle, Charles took up his commission on HMS *Forte*. But in May his morale was dashed again, this time by 'a very frigid reception' from her captain, Jeremiah Coghlan, a celebrated hero of the French Wars and a close friend of Admiral Pellew. It took fresh encouragement from Sir George and another comforting period of leave to stiffen Charles's resolve.

Charles to his father, HMS *Forte*, Devonport, 2 May 1826:

Thank you for your letter of condolence. It affords me much satisfaction to reflect that my conduct and exertion have obtained your approbation. It would have given me much joy to have relinquished my mission as it is most difficult to execute in a satisfactory manner.

As above, 20 June 1826:

> And now my dear Father that the pain of separation is past in
> some measure, I can more readily express my gratitude for your
> unparalleled forgiveness and generosity towards me who so greatly
> needs it and so little deserves it, extending as it does to the past,
> the present and the future and it will ever be to me a wellspring of
> motives to conduct myself so as to meet with your approbation.[43]

It was a suitably fortified Lieutenant Barlow who sailed on *Forte* for
South America. Her task was to uphold Britain's trading relations with
countries which had recently won their independence from Spain and
Portugal – thus, in the words of Foreign Secretary George Canning,
calling 'the New World into existence to redress the balance of the Old'.[44]
Forte's contribution to this enterprise was to recapture a passenger ship
from privateers at Montevideo and help to break a French blockade of
Callao on the Pacific coast. She returned home in June 1830 carrying a
load of gold and silver bullion on behalf of British merchants.

All we know of Charles's experiences in South America is that he
enjoyed such good health in these seas that he was disappointed when
his next posting, as lieutenant on HMS *St Vincent*, took him back to the
Mediterranean, where he found the climate 'too warm and relaxing'. He
was followed there by letters from his devoted sisters, whose anxieties for
his health and safety increased when Charles suffered a serious accident
a year later.

Fanny Barlow to Charles on HMS *St Vincent*, May 1831:

> I thank you for your kind present of coco [cocoa from South
> America?], which will form an ample provision for my wayward
> appetite when suffering under my troublesome rather than painful
> indisposition. … I do beg you and intreat that you will have too
> much regard to your own health on our account to confine yourself
> to the ship in the manner in which you sometimes threatened to do.
> I am induced to say this because when you were last with us it struck
> me that you looked as if you had been over exerting yourself and

much mischief often arises from this cause in an ardent and active disposition like yours.[45]

Samuel Irvine, surgeon HMS *St Vincent*, 10 June 1833:

This is to certify that Lieut. Charles Barlow of HMS St Vincent was confined in the sick list on board that ship from the 19th April to the 7th August 1832, for the cure of a severe contused and lacerated wound of the right leg which he received in Fort Palamede, at Napoli di Romania [old name for the Greek port of Nafplio], whilst employed in transporting large guns from one part of the Fort to the other. One of the guns in rolling down a declivity grazed his leg and crushed the bone severely, so that he was a bedridden patient for nearly two months.[46]

Anne Barlow to her brother on HMS *St Vincent*, 16 June 1832:

The great distance that separates us, and the impossibility of personal attendance, are sufficient aggravations of grief without the painful thought, that we know not the real state of the case. ... We trust that you will come home, as soon as you are able to undertake the passage; ... we will promise to be as good or better nurses than your kind messmates. We had all been thinking of preparing a box. It will contain three mutton hams, gingerbread, three bottles of cherry brandy and some books which we hope may prove a solace and consolation to you, for religion alone can sustain the human mind in such seasons of adversity. Papa has likewise added his contribution of ½ doz of Constantia [sweet wine].[47]

These delicacies from home no doubt aided the improvement which Charles was able to report in the autumn.

Charles to his father, HMS *St Vincent*, Napoli di Romania, 6 October 1832:

My leg is still gradually getting larger and stronger. Most happily nothing has happened to retard its progress of recovery except a slight blow I struck myself with my own sword. … I have procured four 'Tespich' (in Greek 'Combolsio' in English 'Rosary') made at Jerusalem of Aloes wood cut in Syria whence they are exported to Constantinople. Three of one size I intend for my dear Sisters, the fourth a large one for Maria [his niece]. I shall forward them by the first opportunity. … I have also some Arcadian crooks or pastoral walking sticks used by the shepherds in their native hills, made from the wild olive, one of which I have selected for my uncle, also one small enough for a riding whip for Fanny.

As above, Malta, 1 June 1833:

I shall be very glad if our removal from this place takes place as the Mediterranean climate does not suit my constitution. Having suffered much from a complicated attack of Febrile Catarrh and total derangement of the biliary system, I fancied myself better before I really was, and went to duty on the following day. However I received a stroke of the sun which produced congestion in the brain attended by other symptoms that induced it necessary to bleed me and adoption of a reducing system.[48]

Like Jane Austen's sailor brothers and her fictional William Price, who brought his devoted sister Fanny a 'very pretty amber cross from Sicily',[49] Charles delighted in buying exotic presents for his family. An additional bonus for Charles on *St Vincent* was the 'brotherly kindness' of his messmates, who attended him during these various illnesses 'with as much assiduity as if indeed of the same family'.[50] But this close companionship made it all the more painful for him to take his leave in February 1834, when he was posted to HMS *Malabar* as first lieutenant under his friend, Henry Shovell Marsham. One of his erstwhile shipmates took note of Charles's anguish.

Morris Scott to Charles Barlow on HMS *Malabar*, HMS *St Vincent*:

I could not help observing my dear Barlow how anxious and depressed you appeared yesterday and had in my own mind attributed it to the very cause you assign. The feelings under which you at present suffer do honour to your Heart and show how worthy you are of those sentiments of regard and esteem with which you have inspired all those who have had the happiness to know you, and had good sense enough to appreciate your good qualities. It must always be painful to part with people who have been living on terms of intimacy. ...

Your attached friend, Morris Scott

Scribbled note from Charles to unidentified recipient on HMS *St Vincent*:

Dear Sir,
I had intended to write to you a very long letter before we parted company but as it is so soon I have no time. Let me once more thank you for many very great kindnesses to me and wish you goodbye and all the good wishes for your happiness and promotion that I poor wretch can wish you. ... The boat is leaving now so goodbye my dearest and best friend and I send you the best love of a now unhappy youngster,

Charles Barlow.
Remember me to all hands.[51]

It is not clear whether Charles dispatched this hasty note but the ardent sentiments it expresses were not unusual between young men in the early nineteenth century and are not evidence of a homosexual relationship. At about the same time Dickens, for example, regularly wrote to his friend John Forster of an 'attachment which no ties of blood or other relationship could ever awaken', and which would last 'till death do us part'.[52] Such intimate ties were particularly likely to form in the close quarters of shipboard life but had often to be abruptly broken. In December, Barlow had to make more sad farewells when he was at last given his own command, albeit on a small 10-gun schooner, HMS *Royalist*, and as a mere lieutenant-commander.

*   *   *

Sad to be leaving home just before Christmas, bitterly dissatisfied with his rank, and dismayed to be returning to seas he thought harmful to his health, Charles prepared his ship for an expedition to Spain where civil war was raging. Britain was part of a Quadruple Alliance (with France, Spain and Portugal) supporting the liberal Queen Isabella against followers of the absolutist Don Carlos.

Charles to his father, HMS *Royalist*, Devonport, 22 December 1834:

> Although not present with you at this season of peace and good will, yet are my strongest affections so firmly rooted in the society of you my dear Father and Sisters, where alone I have ever been truly happy, which time nay even eternity will never eradicate … nor can distance weaken the nourishment that is thrust from the root to the branch.

Charles to his sister Anne, HMS *Royalist*, Lisbon, 20 June 1835:

> We had better allow matters [about promotion] to take their ordinary course. … I care not if my eyes ever settle on the blue deep again, not that I am in any way disgruntled with my profession on the contrary much attached to it and if there was a hope however distant of advancing myself would continue therein, but at 38 years of age to be still on the first grade of a profession wherein a man has spent 26 years of his best days is not either prospectively or introspectively gratifying or inciting.[53]

Despite these regrets and a recurrence of his 'old attack', Charles soon busied himself with the task of giving naval support to the Spanish queen's troops who were under siege from the Carlists in Bilbao. In fact his conduct there 'gave so much satisfaction to the Cabinet at Madrid' that he was awarded the Order of the First Class of San Fernando in 1839. What is more, he was pleased to be in action, glad to uphold the rights of the 'industrious and labouring community' and proud of Britain's contribution to 'the cause of moderation and happiness'. He also appreciated the scenery of the Spanish coast, marred though it was by the 'presence of ships of war, the shrill pipe or the hoarse voice of the Boatswain'. Finding it 'romantic and beautiful beyond my powers of description', he commissioned a friend to make several sketches of the Bilbao River for his sisters. Even so, Charles continued to 'repine sometimes' about his unsatisfactory naval career.[54]

Assiduous efforts by Sir George on his son's behalf were eventually rewarded when Charles was promoted to the rank of commander in January 1837. Soon after this he left *Royalist* – though the 'desolating war' in Spain continued until 1839. He seems to have spent the next two years at home, where he commissioned a portrait of himself in his commander's full dress uniform, to which were added the medals he was later awarded. He appears as 'the handsome creature' described in his childhood with a slim figure, dark hair, serious eyes, aquiline nose, sensitive mouth, fashionable side-whiskers and the cleft chin which was much admired in his day.[55]

The culmination of Charles's career came in December 1839 when he assumed command of HMS *Nimrod*, which he considered 'the perfect ship of her class in the Navy', combining her force of twenty guns with 'magnificent accommodation for officers', including an extra poop deck cabin 'for hot weather'. Altogether, the ship was 'such as might be selected for the king's sons'. It was in this enviable vessel that Commander Barlow sailed for Singapore to conduct, as he explained to his father, 'the duties of suppressing piracy and protecting British Trade in these seas'. He admitted to being in the dark 'as to the sense or mode of operations', which have indeed been much debated ever since.[56]

The 'Opium War' in which *Nimrod* was to be engaged was the outcome of a long quarrel over Britain's lucrative Chinese trade, which involved her illegal exporting of opium from British India to balance the ever-growing British demand for Chinese tea. Whig politicians, typified by the current Foreign Secretary, Lord Palmerston, saw free trade (even in opium) as the 'best pioneer of civilisation' which would 'render mankind happier, wiser, better' – as long as 'half-civilised governments' were given 'a dressing every eight to ten years to keep them in order'.[57] For his part, the Chinese Emperor, who viewed Western merchants as red-faced barbarians intent on exploiting, corrupting and demoralising his people, encouraged the restrictions and humiliations to which they were increasingly subjected. Matters came to a head in 1839 when the Emperor's agents in Canton seized and destroyed over 20,000 chests of opium and closed the Pearl River estuary to shipping. It was time, said one Whig MP, for Britannia to redress 'the wrongs of her children' as she had done with the Dey of Algiers.[58] Thus Charles Barlow found himself taking part in a second punitive expedition, which has attracted 'almost as much moral opprobrium as the Atlantic slave trade'.[59]

His first task was to assist in the seizure of Chusan Island at the mouth of the Yangtze River. It was captured in nine minutes but 'would quietly take its revenge', as occupying troops were 'struck down in their thousands by malaria and dysentery', making the island 'a great British graveyard'.[60] Prone though he was to ill health, Charles did not apparently fall victim to these scourges. Rather, he was worried that his presence there had deprived him of opportunities for participating in more important action further south.

A blackened and torn letter from Charles to his sister Anne, HMS *Nimrod*, off Whampoa, 14 March 1841:

I take advantage of the only direct communication we have had to Calcutta and answer all your letters which came to me in a heap as we were at Chusan from October till February. Oh that vile place! The retention of it by us has deprived me and our other ships of the honour and glory gained by the total destruction of Bocca Tigris [the Tiger's Mouth, i.e. the forts which guarded the mouth of the Pearl River]. ... We are now in sight of Canton and came along to take possession of it but we are told that the occupation of it is strictly forbidden from home.

Dear Fanny will have something to pride herself on when I tell you that among the pictures I gave to the King of Loo Chow is her picture of the Madonna hanging in my cabin. Knowing that dear Fanny will paint another Madonna I consented to part with it. I left with them also a complete run of the Saturday Review and an English Bible and Prayer Book.[61]

Charles to his father, HMS *Nimrod*, off the walls of Canton, 24 March 1841:

> Although I was not in time to take part in the destruction of the Bocca Tigris batteries by persevering I managed to get the command of a Division of boats and assisted at the capture of all the other defences and was in the melee when we hoisted the British Union on the Factory flag staff with the cheers from all the boats crews. ... Although we fought up to the very walls of the city and actually took possession of the suburbs not an instance occurred of straggling or disorder among our sailors or marines. The casualty on our side was not worth mentioning indeed if not presumptuous one might almost pronounce a palpable interposition of Providence on our behalf from the commencement of operations to the surrender of the provincial authorities. The loss on the part of the Chinese is truly shocking amounting to three thousand. ...
>
> I was in quest for two chests of the best black tea. Neither will I forget dear Fanny's order for the preserved Ginger which is both good and cheap. GOD be thanked, my dear Father, for his goodness in preserving you in health and happiness, may it continue. Dear Harriet I find is the chief sufferer. I think I must cut off a Mandarin's head and send it to replace her troublesome one.

As above, Hong Kong 5 May 1841:

> I have fallen on my legs this time. ... We are about organising an expedition to the North [to the Yangtze River] and Nimrod is one of the ships destined to go. I am appointed to the command of ... four or five hundred men, who are to act in conjunction with the land force.[62]

Thus Charles was able to render himself 'conspicuous by his zeal' in the capture of Canton and then of Nanjing on the Yangtze.[63] As a result he was promoted to the post of captain in June 1841, even without the patronage of his friend, Sir Humphrey Senhouse, second-in-command of naval forces in China, who died of fever on board his ship in May.

Despite the good it had done to him personally and to his country's trading interests, the 'immense loss of human life' to China and the high financial cost to Britain led the peaceable Charles to regret a war caused, he thought, by a failure of diplomacy.[64] He might have deplored it even more had he known of the true extent of pillaging and misbehaviour among British troops. Their 'foraging' at Canton included not only an orgy of plunder, but the desecration of ancient burial grounds and the rape of many Chinese women. Nanjing 'became an open-air Aladdin's cave: a sea of porcelain, bronzes, satins, silks, embroideries and wax-encased balls of opium'.[65]

Charles returned to Britain bearing no such precious booty, not even a Mandarin's head. Instead he was deputed to carry despatches announcing the final conquest of Canton, delivering them to the governor general of India in Calcutta before taking them on to London. Arriving off Ryde harbour in October 1841, he was promptly made a Companion of the Bath in recognition of his services and was then all too happy to 'return to the society of those most dear' to him, his father and sisters. Up to his own death in 1846, Sir George continued to write 'handsome commendations', accompanied by painstaking summaries of his son's career, to influential friends and relations. These included his niece, Lady Hilaire Nelson, Sir Robert Barlow's daughter, who married Horatio Nelson's older brother after the death of her first husband, George Barlow junior. Charles was even prepared to take up positions in Canada or India, swallowing the 'bitter ingredient' of further separation from home. But 'the great reduction in our naval force' meant that he remained out of employment on half-pay until his death in 1855.[66]

Instead he served as a comfort to his family. With his three spinster sisters he leased a handsome classical villa on Balham Hill near the Streatham house where they had all lived as children. There, as the 1851 Census reveals, they looked after three of their brothers' offspring, who in their turn had been sent over the sea from India. Letters written by Fanny describe a holiday in Hastings where her nephews and niece were learning to swim and (with help from Charles) to 'handle a gun in a gentlemanly and safe way'. They sound benign guardians who 'cannot get the children to keep in except to their meals', and consider that 'they are better out'.[67] It may have been here that Charles painted accomplished watercolour scenes which recalled his years at sea: frigates depicted 'in front of the wind', in 'a fresh breeze off Mt Etna', 'at anchor off Dartmouth', or in moonlight.

These paintings were no doubt among the 'personal property' cited in his will, which reveals a childless bachelor lacking the affluence of his Pellew in-laws, but well able to support his comfortable Streatham ménage.

Will of Charles Anstruther Barlow, 6 February, 1853:

> Ist I direct that all my debts be paid and that my funeral be executed with the least possible expense the regulating of which is to rest with my sister Miss Frances Barlow 2nd I give and bequeath to my sister Frances Barlow ... all my real and personal property ... for her absolute use and disposal. Herewith I annex a list of my possessions and expectations: 3 per cent consolidated funds £700, 3 per cent resources £216.4.10, a legacy in reversion by my late Uncle William Barlow Esq £500, my plate consisting of spoons forks and sundries, a gold watch, my decorations of the Bath and St Fernando and my medals for service in China and Algiers, my library being those books in which my name and crest are inserted, my interest in the lease of this house No 3 Devonshire Place Balham Hill.[68]

The direction that his funeral be conducted cheaply is typical of this modest man, anxious to provide as well as he could for his sisters, all of whom lived on as single women into the 1880s. His had been an honourable naval career, during which he had neither sought nor shirked danger, but it had not brought him great riches, high rank or even a sense of fulfilment. The child, as Wordsworth wrote, 'is father of the man', and Charles Barlow had been shaped by the far-flung separations of his early years. They had made him fearful of further partings, over-dependent on father-figures, anxious to please and averse to risk – attributes quite unsuited to the seafaring 'life of enterprise' which Admiral Barlow recommended to Charles's brother William. His wayward mother, as unbuttoned as the Prince Regent himself, had produced not the 'great man' she envisaged, but a respectable Victorian – a dutiful son, loving brother and loyal friend who was only truly happy at home.

Chapter 7

Sydney Dickens 1847–1872:
A Life Illuminated by his Father's Fiction

T he seventh child and fifth son of Charles and Catherine Dickens was born in London on 18 April 1847 after a prolonged breech delivery during which, her husband wrote, 'dear Kate suffered terribly'. He was christened Sydney Smith Haldimand after the Rev. Sydney Smith, a writer his father judged 'one of the wisest and wittiest of this age', and the wealthy banker and philanthropist, William Haldimand.[1] Sydney was not as welcome as these illustrious names suggest. Having already sired Charley, Mary, Katey, Walter, Frank and Albert, Dickens felt that there were 'too many Dickenses in the world', and in any case he was more 'partial to girls'. It was only half in jest that he said of his sons: 'Take 'em away to the Foundling.'[2] But at least he didn't take such precipitate action as David Copperfield's aunt, Betsey Trotwood, who on learning that the baby born to her sister-in-law was a boy, 'vanished like a discontented fairy … and never came back any more'.[3]

The ten years which had produced seven children had also seen the publication of Dickens's first eight novels. At the time of Sydney's birth he was engaged in writing monthly instalments of *Dombey and Son*, a book permeated by images of the 'dark and unknown sea that rolls around all the world'. As the delicate little Paul Dombey sat on the beach at Brighton with his sister Florence, he 'would try to understand what it was that the waves were always saying and would rise up in his couch to look towards that invisible region, far away.' The sea, indeed, became a metaphor for mortality. As Paul lay dying in London, 'his fancy had a strange tendency to wander to the river … and he thought … how steadily it rolled away to meet the sea.' As Florence worried about the fate of her sweetheart Walter, who had been sent on a voyage to the West Indies, uncertainty and danger seemed written upon everything. The weathercocks on spires and housetops were mysterious with hints of stormy wind, and pointed, like so many ghostly fingers, out to dangerous seas, where fragments of great wrecks were drifting, perhaps, and helpless men were rocked upon them into a sleep as deep as the unfathomable waters. ... The smoke and clouds, though moving gently, moved too fast for her apprehensions and made her fear there was a tempest blowing at that moment on the ocean.

And when she returns to Brighton and remembers the time she and Paul spent there as children:

The waves are hoarse with repetition of their mystery; the dust piles upon the shore; the sea-birds soar and hover; the winds and clouds go forth upon their trackless flight; the white arms beckon, in the moonlight, to the invisible country far away.[4]

These scenes were surely on Dickens's mind when he gave the infant Sydney his special pet name, Ocean Spectre, or Hoshen Speck in baby language. He was thus called when, during the family seaside holiday of 1847, Catherine's sister Georgina Hogarth noticed him 'cupping his tiny hands under his chin and casting a faraway look over the ocean'. The nickname was to prove more prophetic than the names with which he was christened. No literary fame or banking fortune would come Sydney's way but he went to sea while still a boy. He took with him a surname 'widely and uniquely loved' wherever he travelled in the world. He would carry too the burden of growing up with a father who was, in his own words, 'admitted into many homes with affection and confidence [and] regarded as a friend by children and old people', but who did not always understand the emotional needs of his own sons.[5] Any evidence of their feelings was later destroyed by Dickens, while his own correspondents and publishers preserved his every word. Fortunately, the great writer's letters, articles and novels throw light not only on the human condition in general, but also on the conflicting experiences of Sydney, all at sea by the time he began his life on the ocean wave.

* * *

As the diminutive toddler with 'large wandering eyes' portrayed by the artist Frank Stone, Sydney was for a time his father's 'particular protégé among the smaller fry'.[6] And with all his children in their engaging early years, Dickens was often as 'bright and jolly as a boy', in the words of his sixth son, Henry. He would organise running races on the sands, cricket matches in the garden, round games of an evening, theatrical productions at Christmas, or dancing, conjuring tricks and cake on Twelfth Night, which was also Charley's birthday. These were magical times. But Henry also remembers his father's 'heavy moods of dark depression', his 'strange reticence' and an obsessive tidiness which failed 'to meet with the entire approval of us small boys'. His system of 'Pegs, Parade and Custos' allotted each boy a peg for his hat and coat, required regular parades to check for stains on their clothing and deputed each boy in turn to be the custodian of their games equipment. Though the boys dared not complain openly about these rules, they muttered among themselves about the 'slavery and degradation' to which they were subjected.[7]

The quixotic style of Dickens's fatherhood is well illustrated by an episode he recounted to Catherine in September 1850. He and the children were staying at Broadstairs in 'a good bold house on the top of a cliff, with the sea Winds blowing through it', while she recovered from another childbirth in London.[8] As they awaited the arrival of family friend John Forster, Dickens jokingly asked 3-year-old Sydney to 'go to the Railroad' (which was some distance away) to see if their guest was coming. The child set off 'alone, as fast as his legs would carry him', but was pursued and 'brought back in triumph'. This game was repeated several times before Sydney and Alfred ran off together.

> Instead of running after them, we came into the garden, shut the gate, and crouched down on the ground. Presently, we heard them come back and say to each other with some alarm, 'Why, the gate's shut, and they are all gone!' Ally began in a dismayed way to cry out, but the Phenomenon [Sydney], shouting 'Open the gate!' sent an enormous stone flying into the garden (among our heads) by way of alarming the establishment. I thought it a wonderful piece of character, showing great readiness of resource. He would have fired a perfect battery of stone – or very likely have broken the pantry window, I think – if we hadn't let him in.[9]

Thus young Sydney earned his father's admiration, but only after he and his 4–year-old brother has been frightened into believing themselves abandoned. This unkind prank is hard to square with a writer renowned for his ability to understand the child's point of view. Here, for example, he brilliantly conveys the terror Pip felt on returning home after his encounter with a convict in the graveyard.

'And please what's Hulks?' said I.

'That's the way with this boy!' exclaimed my sister, pointing me out with her needle and thread, and shaking her head at me. 'Answer him one question, and he'll ask you a dozen directly. Hulks are prison- ships, right 'cross th' meshes.' We always used that name for marshes, in our country.

'I wonder who's put into prison-ships, and why they're put there?' said I, in a general way, and with quiet desperation.

It was too much for Mrs Joe, who immediately rose. 'I tell you what, young fellow,' said she, 'I didn't bring you up by hand to badger people's lives out. It would be blame to me, and not praise, if I had. People are put in the Hulks because they murder, and because they rob, and forge, and do all sorts of bad. Now, you get along to bed!'

I was never allowed a candle to light me to bed, and, as I went upstairs in the dark ... I felt fearfully sensible of the great convenience that the Hulks were handy for me. I was clearly on my way there. I had begun by asking questions, and I was going to rob Mrs Joe.

Since that time, which is far enough away now, I have often thought that few people know what secrecy there is in the young, under terror. No matter how unreasonable the terror, so that it be terror.[10]

* * *

For the first six years of his life Sydney regularly spent August and September at Broadstairs together with his siblings, various nurses and governesses, Aunt Georgina and (intermittently) his parents. From 1853, however, the family decamped for the summer to Boulogne, described by his father as 'a bright, airy, pleasant, cheerful town', 'wonderfully populous in children'. Many of them were the offspring of the town's 7,000 English residents but Dickens did his best to avoid these 'bores from the shores of Albion'.[11] However, his childless friend J.T. Delane, editor of the *Times*, recommended to him one of the many schools for English boys in Boulogne. Thus, when the family departed for home in September 1853 'two small representatives', Frank and Alfred, were left in the charge of its joint headmasters, the Revs Matthew Gibson and James Bewsher. 'Nothing could be more satisfactory', pronounced Dickens. And later he recommended the school to other parents as a 'perfectly honest establishment' providing a 'French and Classical education and the usual branches of knowledge' for ten months of the year with no vacation at Christmas 'unless the parents wish', and charging only £40 a year. The boys' manners and clothes were 'well looked after', and he thought they were 'very happy' in the charge of 'a gentleman so perfectly acquainted with boy-nature as [Rev. Gibson]'.[12]

Frank and Alfred were joined in 1855 by 8-year-old Sydney, described by his father as 'an odd child, with a great deal of originality and character'. He had 'learned from his Aunt to write very well [and] has for some time conducted a large imaginary correspondence with scores of people.'[13] Sadly, neither these interesting letters nor any written by the schoolboys have survived, so that we have to rely on their father's word for their happiness. Only the cleverest Dickens son, Henry, a Boulogne pupil from 1857, recorded his memories of the school and it was not 'with any degree of pleasure'. He felt 'sad and forlorn' there, despite the presence of his brothers. In particular, he disliked the 'very pale veal with very, very watery gravy and the usual stick-jaw pudding' served up on tin plates and the practice of forcing the boys to speak French all the time, each boy acting as 'a spy upon the others'. He developed a particular hatred for the school's regular parades (which sound remarkably like the Brighton cliff walks endured by Paul Dombey at Doctor Blimber's academy) 'in a body of two by two round and round the ramparts'. This same peregrination was described by his father as 'a charming walk, arched and shaded by trees, on the old walls … [with] views of the river, and of the hills and of the sea'.[14]

The sea can hardly have added to the attractions of the school from the boys' perspective, as Dickens's friend Wilkie Collins sensed when Sydney set out from Folkstone in September 1855, looking 'very small and flushed', but accepting 'his fate like a hero [with] a threatening sea before him, and the horrid perspective of the schoolmaster awaiting him on the opposite shore.' Dickens himself often described the 'floundering and knocking about' involved in crossing the Channel when passengers could only submit to 'the unreasonableness and hopelessness of the Ocean'. He had 'a most miserable passage' in September 1853: 'the sea very high washing over us the whole way: nearly everybody ill (I among the number) and the boat so intolerably crowded that nobody had room to be ill in.' The boys would often arrive after a crossing 'in every stage and aspect of sea sickness', 'miserable objects ... all manner of toad-like colours'.[15]

For a few years the necessity of summer crossings was avoided by their simply joining the rest of the family at a rented villa in Boulogne, a boys' paradise as described in Dickens's letters. In 1854 they could watch thousands of French troops who were encamped on the cliff tops before embarking for the Crimea. They also joined in the celebrations their father organised to honour Prince Albert's visit to the town: 'In our own proper illumination, I laid on all the servants, all the children now at home, all the visitors ... one to every window, with everything ready to light up.' Each year there was a grand fête with 'a puppet-theatre, and a lottery, and a fire-balloon, and a capital display of fireworks, and a donkey-race ... and a match of jumping in sacks'.[16]

When the boys came home in 1856 'with a prize apiece', Dickens 'made rejoicings with five franc pieces, running races, and cricket ditto'. The villa rented for that year had 'a field in which they tear themselves to pieces all day long' and a little cottage in the garden where they slept. But they also had to put up with the ship-shape standards imposed by their father: 'The washing arrangements and so forth are conducted on the strict principles of a Man of War. Nothing is allowed to be out of place. Each in his turn is appointed Keeper for the week, and I go out in solemn procession (Georgina and the Baby forming the rest of it), three times a day, on a tour of inspection.' Thus Sydney had a foretaste of the naval discipline he was to experience later in his life when his father caught him out in a misdemeanour: 'The man on duty in the Man of War broke down this morning at Inspection-time, and was found guilty of having omitted to open one of the windows. In consideration, however, of previous good character and this being the first offence on board he was not superseded.'[17]

These 'pleasant summer-quarters' were prematurely broken up in late August by an epidemic of diphtheria in Boulogne which caused the death of many children. As soon as he heard of it, Dickens sent the younger boys off with Catherine on a rough passage to England and then wrote to her explaining why they should not return to school on the regular day: 'The interval I propose will enable us to see (I hope) that there are no dangers behind or facts behind, which are unknown to [Rev. Gibson] … All unite too in love to you and Frank, Alfred, Syddy (Giant I mean) and Harry.' It was mid-September before it was thought safe for the boys to travel to Boulogne. They went aboard a General Steam Navigation Company boat at 9 pm one Thursday evening, ready to leave London Bridge Wharf at 3 pm the next day. Dickens's letters make no further reference to them until 10 July 1857, when he wrote from Gad's Hill (the family's new holiday house in Kent) that they were 'just home from Boulogne after a year's absence'. They had clearly spent Christmas at Rev. Gibson's school.[18]

It is easy to imagine the boys' yearning for the Christmases of former years as captured in Dickens's essay about a Christmas Tree decorated with a 'motley collection of odd objects, clustering … like magic fruit, and flashing back the bright looks directed towards it from every side'. To share such delights, he wrote, 'We all come home, or ought to come home, for a short holiday – the longer the better – from the great boarding-school, where we are for ever working at our arithmetical slates, to take, and give, a rest.' Over the Christmas of 1854 the nine children had been 'all agog about a great Fairy-play' to be performed on Twelfth Night and in 1855 the family had gathered in 'brilliantly lighted' Paris for Christmas and New Year, returning to school with a large cake.[19] How the absent schoolboys must have longed in 1856 to share the 'tremendous excitement' in their London house as all the older children as well as many friends prepared for another legendary Dickensian Christmas. The following year saw the boys, now including Henry, once again left in Boulogne for the festive season. Back in Kent their father kept a Rochester audience spell-bound by his 'magic voice and manner' as he recited *A Christmas Carol* on 22 December.[20] But there is no evidence that he thought of his own sons as he read about the First Spirit taking Scrooge to visit Christmas Past.

'The school is not quite deserted,' said the Ghost. 'A solitary child, neglected by his friends, is left there still.' Scrooge said he knew it. And he sobbed. They left the high-road, by a well-remembered lane, and soon approached a mansion of dull red brick, with a little weathercock-surmounted cupola, on the roof, and a bell hanging in it. ... Entering the dreary hall, and glancing through the open doors of many rooms, they found them poorly furnished, cold, and vast. There was an earthy savour in the air, a chilly bareness in the place, which associated itself somehow with too much getting up by candle-light, and not enough to eat.

They went, the Ghost and Scrooge, across the hall, to a door at the back of the house. It opened before them, and disclosed a long, bare, melancholy room, made barer still by lines of plain deal forms and desks. At one of these a lonely boy was reading near a feeble fire; and Scrooge sat down upon a form, and wept to see his poor forgotten self as he had used to be. [21]

* * *

One reason for the boys being abandoned like young Scrooges over Christmas was no doubt the danger and discomfort of crossing the Channel in winter. By 1858, however, Dickens had another motive for wanting his children out of the way. For this was the time during which he fell in love with the young actress Nelly Ternan and brought an end to his marriage. In June, while the schoolboys were still absent, he arranged a Deed of Separation from Catherine, by which she was to live in Gloucester Terrace; 22-year-old Charley chose to take up his quarters with her while 'the other children still at home' were to stay with him. Dickens specified that she should have the right to see the children whenever and wherever she liked but imposed certain conditions. They must never, for example, have any contact with her mother or sister Helen Hogarth: 'If they are ever brought into the presence of either of these two', he directed Charley 'I charge them immediately to leave your mother's house and come back to me.'[22]

Thus when the boys came back to spend their summer at Gad's Hill they found only their sisters, 6-year-old Edward (always known as Plorn) who had replaced Sydney as the apple of his father's eye and Aunt Georgina, who had lived with the family since 1842 and chose to stay with her brother-in-law. Dickens himself spent most of that summer and autumn on a lucrative and exhausting tour in which he performed readings from his books all over England, Ireland and Scotland. Katey described later 'the misery and unhappiness of our home' that summer, claiming that her father 'did not care a damn what happened to any of us'.[23] For her young brothers it must have been a bewildering time as they heard rumours but never any direct explanation of what had happened. To his friends Dickens justified his behaviour by claiming that the children had never loved Catherine, nor she them: 'She never attached one of them to herself, never played with them in their infancy, never attracted their confidence as they have grown older, never presented herself before them in the aspect of a mother.' He went so far as to claim that 'she is glad to be rid of them, and they are glad to be rid of her'.[24]

All we have of their side of the story is an account Catherine gave her aunt, Helen Thomson, of a visit from her 'dear boys' when they 'thoroughly enjoyed being together' in August 1858:

> I cannot tell you how good and affectionate they were to me. One of them, little Sydney, was full of solicitude and anxiety about me, always asking what I should do when they were gone, and if I would not be very dull and lonely without them; he should so like to stay.

Henry's memoir mentions regular visits to his mother and their 'mutual affection'. While Dickens might dismiss all this as 'a little play' acted out by the boys it is more likely that they felt genuinely confused and guilty about their mother's banishment.[25] The strength of Sydney's particular attachment is borne out by his close relations with Catherine in later years.

Again it is striking that Dickens showed less empathy with his own children than with the offspring of his literary imagination. He enters, for example, into the troubled feelings of David Copperfield who returns from boarding school to a home transformed by his mother's stern new husband, Mr Murdstone, into one where he is no longer welcome.

Ah, what a strange feeling it was to be going home when it was not home, and to find that every object I looked at, reminded me of the happy old home, which was like a dream I could never dream again!

.... God knows how infantine the memory may have been, that was awakened within me by the sound of my mother's voice in the old parlour, when I set foot in the hall. She was singing in a low tone. I think I must have lain in her arms, and heard her singing so to me when I was but a baby. The strain was new to me, and yet it was so old that it filled my heart brim-ful; like a friend come back from a long absence.

I believed, from the soft and thoughtful way in which my mother murmured her song, that she was alone. And I went softly into the room. She was sitting by the fire, suckling an infant, whose tiny hands she held against her neck. ... I was so far right, that she had no other companion.

I spoke to her, and she started and cried out. But seeing me, she called me her dear Davy, her own boy! and coming half way across the room to meet me, kneeled down upon the ground and kissed me, and laid my head down on her bosom near the dear little creature that was nestling there, and put its hand up to my lips.

I wish I had died. I wish I had died then, with the feeling in my heart! I should have been more fit for Heaven than I have ever been since.[26]

* * *

Dickens found it easier to concern himself with the more practical aspects of his sons' lives, in particular with their future careers. He had already sent 16-year-old Walter off to India as a military cadet and made inquiries about similar distant openings for Frank and Alfred. In November 1858 he turned his attention to Sydney's prospects. Apparently, the boy had talked while he was on vacation at Gad's Hill about wanting to go into the navy. Subsequently he had written 'an odd characteristic letter' to one of his sisters saying that he was devoted to this profession 'without any sham'. Dickens accordingly wrote to ask Rev. Gibson whether this idea was 'in-bred in the boy' or just an 11-year-old's whim, inspired perhaps by a young midshipman who had made frequent visits to the house over the summer decked in 'glorious buttons and with a real steel weapon in his belt'. He was happy to set 'the gigantic Sydney' on this path if he was in earnest, believing him to be 'a boy of such remarkable energy and purpose, considering his years and inches, ... [that] he would then follow it out with spirit'.[27]

It seems that the Ocean Spectre really did want to live up to his nickname showing the 'cosmopolitan spirit' he had displayed as a young child. He had, after all, spent much of his life by the shore, and when at Gad's Hill had plenty of opportunity to observe 'great ships standing out to sea or coming home richly laden' at nearby Chatham, one of Dickens's own childhood homes. Like his father, he had received some of his 'earliest and most enduring impressions among ... ships and sailors [and] outgrown no story of voyage and travel, no love of adventure, no ardent interest in voyagers and travellers.'[28] It may also be that the sea represented an escape from the exacting control of home and school. Perhaps a tough navy life was not entirely suitable for a boy who was still, in Dickens's estimation, only about 3ft high and who had never been robust – but it was his own choice and his father was prepared to support him.

Through his friends in high places, Dickens gained his 'very uncommon boy' a place on the Admiralty's list of applicants for midshipman-commissions and then arranged for him to attend a naval school run by the Rev. Ashton Burrow at North Grove House in Southsea, near his own birthplace. He was proud of the 'Little Admiral' he sent off there soon after his twelfth birthday in 1859 and sure that his new headmaster would 'be interested in him'. After a week Sydney was apparently 'as much at home as if he had been born there', a judgement his father based on letters, which were among those he put to the fire in 1860.[29] Only through his own letters to other people do we learn, for example, that he gave the boy permission to visit an Irish nobleman with whom he had become friendly and that Sydney was known in Portsmouth as 'Young Dickens, who can do everything'. His behaviour was reported as 'uniformly correct', and in March 1860 he passed the examination enabling him to be nominated as a midshipman and inspiring a paternal acclamation as 'the boy of the lot, and the one who will be heard of hereafter'.[30]

Father and son were clearly on excellent terms at this time. Sydney was fêted when he came home in September, 'all eyes and gold buttons', and was treated by Wilkie Collins to champagne and a theatre visit as 'one of our naval heroes'.[31] Dickens willingly paid out large sums for his uniform, books and nautical instruments, escorted him to the training ship HMS *Britannia* at Portsmouth and was very anxious when the boy was taken ill in November, and sickened again with a 'low fever' in February 1861. After Sydney graduated from *Britannia* in December he was given a sovereign in 'recognition of his meritorious services'. His father then accompanied him to Plymouth where he would sail for America in one of the new steam-powered, screw-propeller frigates, HMS *Orlando*, pronounced 'one of the foremost ships in the service, and the best found, best manned, and best officered, that ever sailed from England'. It was just before Christmas when the 14-year-old lad 'went away much gamer than any Giant, attended by a chest in which he could easily have stowed himself and a wife and family of his own proportions.'[32]

The joke about the sea chest, which Dickens repeated in several letters to friends, is typical of his comical stories about Sydney's small stature, for which the only other evidence is a photograph of him at 13. The sextant his father bought for him in London, for example, 'entirely concealed him [so that] not the faintest vestige of the distinguished officer behind it was perceptible to the human vision'. As they walked through the city together, 'people turned round and stared at him with the sort of pleasure people take in a little model.' On *Britannia* his shipmates 'good-naturedly helped him, he being so very small, into his hammock at night. But he couldn't rest in it on these terms, and got out again to learn the right way of getting in independently', a feat he accomplished 'after a few spills'.[33] As he awaited sailing orders at Plymouth, Sydney caused further merriment after dining with an officer friend of his father's on board another ship and sleeping in his cabin. The next morning the officer's servant, who was seen to be choking with laughter, explained how greatly the young gentleman in the cabin had amused him: '"Beg pardon then, Sir; hope there might be no offence in my saying" – choking again here "as the young gen'lm'n is so wery small, as I see him a standing on your portmanteau Sir to get himself on a level with the washing stand afore he could wash himself."'[34] Such ribaldry was (and is) common in the Royal Navy and Sydney had proved that he could stand up to it, just as he had stood up to his father's practical joke in Broadstairs.

Where his fictional little people were concerned Dickens was more perceptive about the pain such ridicule could cause. Amy Dorrit, disparaged for being 'so very, very little', sobs 'over that unfortunate defect of hers, which came so often in her way'.[35] David Copperfield (often thought to be a self-portrait) is surprised when he finds Miss Mowcher, the diminutive hairdresser of his friend Steerforth, is a distressed state:

> 'Yes, it is always so!' she said. 'They are always surprised, these inconsiderate young people, fairly and fully grown, to see any natural feelings in a little thing like me! They make a plaything of me, use me for their own amusement, throw me away when they are tired, and wonder that I feel more than a toy horse or a wooden soldier! … I must live. I do no harm. If there are people so unreflecting as to make a jest of me, what is left for me to do but to make a jest of myself, them and everything? If I do so, for the time, whose fault is that? Mine?'
>
> No. Not Miss Mowcher's, I perceived.[36]

Sydney was luckier than Miss Mowcher. He was well-proportioned and seems to have had a growth spurt in his later teens so that his adult height probably approached 5ft. But the mockery he had received at an impressionable age would leave its mark.

*   *   *

As Midshipman Sydney Dickens left Plymouth to spend his first Christmas away at sea, he faced the usual perils of a sailor's life: war, weather and all manner of threats to his physical and moral wellbeing.

The navy had just been placed on a war footing, despite Britain's official neutrality in the American Civil War between the abolitionist United States and the Confederacy of slave-owning southern states. Suspecting, with some justification, that the British government favoured the south, the US had seized two Confederate diplomats from a British mail ship in November 1861. As Prince Albert pronounced on his deathbed, Britain would not 'allow its flag to be insulted and the security of her mail communications to be placed in jeopardy' and thus prepared for action.[37] But even before *Orlando* reached the shores of America, President Abraham Lincoln had apologised and released the prisoners, thus averting war with 'its honours and its evils'. Sydney thus gained a safer tour of duty, but lost any chance of battle medals or prize money.

Orlando's crew did not escape other dangers. About four days out from Plymouth the ship ran into severe gales and squalls, during which Sydney fell from a porthole. He incurred a blow to his head resulting in 'brain concussion', which Georgina Hogarth blamed for the subsequent deterioration in her nephew's health and character.[38] In similar fashion Dickens attributes the eccentricity of Captain Bunsby in *Dombey and Son* to his taking 'many spars and bars and bolts about the outside of his head when he was young'; the taciturn old sea captain seems 'to be always on the look-out for something in the extremest distance', gazing intently at the horizon even when ashore.[39]

Sydney's odd behaviour took a different form. A constant stream of bills in the name of Sydney Dickens soon began to be forwarded to his father from the Naval Agents Banton & Mackrell. Often these were for over £40, the recommended annual private allowance for a midshipman at this time.[40] The demands came from Bermuda, where *Orlando* was stationed from February 1862 to protect British merchant ships from any further Union interference. Partial explanation for them emerges in a story later told by one of Sydney's shipmates, Cunningham Bridgman, about Mrs Dinah Browne, a Bermudan 'bum-boat woman' who sold tuck to the British fleet and beguiled all the young officers. She was especially fond of Sydney (or 'Little Expectations', as he was nicknamed after the publication of *Great Expectations* in 1861). He became her particular favourite because of 'his prodigious purchases of the luxuries she purveyed, such as guava jelly, rahat lakoum [Turkish Delight], bananas, boot-laces etc'. She would also invite Sydney and Cunningham to tea at her cabin on the shore, where they were entertained by her 'humorous anecdotes ... and charming coon-songs'.[41]

Free from paternal control, 'Little Expectations' fell into habits as ruinous as those of Pip, the novel's young hero who, with his friend Herbert Pocket, adopts extravagant habits and contracts 'a quantity of debt'. Pip occasionally does their accounts, ties the bills into a bundle and puts them back into a drawer.

> My business habits had one other bright feature, which I called 'leaving a Margin.' For example; supposing Herbert's debts to be one hundred and sixty-four pounds four-and-twopence, I would say, 'Leave a margin, and put them down at two hundred.' Or, supposing my own to be four times as much, I would leave a margin, and put them down at seven hundred. I had the highest opinion of the wisdom of this same Margin, but I am bound to acknowledge that on looking back, I deem it to have been an expensive device. For, we always ran into new debt immediately, to the full extent of the margin, and sometimes, in the sense of freedom and solvency it imparted, got pretty far into another margin.[42]

*   *   *

Despite continuing calls on his purse Dickens still took pride in his 'born little sailor', to whom he also sent presents such as a gun and a complete set of his own books. He was pleased when *Orlando* returned to Chatham Dockyard in May 1863 and Sydney was 'pretty constantly at home while the shipwrights are repairing a leak in her'.[43] We can glimpse a little of the communication between father and son in a piece of Dickens's journalism of this time. The essay on Chatham Dockyard, which appeared in his journal *All the Year Round* in August 1863, seems to be based on visits he and Sydney made that summer – as well as on his own memories of childhood. He describes meeting at a landing-place near an old fort 'a young boy, with an intelligent face burnt to a dust colour by the summer sun, and with crisp hair of the same hue', an amalgam perhaps of Sydney and his young self. This 'wise boy', whom he calls the Spirit of the Fort,

instructs him in the 'mysteries of seamanship', and together they watch
the building of an iron armour-plated ship, the *Achilles*, marvelling that
'this monstrous compound of iron tank and oaken chest, can ever swim
or roll!'.[44]

A letter of Dickens's evokes other agreeable times which Sydney spent
on shore leave – albeit subject to the familiar jokes about his height.
Writing of his late friend and illustrator John Leech, Dickens remembers
his fondness for this 'extraordinarily small boy of great spirit'. Leech used
to take Sydney to the theatre and to dinner at the Garrick Club, but on
one occasion was 'filled with horror' when he saw his 'frightfully small'
guest struggling with a very large knife. Not wanting to single him out
he complained about the 'enormous and gigantic' knives they had been
given and ordered smaller ones. 'After which, he and the officer messed
with great satisfaction and agreed that things in general were running
too large in England.'[45] But Sydney did not spend all his periods of leave
in such literary company. Catherine saw her Gloucester Crescent house
as 'his Home when on shore', and treasured the presents he brought her
from foreign parts – a case of stuffed birds, a pair of silver candlesticks,
a picture of Mary Magdalene, a bronze inkstand or a pair of white and
pink china flower vases.[46]

Back on the high seas but now cruising in the Mediterranean, the
17-year-old midshipman fell into bad company. He and several others
were found guilty of misconduct in May 1864 and 'deprived of one
year's time' (meaning that promotion would be delayed). This appears
on Sydney's naval service record but his father seems not to have known
about it, being preoccupied by the 'wretched affairs' of Walter, who
died in India earlier that year leaving large debts.[47] Sydney, despite his
extravagance, was still considered an asset; the Christmas Eve edition of
All the Year Round contained a stirring naval story, 'The Spirit of Nelson',
contributed by 'a very young officer' known to the editor.

It concerns a party of officers and seamen who went ashore for a
shooting picnic from Sydney's old ship, *Orlando*, while anchored in
the Bay of Tunis. On the return journey their small boat was caught
in a violent squall and capsized, after which Kemble, the youngest
midshipman, twice demonstrated his 'heroic Spirit'. First he swam to
rescue the captain of the marines and brought him back to cling with

the others to the upturned boat. Then, although he was an excellent swimmer, he gallantly resisted the temptation to swim ashore with the coxswain saying that it was his duty to set an example by staying with the boat. The coxswain managed to save his own life, but the 'little midshipman' and all the rest drowned during the night. The essay ends with the narrator expressing his special sympathy for 'poor little Kemble … as he had so many sisters, and seemed so loved and so much adored by all his friends.'[48]

Sydney gave his own relations no special cause for concern in 1865, when Dickens was pleased to hear him described as 'a highly intelligent and promising young officer'.[49] But the next year they were all worried when he joined HMS *Antelope* bound for the west coast of Africa as part of a squadron engaged in showing the British flag against hostile Asante chiefs. 'We will not see him again for three years', lamented Georgina, while Dickens noted that this station was 'unlucky in losing members'.[50] He was putting it mildly. The *Antelope* alone lost three captains on that coast between 1865 and 1870, and the captain of HMS *Bristol* (which Sydney was supposed to join at Lagos) wrote gruesome reports of conditions on board: 'The fever laid on us very hard. We had thirty new cases, and lost twenty men, all dying of yellow fever. … This is not a place that anyone would wish to stay if he could get away.' Sydney himself was dismayed by the posting. He went off bravely in August according to his aunt, but his early letters home were 'very dejected indeed'. Later Georgina was able to report that he was 'in better spirits [and] cheerful as to his prospects'.[51]

Sydney had good cause to be optimistic about his career in November when eight months of the time he had lost were restored as a result of 'perfectly satisfactory conduct'. But before he had a chance to take the promotion exam aboard the *Bristol* he fell victim to African Coast Fever, as his worried father called it, and had to be sent home in March 1867 'for preservation of life'. He must have had a miserable voyage on a mail steamer bound for Liverpool and it took him some months to recover his health. By the end of August, however, he was well enough to be successfully examined, appearing at Gad's Hill as a sub-lieutenant, 'with the consequent golden garniture on his sleeve'.[52]

He was still on leave in October when he attended a farewell dinner for Dickens who was about to depart on his second visit to America. It would not be long before Sydney was bound for the same continent on a posting which was to make a shipwreck of his fortunes. He was approaching the age of majority and was to find his father less forgiving now that he had moved from the 'beautiful and engaging' stage of childhood into 'that perplexing state of immaturity' when, 'in mercy to society', a boy should be put into a barrel for six years.[53] Or, as Mr Chester explains to his son Ned in Dickens's early novel *Barnaby Rudge*, he can simply be sent elsewhere.

A son, Ned, unless he is old enough to be a companion – that is to say, unless he is some two or three and twenty – is not the kind of thing to have about one. He is a restraint upon his father, his father is a restraint upon him, and they make each other mutually uncomfortable. Therefore, until within the last four years or so ... you pursued your studies at a distance, and picked up a great variety of accomplishments. Occasionally we passed a week or two together here, and disconcerted each other as only such near relations can. At last you came home. I candidly tell, my dear boy, that if you had been awkward and overgrown, I should have exported you to some distant part of the world.[54]

*   *   *

In August 1868 Sydney joined HMS *Zealous* stationed at Esquimalt Harbour on Vancouver Island, a British colony off the western American seaboard. By that time his father had completed his exhausting reading tour of the United States, commanding 'full houses and ecstatic applause'.[55] It is true that declining health had prevented his going west as he had planned, but the magic of his name had travelled far across the continent. Thus Sydney was 'made a good deal of' on his arrival – just as he had been 'shewn to visitors as one of the curiosities' of Portsmouth when he was 12 years old.[56]

Of course it was exciting for a young man to be the centre of attention and it is clear that Sydney responded eagerly. On board *Britannia* he had led choruses on Saturday nights and taken tea with the captain, while on *Zealous* he was given the principal role in dramatic productions put on by the ship's crew for local inhabitants. The 'talented young gentleman' was hailed in the *British Colonist* as a true 'chip off the old block' and praised for the 'merriment' his performances aroused. The editor of this newspaper remembered that he was fond of 'riding out with ladies', who liked him despite his 'short and spare' physique and the fact that 'on horseback he resembled a groom rather than a gentleman'. He tells a comic tale of Sydney's getting some of these 'fair companions' lost in the woods and showing 'great gallantry' by staying with them all night.[57] Sydney also enjoyed shooting expeditions, though he was not exactly expert with a gun according to Admiral Sir Frederick Fisher, who had served as a midshipman on board *Zealous*. His *Reminiscences* report that after Sydney and another officer had returned from such a jaunt, a local resident came on board to accuse them of having killed his horse. The two young men had to explain to the captain that they had mistaken the horse's ears for 'a snipe getting on the wing', a story which greatly amused not only the captain, but also the accuser who 'invited the two famous shots to dine with him, adding that horse-meat would not figure on the menu'.[58] It seems that the 'Little Admiral' was still the object of affectionate mockery.

In his professional life Sydney gained more respect. He had good testimonials as an officer and was several times promoted to acting lieutenant when a death vacancy arose on his own or a neighbouring ship. But the navy seems to have been somewhat under-employed on the Pacific station, where its role was to safeguard Queen Victoria's sovereignty over Vancouver and British Columbia, during a period of gold rushes and boundary disputes with the US such as the bloodless 'Pig War'. There was all too much leisure in which officers could run up large wine bills on board and take leave on shore where on both sides of the border, Sydney explained to his father, 'dollars are spent as shillings'. In these newly settled communities of miners and lumberjacks, taverns, gambling saloons and brothels abounded, presenting as much temptation to young sailors as did Bermudan bum-boat women: 'You know what American people are – you know their customs – you know their habits of drinking – that has led me into debt.' Sydney's debts now mounted to such an extent that in March 1869 he confessed to his father with 'shame and regret' that he faced 'utter ruination' unless he received assistance. Even though Dickens had previously instructed Banton & Mackrell that he would no longer settle Sydney's bills, he paid out about £200 in May and June alone to prevent 'hostile legal proceedings' against his son.[59]

But by the summer he had lost patience and, according to Georgina, he wrote to Sydney to say that he would not be received at Gad's Hill on his return to England. This letter has not survived but a later, even more drastic paternal rejection has. In May 1870, while Sydney was still in the Pacific running up more debts than he could ever hope to pay, Dickens wrote to his son Alfred in Australia: 'I fear Sydney is too far gone for recovery, and I begin to wish that he were honestly dead.'[60] Since Dickens himself died a month later, we can only guess what might have happened had Sydney been able to seek a reconciliation on his return from the Pacific. Would his father have rebuffed his advances as heartlessly as Mr Dombey does those of his daughter Florence as she tries to console him after his wife's desertion?

> Yielding at once to the impulse of her affection, timid at all other times, but bold in its truth to him in his adversity, and undaunted by past repulse, Florence, dressed as she was, hurried downstairs. As she set her light foot in the hall, he came out of the room. She hastened towards him unchecked, with her arms stretched out, and crying 'Oh dear, dear papa!' as if she would have clasped him round the neck.
>
> And so she would have done. But in his frenzy, he lifted up his cruel arm, and struck her, crosswise, with that heaviness, that she tottered on the marble floor; and as he dealt the blow, he told her what Edith was, and bade her follow her, since they had always been in league.
>
> She ... saw that she had no father upon earth, and ran out, orphaned, from his house.[61]

* * *

Unlike many Victorian fathers Dickens rarely struck his children, but he delivered blows of a subtler kind. Following the advice voiced by his own Mr Chester, he had in turn dispatched the awkward sons who disappointed him by their 'limpness', Walter, Frank, Alfred and even the cherished Plorn, to make their own way in India or Australia. In each case he wept at the parting but, like Martin Chuzzlewit leaving his sweetheart as he goes off to America, he took little heed of anyone else's 'share in the separation'. Nor had Dickens paid attention to filial feelings when he sent the boys' mother away from the family home, doing all he could to discourage them from loving or visiting her. Yet, this is the writer who understood so well the cry of desolation which issued from Florence's heart, or the sobs of Pip as he reached the finger-post at the end of his village, realising that 'all beyond was so unknown' and weeping for his 'dear, dear friend' Joe Gargery. As his oldest son wrote: 'The children of his brain were much more real to him at times than we were.'[62]

Sydney had, of course, done a great deal more than the innocent Florence to deserve his father's anger. Nor did he improve his ways, despite his promises of 'future amends'. Even as he travelled back to England on HMS *Satellite*, mourning his father but aware also that he should inherit a share of his £90,000 estate, he continued to spend recklessly. Admitting to the family solicitor that he did not know how his pecuniary matters stood, he asked for the urgent settlement of his current debts on board, 'which will come to some forty odd pounds'. Leaving a margin in Pip-like fashion, he asked to be furnished with fifty pounds so that he would be 'at ease' until he arrived home in December 1870.[63]

Sydney knew, of course, that he would still have a home with his mother, who treasured a photograph of him 'in a small Oxford frame', with his pet monkey on board HMS *Zealous*, and looked forward to his periods of leave.[64] They probably spent Christmas together. He also visited his aunt who found him in 'a most wretched state', but was pleased that he brought 'a good character as an officer' from his previous ship. This confidence was clearly justified for in June 1871 Sydney was posted to HMS *Topaze*, on which he was later promoted to the rank of lieutenant. But Georgina's prayers that he would keep to the 'good intentions' he expressed were not to be answered. By the following Christmas the trustees of his father's estate had to advance Sydney £300 to clear his debts as well as 'something to go on with until the Estate can be divided'.[65]

There are few clues as to what Sydney spent the money on. No doubt there were plenty of opportunities at Portsmouth's elegant Royal Naval Club, which he joined in November before sailing with *Topaze*. During the voyage ports of call such as Madeira, Rio de Janeiro, and the Cape of Good Hope offered many exotic temptations, while fancy dress balls and grand receptions gave scope for extravagant wining and dining. But before his fleet reached its next destination, Bombay, in April 1872, Sydney had fallen seriously ill with bronchitis; he was transferred to another ship to be taken home on sick leave but died on 2 May, soon after his twenty-fifth birthday, of 'general debility' according to a Board of Trade report. His body was committed to the Indian Ocean 'with all the honours due to him, not only as an officer in the Service – but also as being the Son of one of the most distinguished men in England'.[66]

Georgina thought it 'very, very sad' that the 'poor fellow' should have died so young but echoed the feelings of her beloved brother-in-law by adding that his death was 'probably the most merciful thing ... that could have happened to him'. However it was Sydney's 'natural and lawful Mother' who, as his sole legatee, had to pay off debts which now amounted to over £1,000. Once she had done so she distributed the income she received from his estate to her surviving children. Meanwhile she mourned the loss of 'such a tender loving son' and could hardly bring herself to believe that she would never see 'his dear bright face again'.[67]

It is puzzling that a young man who had shown such promise as a boy should have died with his finances and his health in ruins, 'going to the dogs', as his father would have put it. The many hazards of naval life were no doubt partly to blame: shipboard accidents, damp conditions and tropical diseases weakened a constitution which had already shown 'strong traces' of the 'incurable aneurism of the Aorta' which had caused the death of his brother Walter.[68] And any young man going off to sea ran the risk of turning into the legendary drunken sailor with a girl in every port, as typified by George King. But compulsive spending such as Sydney went in for usually has deeper roots. It is characteristic of someone who wants to impress others, and in Sydney's case may be linked with the small stature for which he was constantly ragged as a boy and as a sensitive adolescent. In addition he shared with his brothers the challenge of living up to a brilliant father's name. Away from his benevolent but overbearing control, it was all too tempting to show off extravagantly.

Dickens himself understood better than most Victorians the influence parents have on the behaviour of their offspring and often demonstrated this in his novels. *Barnaby Rudge*, for example, portrays two fathers who behave inappropriately towards their adult sons. One is Mr Chester and the other is John Willet, landlord of the Maypole Inn, who insists on treating his 20-year-old son, Joe, as if he were a child and making him 'the laughing-stock of young and old'. Finally he provokes an act of rebellion.

Old John ... grew so despotic and so great, that his thirst for conquest knew no bounds. The more young Joe submitted, the more absolute old John became, ... trimming off an exuberance in this place, shearing away some liberty of speech or action in that, and conducting himself in his small way with as much high mightiness and majesty, as the most glorious tyrant that ever had his statue reared in the public ways, of ancient or of modern times.

[After further degradation Joe turns on one of the inn's customers, an ally of his father.] Crowding into one moment the vexation and the wrath of years, Joe started up, overturned the table, fell upon his long enemy, pummelled him with all his might and main, and finished by driving him with surprising swiftness against a heap of spittoons in one corner; plunging into which, head foremost, with a tremendous crash, he lay at full length, stunned and motionless. Then, without waiting to receive the compliments of the bystanders on the victory he had won, he retreated to his own bedchamber, and considering himself in a state of siege, piled all the portable furniture against the door by way of barricade.

'I have done it now,' said Joe, as he sat down upon his bedstead and wiped his heated face. 'I knew it would come to this at last. The Maypole and I must part company. I'm a roving vagabond ... it's all over!'[69]

After this Joe runs away and enlists in the army. Sydney did not have such extreme provocation as Joe and his revolt was not as dramatic or as violent. His escape route into independent manhood was the navy, but he carried with him so much emotional baggage that the sea wrecked him. Far from being elevated as a 'Little Admiral', he regressed to the state of 'Ocean Spectre', first as a lost soul banned from his father's doors and finally as the only one of these children at sea whose corpse was sent to lie full fathom five beneath the waves.

Chapter 8

Ada Southwell 1875–1953: Child Migrant

In the course of his study of the 'London Poor' in the 1840s, Henry Mayhew interviewed a 15-year-old girl who sold flowers in Drury Lane. She had never seen her father but had been told he was a tradesman in County Cork. Since the death of her mother seven years earlier she had supported herself and her brother and sister 'and never had any help but from the neighbours', who were all poor people like themselves. They lived on bread and tea with 'sometimes a fresh herring of a night', often going without food all day. But, she proudly told Mayhew, she had put them all through a Roman Catholic school so that they could all read and her brother could write as well. None of them, she added, 'ever missed mass on a Sunday'. Asked whether she had ever considered emigrating she replied: 'No, sir, I wouldn't like to emigrate and leave brother and sister. Even if they went with me I don't think I should like it, not among strangers.'[1]

Whether they liked it or not, many such children were dispatched to live among strangers as indentured servants in Britain's colonies. At the very time of Mayhew's interview with the flower-seller, Irish girls of about her age were being selected as part of the Earl Grey emigration scheme. The idea was that they would cease to be a 'dead weight' in workhouses crowded with famished victims of the 1845 potato blight by going off to relieve the shortage of domestic servants and marriageable females in Australia. Most of the 4,000 or so chosen girls were apprenticed and, within a year or two, married squatters or ticket-of-leave men, with whom they faced the challenges of a lonely life in the outback, or a nomadic existence in the newly discovered goldfields. Despite this, the scheme was halted after only two years as a result of mounting press criticism in the developing colony. The girls were denounced as 'immoral, useless and ... blindly devoted to their [Popish] religion', with the particularly strident *Melbourne Argus* claiming that they were barely able to distinguish 'the inside from the outside of a potato', and were fit for little more than fetching a runaway pig. It seems, concludes a recent study, that age-old English prejudice had followed these deprived and largely illiterate Irish lasses to the other side of the world.[2]

Over the next ten decades, however, child migration swelled as philanthropists such as Maria Rye, Annie Macpherson and Dr Barnardo took up the cause. Shiploads of lone youngsters left Britain's shores between the 1860s and the 1960s to start a new life in Canada, New Zealand, South Africa or Australia. Few made the return passage. Some were orphans, while others were removed from the 'contaminating' influence of parents to be trained in 'habits of truthfulness, obedience, personal cleanliness and industry'.[3] Most were paupers plucked from Poor Law workhouses, or waifs and strays swept up from mean city streets – though some set off from comfortable homes. Charles Dickens, as we have seen, sent four of his sons to overcome 'the curse of limpness' by making their own way in the colonies.[4] The prevailing opinion was that the best thing to do with all such problem youngsters was to:

> Take them away! Away! Away!
> The bountiful earth is wide and free,
> The New shall repair the wrongs of the Old –
> Take them away o'er the rolling sea![5]

*　*　*

Seven-year-old Ada Southwell became a problem when her father, Henry, took poison on 2 February 1883 in a Whitechapel pub and died the following morning. He had been working as a porter for a leather manufacturer, lugging great hides over the city to support his family of six children. He had recently discovered that for about a year his wife Harriett had not been paying the rent, so that he now owed his landlord £15. 'Debt was the stuff of nightmare' for a poor workman, as the historian Jerry White has written, and suicide was not uncommonly 'the shortest way out of Queer Street'.[6]

Southwell Family Tree

(simplified to include family members mentioned in the text)

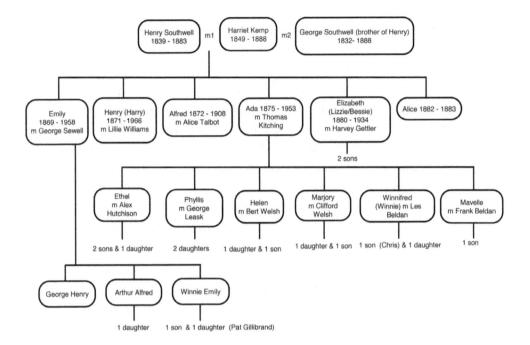

The fatherless family was evicted from the four-room terrace house they shared with a lodger in Bacchus Walk, Hoxton (unless they did a moonlight flit) and moved to an underground kitchen in neighbouring Britannia Street. Harriett took in washing, worked as a charwoman and sold the furniture in her attempt to make ends meet. After receiving a grant from the United Friends Benefit Society, she managed to pay her husband's funeral expenses but was soon reduced to a state of 'the greatest poverty and distress'. On the basis of family visits and neighbourhood inquiries by Miss Macpherson and the governor of Barnardo's, Harriett was judged 'unfit for the care of her children' and the family was broken up in April. Emily, aged 14, went into service; Ada was taken in by the Barnardo's Receiving House in Stepney along with her 12-year-old brother Henry, while Alfred and Lizzie, aged 10 and 3, entered one of the Macpherson Revival Homes. Alice, at just 10 months old, died at around this time.

The conclusion reached by Barnardo's was that the Southwell parents had brought their plight on themselves by his 'intemperate habits', and her being 'much addicted to drink'.[7] But this kind of accusation, as Maud Pember Reeves observed in her study of Londoners' working lives twenty years later, was 'fatally easy to throw about'.[8] It may well be that the struggle to support six children, including a sick baby, in the grimy dilapidation of Hoxton had driven the Southwells to seek solace in some of the East End's many public houses. In his vivid account of a rough Hoxton childhood, A.S. Jasper suggested that drink was not only a common cause of misery, but also an escape from it. Indeed, a clergyman giving evidence to Charles Booth's 1889 Inquiry, *Life and Labour of the People in London,* attributed women's drinking in particular, directly to 'their slavery at the wash-tub'.[9]

Even so, Henry was described by a colleague as 'a steady, industrious and honest servant' of the firm which had employed him for fifteen years, paying him not much more than a pound a week, and Harriett had been working as a dressmaker to supplement his wages.[10] With great care such a couple could pay a typical rent of six or seven shillings a week and keep their children fed, warm and clean. They could also educate them now that the London School Board had built enough new schools to make this possible – and, indeed, compulsory after 1880. Thus 5-year-old Henry was admitted to Hammond Square Board School in 1875 and his siblings no doubt followed suit.[11] But nearly all working-class Londoners lived on a knife-edge at this time and often ran into debt, most frequently to their landlords. In good times they might be able to afford a two-penny ticket to the Britannia Theatre, spend three ha'pence at an eel and pie shop, or find a few shillings for a dozen of the popular family photographs known as *cartes de visite*.[12]

There are, in fact, several such photographs of the Southwells, which give the impression of a steady family keeping up appearances. In one taken shortly before their marriage in 1868, Henry wears a respectable three-piece lounge suit and holds a Bible while Harriett's dress has the fashionable fitted bodice and bell-shaped skirt. Not long before the family crisis, three of the children posed for a portrait in which they look clean and healthy, dressed up in their Sunday best. Lizzie and Ada wear prettily decorated velvet dresses and Henry has an elaborate lace frill on his jacket – all of which could well have been made by their mother. These images give no hint of the family's swift decline in the wake of Henry's death. By the time Ada was photographed on admission to Barnardo's she was no longer the well-cared-for child enfolded in a family trio.

When disaster struck the Southwells could not obtain, as did many working-class families, support from their relations, for they too were struggling to survive in the precarious economic conditions of the 1880s. Henry had a brother, George, who was a widower with his own four children to support on a porter's wage, one sister in a workhouse infirmary and another in domestic service at an unknown address. One of Harriett's brothers was in a lunatic asylum, another was a travelling salesman and a third was an unemployed compositor with five dependent children. She also had two married sisters: Mrs Gibbs living with six children south of the river in Walworth and Mrs Powell, the wife of a labourer, a few doors down in Britannia Street. Both were presumably too poor to help out. The only way to save the family from the dreaded workhouse was to have the children taken in by one of the Christian charities which, a contemporary noticed, were 'spreading like a network over London'.[13] It would be very difficult for Harriett to keep up any contact once they were admitted to one of their Homes, which kept inmates cut off from the outside world by walls, gates and guards. But she could not have expected them to be separated from her by the rolling Atlantic Ocean, a barrier she would never be able to cross.

* * *

The fate of the Southwell children might have been hidden from view since all their records are held in the Barnardo's Archive, which is now closed to the public for 'reasons of confidentiality'. Access can, however, be given to direct descendants who may pass on their discoveries to others if they wish. It is in this way that I learned Ada's story from her Canadian grandson, Chris Beldan, and he was also able to prove that he is the closest descendant of his childless great-uncle Alfred, whose Macpherson records are part of the Barnardo collection. Chris kindly allowed me to see this evidence as well as giving me the benefit of his further family research. Indeed, he very much wants the Southwell children's story to be told.

Alfred was the first of Harriett's children to leave Britain's shores. On 17 May 1883 he embarked along with twenty-two other boys on SS *Sarmatian* bound from Liverpool for Quebec. His 3-year-old sister Lizzie followed a month later in a batch of sixty-five children aboard another of the Allan Line's steamships. Both voyages were supervised by Annie Macpherson on what she called 'the God-opened way of emigration to Canada', designed to reduce the numbers of destitute children in her homes and to save them from the criminal future she saw 'looming before them' in Britain. She had already conducted over 2,000 children across the Atlantic to the 'pious rural homes' which Canada was thought to offer, and was to carry on indefatigably until her death in 1904.[14]

Miss Macpherson's enthusiasm for child migration inspired Thomas Barnardo to use the same remedy for 'the evils of which child misery and destitution are prominent symptoms'.[15] His first party sailed for Canada in August 1882 and by the First World War nearly 25,000 Barnardo boys and girls had made the same journey. They included Henry and Ada Southwell who were sent separately on SS *Circassian* in June 1884 and SS *Polynesian* a year later, after being officially photographed in new outfits provided by the charity. Ada's last days in her native country were also captured for Barnardo's magazine *Night and Day* just before she set off from Liverpool for 'a Land of Promise' – though it is impossible to pick her out from the group of solemn pinafored girls.

By the time this photograph was taken Harriett Southwell had already married George Southwell, her late husband's widowed brother, an arrangement to which many desperate families resorted in those days.[16] Harriett would have the benefit of George's income from his work as a market porter and he would receive care for his four children under 10, the youngest of whom was another Ada. Did anyone think of rescuing her namesake as she awaited emigration? After all, as Joy Parr revealed on the basis of her access to Barnardo's case records in the 1970s, 'When the institution raised the threat of emigration ... even foster parents, step-parents and neighbours tried every alternative before they let the child go.' But Barnardo's did not usually give prior notice of sailing to parents they considered 'not moral', and there is no evidence that they sent such information to the 'unfit' Harriett.[17] They may not even have known her address after she moved into George's house in Seven Dials, an area of London as poor and disreputable as it had been when George King purchased his sailor's garb there eighty years earlier. In any case, George's children would take priority over hers in a patriarchal society so that he might not have welcomed another mouth to feed. Seventeen-year-old Emily, who was still in the country, must have known of her mother's remarriage but was not in a position to prevent Ada's emigration. She herself travelled to Montreal in July 1886 as the servant of Mrs S.C. Stevenson, though it is not clear whether this was the employer she went to after her father's death or a new one. The move meant, as Emily wrote in November: 'The five of us brothers and sisters are all out here now.'[18]

The voyage they had all made was not a lengthy one compared to those of convicts or Irish orphans to Australia, Raj children to Britain, or Nelson's sailors on the high seas. The Allan Line's iron steamships carried child migrants from Liverpool to Canada in just two weeks, though Andrew Doyle's 1875 Inquiry into The Emigration of Pauper Children to Canada found it to be a 'tedious and fatiguing journey' for the youngsters. They travelled in steerage, the cheapest accommodation on the lower decks, crammed in because they were 'brought out in such large numbers at a time', and with too few attendants. There was so little attention to their cleanliness that they arrived in 'a most filthy condition, their heads swarming with vermin'. The bunks were so arranged that the children could not get in and out without assistance so that in their early days at sea and in stormy weather, one of them told Doyle, 'we all sicked over each other'.[19] This was a particular hazard aboard the ship on which Ada travelled, the *Polynesian*, nicknamed 'Rolling Polly' because of her unsteady motion. As Joy Parr concludes, 'the sea crossing was often hard on a weakened constitution.'[20]

When the sea was calm, steerage passengers were more able to relish the bill of fare on offer. Breakfast consisted of coffee with bread and butter or porridge; for lunch there was soup followed by fresh beef, salt pork or ling fish, with plum pudding twice a week; milky tea and bread and butter would be served in the afternoon and a final bedtime treat was

'Gruel at 8 o'clock every night'. This plain but reasonably wholesome diet was no doubt welcome to under-nourished juvenile passengers. The children could also enjoy romps on deck, games of tug-of-war and watching for whales and icebergs, while an attentive captain might help them to pass the time with jobs like keeping watch and pulling on ropes.[21]

Of course, it was a relief when the rolling billows were replaced by dry land. But the sea passage had parted children from parents, brothers from sisters and all from their wider kin and familiar neighbourhood. It is easy to imagine their confusion and loneliness as they set off to live among strangers in a strange land.

* * *

Most emigrant children, including three of the Southwells, now faced a three-day train journey west from Quebec at the mouth of the St Lawrence River to the charities' Receiving Homes in Ontario. As they looked out on this new country with its wooden houses and 'rocky hills and woods of maple and fir', they must have wondered why they had been sent there.[22] After a few weeks' stay in a home they would find out the answer as they were distributed to houses needing servants, and farms requiring labourers. Their benevolent new guardians saw this as the 'wholesome soil' of a pristine new world, which would replace 'the gutter, the ooze, the slime' of their native cities and help them to 'grow in time into lordly trees'. Yet at the very time when the Southwell children crossed the Atlantic the British Home Secretary himself criticised the practice of child migration as the work of a 'Philanthropist and world-betterer run mad'.[23]

The nature of children's service varied according to their age, with only the youngest being fully adopted into families. The definition of this arrangement given to Andrew Doyle by one shrewd child migrant was that ''Doption is when folks gets a girl to work without wages', and the Doyle Report concluded that it was usually undertaken 'with a view to the future service of the child'. He acknowledged, however, that a few adoptive parents had 'the very highest of motives' in applying for young children to 'fill a void in the household', and that these children could be 'ultimately absorbed into the best part of the population of the American continent, the Canadian yeomen'.[24]

Lizzie Southwell, it seems, was among the lucky ones. Her descendants have discovered that Miss Macpherson had her adopted at the age of 3 by Mr and Mrs Morrow of Varna and later Fullarton, Ontario, who had two boys but wanted a little girl. They are convinced that Mrs Morrow was 'very nice and kind' and that Mr Morrow 'thought the world of Bessie' (as her new parents called her) so that she enjoyed a 'a very happy childhood'. Mrs Morrow took the trouble to write to Harriett Southwell, sending her a copy of a photograph taken near Varna, in which the child looks well cared for against a studio setting very similar to that in which my own grandmother was portrayed. Mrs Southwell thanked her for this kindness and promised to send a photograph of herself as a keepsake – but there is no evidence that she was ever able to afford that expense. For the same reason Emily was unable to travel from Montreal to visit her youngest sister, whom she remembered as 'such a sweet little Dear at home when we were all together'.[25]

Emily had, however, managed to visit her brother Henry whom Barnardo's sent out as a farm apprentice after his arrival in Canada at the age of 12. There are no available records of his placement, but from later references it seems to have been in rural Ontario. The only glimpses of his lonely teenage years come from his devoted older sister and from his mother. In 1886 Emily managed to get leave of absence from the kind Mrs Stevenson and to scrape together the fare for the long journey. After hearing of this visit, Harriett wrote to her daughter from the Boundary Tavern in Stepney.[26] The letter was dictated to an unnamed friend, who explained in a postscript that Mrs Southwell was 'not very comfortable at present'.

I am glad to hear that you have been to see Henry and stop with him for as long as you did, and I am glad to hear that he is getting on alright at present. And I hope as a Sister that you will go as soon as you can to look to him and be as Brother and Sister to each other. … I hope you will go and see your Brothers and Sisters if you can, and if you want some money I will send you some if you write by return of post and let me no how you are getting on. Dear Emily I hope I shall be with you before long and I am longing to see [you] all once again. And I shall do my best to come to you before long & I will send you more next time I write to you and tell you all the particulars of my mind and heart.

The letter concluded with love and three lines of kisses from 'Your loving Mother and Father', which must be a reference to the children's new but uninvolved stepfather.[27] The hopes she expressed were not realised: Emily could not manage to keep up her sisterly visits (though she kept in touch assiduously with all her siblings) and Harriett was never reunited with her offspring.

                              *   *   *

Thanks to the release of his Macpherson records, more is now known of the middle child, Alfred, than his mother knew at the time. Ten days after he docked in Quebec on 30 May 1883, he was sent to 19-year-old Miss Janet Eastling of Ratho, Ontario, described even today as a hamlet in a dispersed rural community. His was an arrangement halfway between adoption and apprenticeship: he was to receive 'board, clothes and schooling' on the understanding that he would work for the family in due course. After all, as a minister in the Canadian Department of Agriculture commented, 'It costs so little to keep a child which very soon begins to be useful and earns so much more than it costs.'[28] Miss Eastling got married less than a year later to John Lake, a local young farmer, and Alfred remained in her care at the rural abode, which he sketched for his sister Emily in a letter signed off with a line of kisses and 'ten times more' if he could be with her.[29]

Meanwhile his confused and 'anxious Mother' wrote to 'Mrs Eastling' giving her address as 'Seabright Music Hall, Gloster Street, Hackney'.[30] She pleaded for news of Alfred and also of Lizzie (who was in fact 90 kilometres away):

I have never had but one letter from you and that was in November & you stated in that letter that you would forward his photo & I have been anxiously waiting but finding it did not come I thought I had better write to you to know whether you had sent it to the wrong address. ... I sincerely hope that they are both quite well and that they are good children as I have never found either of them bad tempered. ... I have not the slightest thing to remember them by & could not afford to have them taken before they went away. I can hardly bear to think of it for it seems that they are lost to me forever.[31]

The promised photo of Alfred seems never to have arrived as there is no surviving image of him. Perhaps that was just as well, for reports by Macpherson inspectors suggest that he would not have looked in good shape. In 1884 they said that he 'had not been at all well, first from weakness in the spine and then a breaking out in his face'. They advised that he should not be sent to school, but be allowed to 'roam about in the fields'. The next year he was 'the same as ever' and had not grown much. There is no further report until 1888, when he was 15 and had 'at last begun to grow', but this spurt was not sustained and in 1891 he remained 'a wee lad'. The reports also commented briefly on Alfred's treatment, noting that the Lakes were 'very fond of him', that he attended school, church and Sunday School when he was fit enough and that altogether he had 'a good home'. His mother would have been pleased to learn that he was always described as 'a well disposed boy' or 'a good lad'.[32]

It must have been a difficult time for Alfred. Three of the Lakes' nine children were born during his stay with them and, as a 'Home Child', he would take second place to sons and daughters of the house. This must have been all the harder to bear after he heard of his own mother's death in July 1888 at the age of 40, her last words being of 'her dear children'. She died of 'exhaustion', brought on by tuberculosis, in the Southwark boarding house to which she had moved with her second husband, who died of the same disease six months later.[33] Alfred's own poor health meant that he found it hard to cope with the heavy farm work he was expected to undertake as he got older. As the inspectors observed, he was 'too light' and 'not strong enough'. In the end, after he had done his best to please both the Lakes and their German neighbours, the Morganroths, the inspectors decided that he was 'not well adapted for farming' and might 'do well for a trade'. So, in May 1891, he was sent to work at Doon Twine Mill, earning 50 to 60 cents a day and possibly living in its own lodging house. The inspectors found him 'well and very happy' in October. He was still there in January 1892 when he wrote 'a nice note of thanks for his Xmas package', and said that he was doing 'fairly well'.[34]

But how well and happy was he in truth? The inspectors had visited once a year at best and they had not always seen Alfred. In any case children were most unlikely to reveal any maltreatment they had suffered or to say how they felt about their situation. Joy Parr's study of a sample of Barnardo's children shipped to Canada between 1867 and 1917 calculated that 9 per cent of boys and 15 per cent of girls had 'excessive corporal punishment', and that 11 per cent of the girls became pregnant while they were wards of the homes.[35] Many of the post-Second World War child migrants who have recently given evidence to the Independent Inquiry into Child Sexual Abuse 'described care regimes which included physical abuse, emotional abuse or neglect, as well as sexual abuse'.[36] There is no way of knowing whether Alfred suffered in such ways. The only clue to his state of mind is an undated letter written to Emily some time between 1891 and 1893 – after she had returned to England and he had moved to Doon, where he could write more freely.

The letter (which betrays the effects of the patchy education typical of child migrants) is entirely preoccupied with family matters. He thanks Emily for her picture – though she had changed 'an offel lot'. He asks after aunts, uncles and cousins back in England and remembers a Christmas spent with the Gibbs family in Wandsworth. He expresses concern for his brother Harry, whom he had visited recently: 'He is very lonesome without me he is well and getting along nice But I think he will come and work in the rope factory after his time is up.' He reports that Harry is planning to visit Lizzie who is 'getting a long fine and never sick', and that he has heard that Ada is about to move into Ontario. He tells Emily that he is saving up so that he and Harry can come to London 'on surprise'. The most poignant passage deals with his memories of life at home with his parents.

It makes tears come in my eyes when ever I think of [Dear Mother] for she was such a good and kind Mother and I often wish I had been a good boy to her I was a very bad boy and many a good cry I have had over it. And Dear Father I can mind the last time I saw him alive. He was a good father to us and I hope we will all meet him in heaven.

Despite Charles Booth's judgement of Hoxton as the leading criminal quarter of London, there is no reason to think that 10-year-old Alfred had been involved with its warring, thieving gangs. He was rather remembering times when he was cheeky or disobedient and assuming, as do many children sent away from their parents, that he had deserved his banishment. He blamed himself for the break-up of the family and no doubt thought he deserved any harsh treatment meted out to him subsequently. He wished with all his heart that the Southwells 'were to geather again'.[37] And he sounds utterly miserable. Written about ten years after he left England's shores, this letter echoes those discovered in Roy Parker's research which 'belie the contemporary belief that once in Canada children would find a new life and put the past behind them'.[38] Alfred had been bodily transported over the sea, but his heart remained in the old country.

It is clear from Alfred's letter that he, Henry and Lizzie had ended up in the same part of rural Ontario, between Lakes Huron and Erie. Thus they were occasionally able to visit each other – though it is difficult to imagine how they made the journeys. Ada, however, remained in the province of Quebec for the rest of her childhood, as had many Irish Famine orphans, whose parents had died crossing the Atlantic on the notorious 'coffin-ships' of 1848–9.[39] Quebec City itself often struck juvenile immigrants as 'very foreign' with its 'little narrow streets, cobbled and very steep', and its French-speaking inhabitants.[40] But Ada was sent some distance away, to Odelltown, a small English enclave to the south of Montreal with a strong Methodist community led at that time by an English minister, George Poyser. The 10-year-old was placed in his household, which included his wife and a new baby daughter. Undoubtedly, she performed domestic chores in return for her keep, but she may also have attended school. Rev. Poyser's preaching at the local chapel clearly had an effect, for in later life Ada described herself as a Methodist.

Despite Thomas Barnardo's promise that his young migrants would be supervised by 'systematic visitation', there are no reports to show how Ada fared in this or in any of her placements. Since less important pieces of evidence have survived, it is unlikely that inspectors ever made the long journey from Barnardo's headquarters in Toronto into Quebec province. Thus there was even less likelihood of any ill-treatment coming to light than in the case of Alfred. The next we hear of Ada is that in June 1888 she was moved from Rev. Poyser's house to 'the care of her sister with Mrs S.C. Stevenson of 73 Mansfield Street, Montreal'.[41] It is difficult to know why this move happened. A likely explanation is that it was arranged by correspondence at the suggestion of Emily, who felt responsible for the welfare of her younger siblings and thought that Ada was lonely or even unhappy in Odelltown. Mrs Stevenson and her husband, affluent inhabitants of one of the 'resplendent mansions' in Montreal's 'Golden Square Mile', were clearly able to facilitate this reunion, by which they gained a 13-year-old home help.[42]

This mutually beneficial arrangement lasted until Emily returned to England in November following her mother's death. Unlike her siblings she was not bound as an indentured servant and must have managed to save enough money to make her passage back across the Atlantic, complete with Mrs Stevenson's testimonial to a 'trustworthy' employee who had attended to her duties 'in a tidy efficient manner'.[43] There was no family to welcome her – but perhaps she could keep the home fires burning. She clearly managed to gather up her mother's photographs and letters, some of which survive to this day.

Ada may have stayed on for a time to continue her sister's work, but by 1891 she had joined a third Canadian home, a typically peripatetic experience for a Barnardo's child. Walter Cottingham had just set up his own paint manufacturing business in Montreal and could afford a 'general servant' to help his young wife Gertrude look after the house and their baby daughter Gladys. The evidence suggests that Ada was as useful as her sister: her future husband described his 'tiny and dainty' wife as 'a wonderful housekeeper ... [who] couldn't be beat for cleanliness and orderliness'.[44] A studio photograph taken in Montreal when she was about 16 bears out this characterisation: looking shyly away from the camera, she wears a high-necked blouse decorated with intricate embroidery which might well be her own work.

Most young migrants followed in the footsteps of the Irish famine orphans by leaving their Canadian families once the opportunity offered, often to unite with siblings from whom they had been separated.[45] The Southwells were no exception. In 1893 Alfred left Doon to work in the Forbes Woollen Mill, Hespeler, the largest of its kind in the British Empire. Harry either accompanied him or followed soon after. Ada then joined her brothers in this small Ontario town on the Speed River to take up her first independent employment in the same mill. Here the three siblings could try to rid themselves of the shaming stigma of being 'home children', whom many Canadians viewed as 'street arabs' or 'gutter rats'.[46] On her wages from the Forbes Mill, Ada was able to rent a room in a respectable house and to dress herself smartly in clothes which she probably made herself. It was this, as well as her 'jokes and smart answers' and an enduring English accent, which attracted Thomas Kitching. He was a farmer's son who had recently bought some land in Hespeler and was setting himself up as a market gardener. He met Ada in 1896 through his sister, who also worked at the mill, and in June 1897 the couple were engaged. Ada had already agreed to take up a housekeeping post with a Presbyterian minister in Brockville but they were able to marry in April 1898 after 'a long winter' of separation. Thomas 'sure was proud' of Ada in her stylish cream wedding dress and honeymoon outfit of 'a bright green suit with a hat to match'. At the age of 21 she was embarking on a family life of her own and hoping to put the past behind her.[47]

*   *   *

The details of Ada's courtship come from the reminiscences of her husband, which were recorded by their youngest daughter in 1955, two years after Ada's death. Thomas tells the story of their married life but never mentions the fact that she was a British Home Child; indeed it was not until the 1990s that Ada's origins became known to her descendants. Such shamefaced secrecy was typical among the 100,000 or more child migrants sent to Canada over seventy years. The 11.5 per cent of the

Canadian population who are descended from them are beginning to piece together their family histories but, as was demonstrated in a recent Canadian television documentary, this is still 'an unknown story' in the country as a whole.[48] The Atlantic Ocean has continued to separate the child migrants from their British roots.

It was clearly very important to the five Southwell siblings to keep in touch with each other, though not much of their correspondence survived their unsettled lives. Towards the end of her life Emily decided that it was 'no use saving any old letters now', and burnt most of those still in her possession. Even so, their children and grandchildren have managed to reconstruct some of their histories, through which it might be possible to judge to what extent they were affected by their fractured childhood.

Seven years after her return to England Emily got married to George Sewell, he smartly suited and she looking very elegant in her leg o' mutton-sleeved dress. The couple went to live in Barking and had four children, one of whom died as a baby. Emily always yearned to see her siblings again but it was difficult to spare money for the transatlantic fare. A letter of 1954 records her gratitude to George who 'saved all he could' to enable her to visit Ada and Bessie in Canada in 1903, the first time she had seen them in about twenty years. She must have been pleased to find them both happily married: Ada was in Toronto by then with three daughters and Bessie still lived in Fullarton, 'just across the road from the big general store that Mrs Morrow and Joe looked after', with her adored husband Harvey Gettler. She was to lose 'poor Harvey' in 1931, and when 'bad health came she had no one to look after her of her own people'. Emily outlived her own husband by eight years, after which she spent a rather lonely old age, wishing that she 'did not remember so much' of her earlier years: 'You never forget it as long as you live.' She died in 1958 of gas poisoning which an inquest judged to be accidental.[49]

If Emily had been able to travel to Canada two years earlier she would have found both Harry and Alfred living with their married sister in Hespeler.[50] Thomas Kitching's own rural childhood in a family of ten children had been hard but happy, 'with nothing but our hands and our love for each other forcing us on'. In addition, they were sustained by their strong Mennonite faith, which Thomas kept up all his life. Whether or not he knew at this time about the break-up of the Southwell family, he was clearly content to accommodate his wife's brothers. Alfred helped out in his greenhouse until 1902 when the Kitchings moved to Toronto. There is no further mention of Alfred until 1906 when he married Alice Talbot, 'a girl of a different faith – Catholic', after going to live on the American side of Lake Ontario in Auburn, New York State.[51] Chris Beldan has managed to trace the remaining two years of his great-uncle's life through newspaper cuttings.

In September 1906 the *Auburn Citizen* reported the 'very pretty wedding' which took place at the bride's home in Auburn, and also the couple's return from a two-week honeymoon in Toronto 'with Mr Southwell's brother' – which suggests that the inter-faith marriage had not split the family. Alfred was spotted a year later, as crowds gathered to watch him painting the 'very pinnacle' of a church spire in Auburn, suspended at the 'dizzy height' of 175ft from the ground and supported only by a rope about his waist. Another year on he was still a painter, though he may not always have been engaged in such 'perilous work'. When he died 'suddenly' on 11 November 1908, the newspaper's announcement made no reference to any accident and the use of this word was more likely to be a coded reference to a suicide. Since Alfred's death certificate has not been made available, it can never be known whether he shared his father's fate. There is no reason to suppose that he had financial difficulties, as he lived in a pleasant street near Owasco Lake. He was also a popular member of the Painters' Union, which turned out in force to escort the remains of their 'late brother' to the grave. The only one of Alfred's own relations reported as present at the 'very largely attended' funeral (conducted by a Presbyterian Minister) was a brother from Canada, which may refer to Harry or to his brother-in-law, Thomas Kitching. The fact that Alice informed the journalist that 'his parents reside in the old country' suggests that Alfred had been too ashamed to tell her of his true origins.[52]

Harry's adult years remain as shadowy as his undisclosed Barnardo's childhood, but his great nieces and nephews have managed to piece together some of his life. In 1901 he married Lillie Williams while he was still working in Hespeler, but there is no record of any children. His enlistment at the age of 45 in the Canadian Expeditionary Force for the First World War is proved by his 1916 Attestation Paper in which his age is reduced by five years. There is also a picture of him in uniform standing proudly beside Lillie, who seems to be blowing his military bugle. It is clear that he remained part of the family circle after the war, as one of his nieces recalled that 'he would come over for meals once a week and was kind to her'. Thomas Kitching recounts that in 1941 Lillie had 'a stroke which left her paralysed on one side and Harry took over all the housework in addition to looking after Lillie'. After her death Harry went back to Britain, the only one of the four migrants to make the return passage, and saw something of his sister Emily. At the time of his death in 1966 he was working as a rigger in Cardiff Bay.[53]

*   *   *

Meanwhile, Ada was keeping house and looking after a growing family which finally included six daughters, Ethel, Phyllis, Helen, Marjorie, Winnie and Mavelle. Thomas was always able to support them all, even during 'hard depression years'. He worked for a coal company, hauled sand and spray-painted buildings but soon returned to his first love of growing flowers and vegetables, in which he achieved some commercial success. The family moved quite frequently in Toronto, progressing from a rented six-room house with running water but no electricity or inside conveniences to their own brand-new home on Milverton Boulevard with a 'three-piece bathroom'. In 1926 Thomas bought his first car, a Chrysler coach in which he would drive the family to church each Sunday – clearly he was not one of those Mennonites who rejected the modern world and would travel only by horse and carriage.

It sounds as though the Kitchings might even have been able to afford a general servant (such as the young Emily or Ada had been), but I suspect that Ada's pride would not have allowed her to resort to that. Thomas records that she was 'a wonderful housekeeper' who was constantly washing, ironing, mending, preparing home-cooked dinners 'that would just melt in your mouth', and nursing the children through such illnesses as diphtheria, scarlet fever and infantile paralysis. There were times when Ada was 'quite run down' and she developed high blood pressure – 'her body just couldn't take it'. Such physical strain was not, of course, unusual in the days before automatic washing machines, domestic refrigerators, central heating and antibiotics. But Ada had also to cope with the emotional repercussions of her uprooted childhood, which seemed to catch up with her as her own children began to leave home.

The first to depart was Ethel who got married in 1921, after which, her husband writes, Ada 'took quite sick ... and went to stay with Ethel for about three weeks'. Thomas does not go on to say that, as more of the girls left home during the 1920s, his wife suffered a nervous breakdown. The evidence for this is that Winnie, the second youngest daughter, 'lost some of her high school years home caring for her mother'. By 1930 Thomas was 'becoming quite accustomed to walking up the aisle' and only the two youngest girls were still at home. After Mavelle married in 1941 and left to join her husband on war service in British Columbia, the 'house was very lonesome'. 'At all hours of the night', her husband recalls 'Mama would be writing long letters to be mailed by me the next day.' When the last remaining daughter, Winnie, left to be married in 1944 Ada 'really was broken up':

> Time seemed to drag and instead of the heavy washing and ironing, she began to have time on her hands. Now she was having the rest she had always looked forward to, and she was utterly miserable. I believe this was the beginning of the end for her. She was seventy now, and felt her days of usefulness were over, but I tried to pull her out of it. Her bluest time was around six o'clock at night, the hour when Winnie used to come home, and I'd often see her looking out of the door longingly.[54]

We cannot tell to what extent Thomas was able to pull his wife out of her depression in the remaining nine years of Ada's life because he did not complete his reminiscences before his own death in 1955. Such was the taboo about mental illness in those days that he is unlikely to have sought medical help for her.

Ada may well have taken some comfort in the fact that all her daughters were living in Toronto, for they too did not like to be too far from their 'folks and friends'. So strongly did they feel this need not to be separated that two pairs of them married brothers, and in 1946 all six families built homes side-by-side on seven acres of land they had acquired in eastern Scarborough, a pleasant area to the east of the city. Thomas and Ada built a small summer cottage on one of the lots and were able to spend time there with daughters, sons-in-law and grandchildren. The families would share suppers in one of the back yards on summer evenings and spend Christmas all together, as well as helping each other out at other times. It was, writes Winnie's son Chris Beldan, 'the very antithesis of the dispersed Southwell family.'[55]

*   *   *

Take them away! Take them away!
Plant them anew upon wholesome soil,
Till their hearts grow fresh in the purer air,
And their hands grow hard with honest toil.

Ada died in 1953 and was buried near the family plot in Scarborough where, as Thomas said, 'the air is very fresh off the lake'. Just as the charity had promised, the 'wholesome soil' of this country beneath which she was interred had provided her with a good living during her adulthood in return for 'honest toil'.[56] Thomas had grown his market produce in it; the couple had been able to buy some cheap land to house their family; and in their old age they had the benefit of a summer cottage in what is now a comfortable middle-class neighbourhood of Toronto. Ada also dressed herself and her daughters beautifully, was able to take a few holidays on the Lakes and in the Canadian Maritimes and lived to a good age. All this suggests that she was materially better off there than she would have been in Britain, as is true of most child migrants planted anew in Canada – and even of the Irish girls who were made to feel so unwelcome in Australia.[57]

It is harder to judge whether their hearts flourished in the wake of their journey over the sea. As children they could rarely find the words to explain how they felt and were often too frightened to do so. In adult life migrants were loath to reveal that they were home children, let alone to explain how the separation from their own parents and siblings had affected them. There are clues, however, in the case of the Southwell siblings. Their mother's letters express her enduring grief for her lost children. Emily wrote of the memories which haunted her old age. Alfred's anguished teenage letter to Emily shows that the 'guilt and shame' he was supposed to have left behind stayed with him – yet he clearly did not speak of this to his wife. Ada left no correspondence, which may have been lost in the many moves she made in her life or destroyed as evidence of a past she did not wish to reveal. But her husband's account of the heartache she felt at parting from her daughters is evidence enough. It echoes that of many separated youngsters.

Above all, the efforts made by the Southwell siblings to keep in touch testify to their need for each other. Only they could understand what they had lost in being taken across the sea. It is true that they had been rescued from acute poverty and that their mother's early death can be attributed to the slum dwellings and public houses in which she spent her remaining five years. But the migrants' early childhood had not wholly been passed in 'the gutter, the ooze and slime' described by the Children's Society. Guilty as Alfred felt, he knew that he and his siblings had not been 'little vermin' who 'paddle and crawl till they grow and ripen into crime'; they had attended school, posed for family photographs and looked after each other. If they had stayed in the old country, Harriett might have contrived to visit them in a Barnardo's or Macpherson Home. She, or a relation, might even have been able to take them out of care, as often happened after a family crisis. The Atlantic crossing imposed a tyranny of distance which made any such reunion impossible. All the young migrants could do was to try to 'be as Brother and Sister to each other'. Unwittingly, but sensing what their mother had suffered, Ada's daughters and sons-in-law followed suit. Thus, her grandson concludes from his family's experience, the distress of Canada's uprooted migrants, 'ripples out through generations'.[58]

*　*　*

The migration of children from Britain's shores to Canada and Australia ended in 1967, by which time the supply of waifs and the demand for their labour had decreased. Since then both the Old and the New Worlds have sought to repair past wrongs. The prime ministers of Britain and

Australia (but not yet Canada) have apologised for 'the physical suffering, the emotional starvation and the cold absence of love, of tenderness and of care'.[59] Barnardo's now tries to reunite separated families and provide former migrants with counselling.

At the same time, child charities offer support to the thousands of children who are still forced or encouraged to make long journeys unaccompanied by parents or carers. In 2015, for example, about 90,000 lone child refugees arrived in Europe from Asia and Africa after long hikes over land and perilous sea journeys in frail rubber boats. Some had lost their homes in war-torn countries or in natural disasters; some were sent by parents to seek a better life; some were smuggled off into forced labour or prostitution; some left with parents who died or were detained during the journey; some were trying to join families who had already migrated. As children they are especially vulnerable both en route and in their host countries to exploitation, violent treatment, sexual abuse and criminalisation. And, like the young slaves, migrants, transportees and sailors of earlier years, they also suffer the less obvious pains of homesickness, separation anxiety and culture shock. Thus Athari Bassim, a 15-year-old Iraqi girl dispatched to the Netherlands by her parents after her brother was kidnapped and tortured by militias, has repeated nightmares and thinks constantly of her parents and little sisters: 'We were a close family and enjoyed being at home.' Fahmi Ali, a 16-year-old Syrian, asks himself all the time why he agreed to leave his parents in Damascus and when he will be able to get them to his Dutch camp. A 10-year-old Syrian child, Aseel Ahmed, left her country believing her parents had died in the bombing, only to find out later that they had survived: 'I go to sleep so that I can be united with my family in Damascus in my dreams.' Kawkeb Hassan, aged 9, bursts into tears whenever she sees a scene in a cartoon film where children are eating a meal with their parents, begging her older brother to take her back to Lebanon.[60]

Most unaccompanied child migrants are also undocumented as well as unaccompanied. But nowadays there are at least sympathetic journalists and human rights representatives who listen to some of their stories. These accounts might prove useful to historians of the future when they come to write of these forlorn travellers. Even so, many will be lost to history, their fates and their feelings buried by criminal traffickers, evasive governments, exploitative employers and poor, illiterate parents. The twentieth century saw numerous attempts to guarantee the Rights of the Child to special protection, to education, to a name and a nationality and to love and understanding.[61] It seems that these compassionate intentions have not been able to prevent thousands of children embarking on journeys which break family ties as effectively as the slave ships, convict transports, navy frigates and migrant boats which carried children away in the eighteenth and nineteenth centuries.

Chapter 9

Sea Fever: Lives Changed by the Sea

No more thy tender frame, thy blooming age,
Shall be the sport of ocean's turb'lent rage.[1]

Thus wrote John Gabriel Stedman, the grieving father of 17-year-old Midshipman Johnny Stedman, who was drowned off Jamaica in 1792. Stedman had doted on his oldest son, a 'mulatto' born in the Dutch colony of Surinam to Joanna, the slave woman he had married there as a young soldier. When Joanna died Stedman purchased his son's freedom and had the 8-year-old sent to join him and his new wife in Holland. For Johnny, as for Joseph Emidy, a trans-Atlantic journey bestowed emancipation and the chance of a better life – but also the risk of being rebuffed in a new land. Stedman's journal tells of some ill-treatment of his Caribbean son by his Dutch wife and mother. The family settled eventually in Devon, where Johnny was educated at Blundell's School, Tiverton, and like my great-grandfather on the Isles of Scilly, received lessons in navigation. Indeed, he was so interested in the subject that he bought himself Hamilton's *Practical Navigation* to sit on his bookshelf with *Robinson Crusoe*, a present from his father. Convinced that Johnny had the 'active enterprising spirit' lauded by naval officers like Admirals Barlow and Collingwood, Stedman launched him on a sea-going career when he reached the age of 13.

He rejected the first offer of a place on the *Scarborough*, which had recently returned from conveying the London lads featured in Chapter 1 to Botany Bay and was scheduled to be part of the second transportation fleet. Stedman clearly felt that the '300 convicts on board' would not be fit company for his son, but he could not have wished on them the abuse and neglect which caused a quarter of them to die on that voyage. Instead Johnny joined the *Southampton*, whose captain soon gave him 'an excellent character'. Even so, he returned with his sea-chest 'nearly empty, having sold all his clothes and even his bed'. He had lost all his money 'by generosity' as free as that lavished by George King on his shipmates. For this he was given 'a severe lecture' and put on a shorter allowance, as well as being made to beg his father's pardon on his knees. But, like the Barlow uncles and Charles Dickens in similar circumstances, Stedman gave his young sailor a second chance and was proud of the 'manly boy' who boarded the *Amity Hall* in March 1791, dressed at his expense in full midshipman's uniform and a gold-laced hat. It seems, however, that the boy's 'olive beauties' became the subject of some scorn 'on the waves' – in much the same way as Sydney Dickens's short stature made him the butt of shipboard ragging. It can never be known how Johnny's character would have developed, for only a year later he met his death 'while discharging his duty in commanding a pinnace'.[2] Just as the manner of his death strikingly resembles that of Othnel Mawdesley, the shipboard experiences of Johnny's short life echo those of many other children at sea. He migrated to a land of opportunities, but not to an entirely warm welcome. Led astray as a raw midshipman he yet remained 'true to his duty'. Endowed with the spirit to 'shine on board a man of war with honour', he lost his young life to the 'ocean's turbulent rage'.[3]

Rather different sea-changes affected another motherless young sailor, the poet John Masefield. His mother died in 1885 when he was 6, after which he was looked after by an intimidating governess before being sent to board at Warwick School at the age of 9. Masefield looked back on his first year there as wretched:

> I was too young. And they discovered that I wrote poetry. I tried to kill myself once by eating laurel leaves but I only gave myself a horrible headache. Once I ran away, and was brought back by a policeman and flogged.[4]

He eventually settled at the school, but was removed after the nervous breakdown and death of his father. The sternly dutiful Aunt Kate, who now took charge of John and his siblings, scorned the boy's addiction to books and decided that he should be toughened up by a career in the Merchant Marine – the Royal Navy being too expensive. Reassured by rosy reports of the moored training-ship HMS *Conway*, and by an article he had read in the *Boys' Own Paper*, the 12-year-old boy agreed to this course of action.

A more dutiful student than William Barlow in Portsmouth, John enjoyed the two-year course in Liverpool, during which he mastered practical navigation and nautical astronomy, won a telescope for 'Proficiency in Writing, Spelling and Composition', and qualified as a midshipman. But the true test of his seaworthiness came when he boarded a sailing vessel bound for Chile. His journal of that thirteen-week voyage across the South Atlantic records frequent prostration with seasickness and sunstroke, as well as wonder at such natural phenomena as a nocturnal rainbow, phosphorescent water, leaping porpoises and laughing penguins. And he was by turns terrified and exhilarated by the roaring forties off Cape Horn:

> The Horn is a hard place in winter. Seas forty feet high and two miles long, and ice everywhere, on deck, in the rigging, and tumbling into the sea, and we fighting the lot of it.

Knocked into manhood by this 'real naked life', he arrived in port such a nervous wreck that he fell ill and had to be shipped home as a DBS (Distressed British Seaman). He clearly felt, like Charles Barlow at a similar age, that anything would be better than a nautical career. But Aunt Kate, furious that he had 'failed to stick it', packed off her orphan charge as firmly as Barnardo's dispatched its child migrants. By this time, however, John was 16 and beginning to know his own mind. A wretched trans-Atlantic voyage on another merchant ship convinced him that the sea should not have him 'in her grip': 'I deserted my ship in New York and cut myself off from her and from my home. I was going to be a writer, come what might.'[5]

For two years Masefield lived in America as a homeless vagrant, taking on such jobs as he could find during the acute economic depression of the 1890s, ruining his health but also finding the energy to write. The poetry which sprang to his pen, published eventually as *Salt-Water Ballads* and *A Sailor's Garland*, arose out of nostalgia for the life he had escaped; he had left the sea, but it had not left him. He continued to feel the 'Sea Fever' expressed in his most famous poem – a yearning for 'the lonely sea and the sky'. When he had a portrait painted in 1909 he specified the background: 'The sea is behind me, a celestial globe to my right'. And when he set up home as a married man in London's Little Venice, with his heart 'still in the wilds and on the oceans', he plastered the walls of his study with charts.[6] In the prose and poetry he composed there he gave a voice to many a less articulate 'fellow-rover', as he did also in his autobiographical writing and maritime history.[7]

He strove to convey the brutality of the sailor's life as he had experienced it, and also his enduring fascination with ships and their journeys. He describes a Cape Horn voyager lashed by the wind and 'icy-cold rain' feeling 'like a king, like an emperor' on the cross-trees and shouting aloud with the joy of that 'rastle [wrestle] with the sail'. He remembers watching fine ships in harbour, picturing 'young men going to the devil, and mature men wasted, and old men wrecked', and wondering 'at the misery and sin which went to make each ship so perfect an image of beauty'.[8] On the other hand he conjures up the romantic child's dream:

> I'm going to be a pirate with a bright brass pivot-gun,
> And an island in the Spanish main beyond the setting sun,
> And a silver flagon full of red wine to drink when work is done,
> Like a fine old salt-sea scavenger, like a tarry Buccaneer.[9]

In his history of navy life he quotes a 14-year-old boy who witnessed terrible scenes in battle during which he feared that he would soon enter 'the other world', but cheered with the rest when victory came. The same book describes ships' boys from the streets who 'lived the life of dogs', but who 'remained in the service all their lives … because the life unfitted them for anything else'.[10] His poem 'Hell's Pavement', portraying such an existence, conjures up that of George King: a sailor resolves to save his 'bit o' pay', marry 'a pretty little lass' and settle down ashore, but when the ship docks in Liverpool,

> … Billy drew his money, but the money didn't last,
> For he painted the alongshore blue, –
> It was rum for Poll, and rum for Nan, and gin for Jolly Jack.
> He shipped a week later in the clothes upon his back,
> He had to pinch a little straw, he had to beg a sack
> To sleep on, when his watch was through, –
> So he did.[11]

A poem like 'Westward Ho' evokes a ship bound for Spanish waters where

> ... there will be sunshine and the thronged sea piers,
> And merry taverns full of tarry buccaneers,
> And jolly sailors dancing, and songs for our delight,
> And Spanish wine and sweet wine, and red wine and white.

But in 'Christmas 1903', the bells sounding in coastal Devon churches seem to 'ring home wandering sailors who have been homeless long'.[12] With such writing Masefield conveys the trials and the triumphs, the miseries and the joys of those who went to sea when young, leaving 'hearth nooks lit and kindly, with dear friends good to see', for a 'vagrant gypsy life'.[13]

Masefield's view of the sea was drawn both from his own unforgettable experience and from his creative imagination. It was very unusual in the nineteenth century for any systematic inquiries to be made into the effects of childhood sea journeys. The exception is Andrew Doyle, whose research for the 1875 Local Government Board report on the 'Emigration of Pauper Children to Canada' was based on about 400 'difficult and laborious' visits to child migrants. He witnessed many cases of physical neglect and ill-treatment, such as 'bread that was mouldy', 'barns for a shelter', or young girls 'compelled to work in the fields with hired men'. Above all, he was 'painfully struck ... with the sense of loneliness manifested by them', and with their enduring homesickness. 'Nobody knows,' he was told, 'what a girl has to put up with that comes from the old country, for they know we have no parents to take our part, and that they can do as they like.' It was the sheer distance from their old homes which isolated them, just as it did young sailors:

> The little emigrants have been set afloat, and too many of them let to 'paddle their own canoes' until ... some of them have gone over the rapids, and others are already lost sight of in the great human tide of the Western cities.

The Doyle Report ruled that no more Poor Law children should be sent overseas until adequate safeguards were provided – but this did not prevent the dispatch of the Southwell youngsters by private charities.[14]

There was no investigation into the further destinies of such children until Margaret Humphreys set up the Child Migrant Trust in 1987. Ever since then she and her helpers have been tracking down men and women who were sent to Australia as children, listening to their stories and, where possible, reuniting them with their families. Like Doyle, she has heard many accounts of abuse and negligence, but is most conscious of the 'absolute loneliness' which has made it difficult for such migrants to form relationships, a state compared by one to 'having a piece of ice inside you all the time'.[15] John Hennessey, an illegitimate Irish boy shipped away by the Christian Brothers in 1947, was so cut off from his family that he did not even receive a birthday card until 1999 – after he had been put in touch with the mother he had been told was dead. Although he has prospered in Australia, becoming deputy mayor of Campbelltown, that card is still Hennessy's most treasured possession. The work of the Trust continues but there can be no neat tally of happy and unhappy endings.

First-hand evidence is more available for wartime 'seavacuees', British children sent abroad by relations, schools, businesses or by the government's Children's Overseas Reception Board (CORB) to escape bombing and possible invasion. They are more likely than uprooted child migrants to have written memoirs. One of their most vivid memories is of the dangerous sea voyage itself. John Catlin considered his journey 'in the submarine-infested waters of the Atlantic ... the riskiest thing' he and his sister Shirley (later Williams) could have undertaken, even though at the time they both found it 'tremendously exciting'.[16] Indeed many children hoped, like the young Lord Montagu, that they would 'see some action' during the voyage. Montagu would have seen plenty had he been one of over 300 evacuee children aboard the *Volendam*, which was hit by a torpedo at the end of August 1940. No doubt, too, he would have joined in the singing of 'Roll Out the Barrel' as all the children were safely loaded into lifeboats. Ann Harrop (later Thwaite) was less heroic when, in the same month, her ship bound for New Zealand over mine-ridden waters collided with another vessel:

What I didn't tell my father was that I myself, at the last moment, faced with climbing over the side of the ship into a frail lifeboat, suspended from ropes on davits, far above the choppy sea, had panicked and refused to get in. I was seven years old and the Captain himself picked me up like a baby from where I lay on the deck and put me safely into the lifeboat, where I tried to pretend that no such scene had occurred, but wept quietly because, in the confusion of my undignified departure, my Peter Rabbit, in his velveteen trousers, had somehow got left behind on the deck.[17]

Unknown to Ann at the time, her worst fears were realised a few weeks later when the evacuee ship *City of Benares* was struck by a German torpedo in mid-Atlantic. Seventy-seven of the ninety CORB passengers either went down with the ship or died in lifeboats before they could be rescued. The survivors never forgot their experiences, which some have recorded for the Imperial War Museum. Among them is Kenneth Sparks, who joined the Royal Navy as a 15-year-old boy bugler four years later. He said that all but one of the boys on his lifeboat went into the navy: 'We'd already had a taste of what the sea was like and I thought, it can't do any worse that it's done already.'[18] The CORB scheme was abandoned after this disaster, having transported only a tenth of those who had applied; but thousands more children travelled by private arrangement to America, Canada, South Africa, Australia and New Zealand.

Seavacuees often wrote home about the comfortable conditions, new experiences and generous hospitality they enjoyed after their arrival – but did not usually reveal any feelings of insecurity. Alistair Horne, for example, had a kind and affluent American foster-family but admits in his autobiography to his 'dark shame about being away from it all'. On holiday with the host family on Chappaquiddick Island he would 'reflect that there was nothing but the ocean – empty but for its lurking U-boats – between me and home. I would feel beset by a deep wave of melancholia, of homesickness, of helplessness and of worry about my father.' Alistair's letters did not tell his father that in the summer of 1941, when feeling particularly depressed, he strung up a noose in his bedroom. Yet he 'began to pine for America' on his return to 'austere, battered London', where he was shocked to find how his father had aged: 'His whole world had got smaller and poorer.'[19] Other seavacuees didn't even recognise their parents when they were reunited after a four- or five-year separation.

Such personal stories are borne out by the sociologists and psychologists who have investigated the effects of overseas evacuation. Patricia Lin established, for example, that those sent off in the CORB scheme were much more likely than their peers who had stayed in Britain, to remain at school beyond the age of 16 and to 'improve their class standing'. She concluded that theirs had been a 'profoundly positive and transformative experience'. Her claim that most evacuees were very sad to board their ships for the journey home suggests the penalty they paid in terms of emotional maladjustment.[20] One participant in the survey sounded just like a child migrant, comparing herself to the 'snow queen in the fairy tale' with a chip of ice in her heart: 'I dare not love people in case I lose them.'[21]

Questionnaires completed more recently for another survey of British evacuees, when they were all over 60, demonstrate comparatively low 'levels of psychological well-being', with about 30 per cent having had therapy. The study suggests that the effects of separation 'may become more pronounced with age', a view supported by the tears of former children of the Raj I have interviewed. A more clear-cut finding is that an unusually high proportion of seavacuees subsequently went to live abroad.[22] It seems that their early journeys had bred in them a wanderlust similar to that taste for the 'vagrant gypsy life' which draws erstwhile sailors 'down to the seas again'. In one way or another, their lives had been shaped by the waves – they were, as one of them put it, 'all at sea'.

Notes

The place of publication is London unless otherwise stated.

Abbreviations
CSAS Centre for South Asian Studies (Cambridge)
HDNSW Historical Documents of New South Wales
LMA London Metropolitan Archives
NA National Archives
NMM National Maritime Museum
OIOC Oriental and India Office Collections

Introduction: A Historian at Sea

1. Samuel Taylor Coleridge, *Frost at Midnight* and *The Rime of the Ancient Mariner*, Part IV.
2. It is thought that the well-known sea shanty, 'Bound for South Australia', was first used by sailors as they set off on these on these perilous voyages.
3. Basil Lubbock, *The Colonial Clippers* (Glasgow, 1921) 131; *Hobart Mercury*, 25 September 1877 and *Melbourne Argus*, 9 October 1877 quoted in www. aberdeenships.com
4. http://trove.nla.gov.au/newspaper *Melbourne Herald*, 27 October 1877.
5. Advertisement by Anderson, Anderson & Co, 1878, in author's possession.
6. Information from Aline Davis's family history research.
7. http://trove.nla.gov.au/newspaper *Melbourne Argus*, 5 October 1878; Medical Certificate of Death; Lubbock, *Colonial Clippers*, 144.
8. Telegram from Captain George Sherris of Scilly from Melbourne, quoted in *Gibson's Guide*, c.1926, information courtesy of courtesy of Roger Banfield; http://trove.nla.gov.au/newspaper *Melbourne Herald*, 7 October 1878; grave record from Williamstown Cemetery, Victoria.
9. Undated death notice for Jane Davis in the *Scillonian*.
10. Alan Villiers, *War with Cape Horn* (1971) quoted in John Coote (ed.), *The Faber Book of the Sea* (1989), 38.
11. From Lord Byron, *Childe Harold's Pilgrimage*, Canto IV in *Byron*, ed. Jerome J. McGann (Oxford, 1986), 199.
12. Joseph Conrad, *Youth* (Penguin edition of short stories, ed. John Lyon, 1995), 9.
13. Emma Smith, *The Great Western Beach: A Memoir of a Cornish Childhood Between the Wars* (2008), 76–7.
14. Charlotte Runcie, *Salt on Your Tongue* (2019), 18.
15. Bella Bathurst, 'Sea-Towers' in *Granta 61, The Sea: Voyages, Mysteries, Discoveries, Disasters* (1998), 170.
16. Linda Colley, *Captives: Britain, Empire and the World 1600–1850* (2002), 118.
17. John Everett Millais, *The Boyhood of Raleigh*, 1870, in Tate Gallery.

18. Vyvyen Brendon, *Children of the Raj* (2005) and *Prep School Children: A Class Apart Over Two Centuries* (2009).
19. James Silk Buckingham, *Autobiography* (1855), vol 1, 10, 78–80, 132 & 153.
20. Mavelle Beldan typed up her father's words so that they form a memoir, 'I Remember'.
21. See, for example, memoirs cited in D.A.B. Ronald, *Young Nelsons* (Oxford, 2009). In 2008 another rare example of an ordinary seaman's diary was discovered, that of George Hodge written between 1790 and 1833. This was sold to a private American collector for $110,000 and no transcript is available to researchers.
22. Conrad, *Youth,* 12, 17 & 43.

Chapter 1: Mary Branham and the Young Convicts of the First Fleet: 1787
 1. www.oldbaileyonline.org, Trial of Mary Bramham, 8 December 1784.
 2. Trial of John Owen, 10 September 1783.
 3. Trial of George Robinson, John Nurse and George Bannister, 21 April 1784.
 4. Trial of Francis Gardener and William Tuckey, 21 April 1784.
 5. Trial of James Pulet, Nicholas English and Peter Woodcock, 7 July, 1784.
 6. Trial of Joseph Tuso, 7 July 1784 and 23 February 1785.
 7. George Eliot, *Adam Bede* (first published 1859, Penguin 1994), 438–9 & 445.
 8. NA, HO47/3/34.
 9. Maya Jasanoff, *Liberty's Exiles: The Loss of America and the Remaking of the British Empire* (2011), 141; Tom Keneally, *The Commonwealth of Thieves* (2006), 46 & 117.
10. https://www.sl.nsw.gov.au, Ralph Clark, Journal kept on the Friendship during a voyage to Botany Bay and Norfolk Island, and on the Gorgon returning to England, 1787–92, List of Passengers.
11. Trial of Ann Mather, 18 April 1787.
12. Mollie Gillen, *The Founders of Australia: A Biographical Dictionary of the First Fleet* (Sydney,1989), 128 & 277.
13. www.lancastercastle.com/history-heritage/archives
14. https://www.sl.nsw.gov.au, Arthur Bowes Smyth, A Journal of a Voyage from Portsmouth to New South Wales and China in the Lady Penrhyn, Merchantman, 1787–89 (MS fair copy compiled c.1790).
15. Keneally, *Commonwealth of Thieves*, 30.
16. Watkin Tench, *A Narrative of the Expedition to Botany Bay* in Tim Flannery, *Watkin Tench's 1788* (Melbourne, 2009), 17–18.
17. Clark, Journal, 9 March 1787.
18. Tench, *Narrative,* 17 & 19.
19. Trial of John Hudson, 10 December 1783.
20. *Historical Documents of New South Wales [HDNSW]* (Sydney 1892), vol 2, 480.
21. *HDNSW*, vol 1, 108; *The Voyage of Governor Phillip to Botany Bay* (1789), 7 February 1788.
22. Bowes Smyth, Journal, 1 and 10 December 1787.
23. Bowes Smyth, Journal, 27 September and 31 December 1787, 1 and 10 January 1788.
24. Robert Hughes, *The Fatal Shore* (1987), 79.
25. Clark, Journal, 22 July 1787.
26. Bowes Smyth, Journal, 15 August 1787 and https://www.sl.nsw.gov.au, Journal of Lieutenant William Bradley of HMS *Sirius*, 21 August 1787.
27. Bowes Smyth, Journal, 14 August and 10 December 1787.
28. Bowes Smyth, Journal, 19 April 1787.

29. Clark, Journal, 16 May, 6 August and 6 November 1787.
30. See Siân Rees, *The Floating Brothel* (2001), 103-5 and Joy Damousi, *Depraved and Disorderly: Female Convicts, Sexuality and Gender in Colonial Australia* (Cambridge, 1997), 33-5 for a discussion of the 'sexual tensions between the women and their commanders'.
31. Bowes Smyth, Journal, 12 August 1787.
32. See Keneally, *Commonwealth of Thieves*, 76 and Deborah Oxley, *Convict Maids: The Forced Migration of Women to Australia* (Cambridge, 1996), 205.
33. Bowes Smyth, Journal, List of children brought out or born on board. The name Branham is wrongly transcribed as Burnham in the transcribed version of the journal.
34. Damousi, *Depraved and Disorderly*, 30.
35. Bowes Smyth, Journal, 10 December 1787.
36. Clark, Journal, 29 May and 15 November 1787.
37. https://www.sl.nsw.gov.au, John Easty, Journal 1786-1793, 2 January 1788.
38. Bowes Smyth, Journal, 24 and 25 December 1787 and 10 January 1788 and Clark, Journal, 28 December 1787.
39. Clark, Journal, 26 & 28 January 1788 and Bowes Smyth, Journal, 6 February 1788.
40. *HDNSW*, vol 2, 393.
41. Cf. Don Chapman, *1788: The People of the First Fleet* (Sydney, 1988), 81 and Keneally, *Commonwealth of Thieves*, 136.
42. Judge Advocate's Bench, 15 August 1789 quoted in Alan Atkinson, *The Europeans in Australia: A History* (Oxford, 1997) vol 1, 136-7.
43. Keneally, *Commonwealth of Thieves*, 435.
44. 'My Family History', posted by Robyn, November 2010.
45. Review by James Atlas in *New York Times*, 20 September 1987.
46. Thomas Keneally, *The Playmaker* (1987, 2014 edition), 381.
47. Cf. NA ADM 36/11120, Muster of HMS *Gorgon* & Gillen, *Founders of Australia*, 47.
48. Clark, Journal, 26 April 1792.
49. List of known burials at St John's church, Parramatta, 1791 transcribed by Michaela Ann Cameron. It must be this evidence which lies behind Keneally's assertion in *Playmaker*, 381 that 'Willy' Branham died 'of a sudden childhood fever'.
50. NA, PROB 11/1326/204, Will of Captain William Furzer, 3 July 1799.
51. Atkinson, *Europeans in Australia*, vol 1, 95; Gillen, *Founders of Australia*, 128–9.
52. Atkinson, *Europeans in Australia*, vol 1, 132; Gillen, *Founders of Australia, 258.*
53. Gillen, *Founders of Australia*, 169; https://firstfleetfellowship.org.au.
54. Oxley, *Convict Maids*, 230.
55. https://www.sl.nsw.gov.au, David Collins, 'An Account of the English Colony in New South Wales', vol 1, November 1789.
56. Clark, Journal, 10 December 1790 and Collins, Account, April 1790.
57. Lieutenant David Collins quoted in Gillen, *Founders of Australia*, 232.
58. Gidley King's Journal quoted in HDNSW, vol 2, 565 & 569
59. Collins, Account, July 1789 and Journal of John Easty, 28 March 1791.
60. Charles Dickens, *Great Expectations* (Penguin edn 1985), 467.
61. Letter from a female convict, Port Jackson, 14 November 1788 in *HDNSW*, vol 2, 746-7.
62. A Convict's Letter and Letter from an Officer, 9 and 14 April 1790 in *HDNSW*, vol 2, 758-9.
63. Eliot, *Adam Bede*, 445 & 505.

64. Phillip to Lord Sydney, 5 July 1788 and George Bouvier Worgan to his brother, 2 May 1788 quoted in John Cobley, *Sydney Cove 1788* (1962), 134.
65. Cobley, *1788*, 152–3 & 42.
66. Clark, Journal, 25 January 1791. See Robert Holden, *Orphans of History: The Forgotten Children of the First Fleet* (2001), 153–4 for an argument that Hudson was probably abused in this way.
67. Alphabetical list in R.J. Ryan, *The Third Fleet* (New South Wales, 1983); Charles Bateson, *The Convict Ships* (Glasgow, 1969 edn), 138.

Chapter 2: Joseph Emidy c.1775–1835: Slave and Musician
1. Buckingham, *Autobiography*, 167.
2. For West African background see *The Life of Olaudah Equiano*, ed. Paul Edwards (1988), 4–7 and Aminatta Forna, *Ancestor Stones* (2006), 5–6 & 61.
3. http://docsouth.unc.edu/neh, *Narrative of the Enslavement of Ottabah Cugoano, A Native of Africa* (1787), 126 & 121.
4. Daniel P. Mannix, *Black Cargoes: A History of the Atlantic Slave Trade 1518–1865* (1963), 76.
5. Hugh Thomas, *The Slave Trade: The History of the Slave Trade 1440–1870* (1997), 395–6.
6. Eg *Life of Equiano*, 22 and Augustino interviewed in Robert Edgar Conrad, *Children of God's Fire: A Documentary History of Black Slavery in Brazil* (1983), 39.
7. Mahommah Gardo Baquaqua quoted in Conrad, *Children of God's Fire*, 27.
8. See Audra A. Diptee, 'African Children in the British Slave Trade during the late eighteenth century' in *Slavery and Abolition*, vol 27, August 2006.
9. Mannix, *Black Cargoes*, 113.
10. Jennifer Hayward & M. Soledad Caballero (eds), *Maria Graham's Journal of a Voyage to Brazil* (Anderson, South Carolina, 2010), 20 October 1821, 72.
11. Mahommah Gardo Baquaqua quoted in Conrad, *Children of God's Fire*, 28.
12. Stuart B. Schultz, 'Plantations and Peripheries' in Leslie Bethell, *Colonial Brazil* (1987), 85.
13. The same assumption can be made about the previous life in Jamaica of Dr Johnson's black servant, Francis Barber. See Michael Bundock, *The Fortunes of Francis Barber: The True Story of the Jamaican Slave who became Samuel Johnson's Heir* (Yale, 2015), 22.
14. Thomas Lindley, *Narrative of a Voyage to Brasil* (1805), 65,176 & 269–70.
15. Maria Graham agreed with the Scottish philosopher David Hume who thought that another hardship of the house slave was his greater awareness of his own subjection. See Hayward & Caballero, *Maria Graham's Journal*, 23 October 1821, 79.
16. Quoted in Conrad, *Children of God's Fire*, 85.
17. Frances Anne Kemble, *Journal of a Residence on a Georgian Plantation in 1838–1839*, ed. John Scott (1961), 193.
18. William Tuck, 'Reminiscences of Camborne' in *Historical Descriptions of Camborne*, ed. Chris Bond (2013), 70.
19. Robert Walsh quoted in Conrad, *Children of God's Fire*, 56.
20. Solomon Northup, *Twelve Years a Slave* (2013 edn), 128 & 142.
21. Bowes Smyth, Journal, 24 August 1787.
22. Conrad, *Children of God's Fire*, 110.
23. Herbert S. Klein & Francisco Vidal Luna, *Slavery in Brazil* (2010), 248.
24. Life of Equiano, 60–7

25. Hayward & Caballero, *Maria Graham's Journal,* 22 November 1821, 89.
26. James Holman quoted in Peter Fryer, *Rhythms of Resistance: African Musical Inheritance in Brazil* (2000), 43.
27. Fryer, *Rhythms of Resistance,* 18 and John Geipel, 'Brazil's African Legacy' in *History Today,* vol 47, issue 8, 1997.
28. See Cristina Nogueira da Silva and Keila Grinberg, 'Soil Free from Slaves: Slave Law in Late Eighteenth- and Early Nineteenth-Century Portugal' in *Slavery and Abolition,* vol 32, September 2011, 431–46; Lindley, *Narrative,* 259; Conrad, *Children of God's Fire,* 319.
29. Buckingham, *Autobiography,* 167.
30. Buckingham, *Autobiography,* 69.
31. James Murphy, *Travels in Portugal* (1795), 131 & 146; Robert Southey, *Letters Written during a Short Residence in Portugal* (1797), 262-3 & 359.
32. Boyd Alexander (ed.), *The Journal of William Beckford in Portugal and Spain 1787–1788* (Nonesuch, 2006), 9 June 1787.
33. Buckingham, *Autobiography,* 167 and Murphy, *Travels,* 198.
34. See Isabel Castro Henriques, 'Africans in Portuguese Society' in Eric Morier-Genoud & Michel Cahen, *Imperial Migrations: Colonial Communities and Diaspora in the Portuguese World* (2012), 76.
35. Beckford, *Journal,* 26 November 1787.
36. Buckingham, *Autobiography,* 85.
37. Beckford, *Journal,* 10 August 1787, 106.
38. See Fryer, *Rhythms of Resistance,* 3–4.
39. Janet Schaw, *Journal of a Lady of Quality of a Journey from Scotland to the West Indies, North Carolina and Portugal in the Years 1774 and 1776* (Yale, 1923), 243; Southey, *Letters,* 314–6.
40. *Life of Equiano,* 119.
41. Beckford, *Journal,* 30 June 1787.
42. Buckingham, *Autobiography,* 132.
43. Patrick O'Brian, *Master and Commander* (1971 edn), 7.
44. Buckingham, *Autobiography,* 167–8.
45. NA, ADM 36/13/13142.
46. Buckingham, *Autobiography,* 167–9.
47. Buckingham, *Autobiography,* 168–9.
48. Stephen Taylor, *Commander: The Life and Exploits of Britain's Greatest Frigate Captain* (2012), 125–6.
49. Buckingham, *Autobiography,* 169.
50. Rabbi Bernard Susser, 'The Jews of South-West England' (Susser Archive, thesis).
51. All these places of origin are listed in the Muster Book for HMS *Indefatigable* 1795, NA, ADM 36/13146.
52. Buckingham, *Autobiography,* 169, Richard McGrady, *Music and Musicians in Early Nineteenth Century Cornwall* (Exeter,1991), 35–6 and *Oxford Dictionary of National Biography* (2004-13).
53. Taylor, *Commander,* 91–2 and NA, ADM 36/12827, 12828, 13870, 13871 & 13872.
54. See Taylor, *Commander,* 152–7 for an account of the mutiny based on the ship's logs and evidence given in the court martial.
55. NA, ADM 36/13872 and Buckingham, *Autobiography,* 169. There is a discrepancy in Buckingham's account between this reference to Emidy's seven years at sea and the assumption that he disembarked when Pellew took over command of *Impetueux* in 1799.

56. Lord Mansfield's judgement was welcomed by Dr Johnson, whose black servant Francis Barber celebrated the decision along with other members of London's black community. See Bundock, *Francis Barber*, 141.

57. See, for example, a report in *Royal Cornwall Gazette*, 18 December 1819 of a Redruth man selling his wife for half-a-crown.

58. Buckingham, *Autobiography*, 9.

59. Tuck, *Reminiscences of Camborne*, 69-70.

60. Buckingham, *Autobiography*, 40 & 165-6.

61. *Royal Cornwall Gazette*, 7 August 1802, 14 August 1804 and 27 October 1806 and C. Northcote Parkinson, *Edward Pellew, Viscount Exmouth* (1934), 137.

62. Buckingham, *Autobiography*, 169.

63. Susser, 'Jews in South-West England'.

64. The reformer, William Lovett, remembered Penzance fishermen being run down by soldiers with drawn cutlasses. Quoted in Jenny Uglow, *In These Times: Living in Britain Through Napoleon's Wars 1793–1815* (2014), 359.

65. For example, Uglow, *In These Times*, 304: the story of an African servant marrying an English farm girl was cut out of the second edition of Maria Edgeworth's 1803 novel, *Belinda*.

66. Thomas Hutchins is described as a mariner in his own marriage certificate 1775 quoted in Margery Emidy, *The Emidy Family* (privately printed, 2000 & Rosetta online), 24.

67. Susan Gay, *Old Falmouth* (1903), 149.

68. Quoted by Richard Cavendish, 'Josef Haydn Arrives in England', *History Today*, January 2016.

69. See Peter Fryer, *Staying Power: A History of Black People in Britain* (1984), 81–3 for the use of blacks as military bandsmen.

70. Royal Institution of Cornwall, Truro, 'A Musical Club', 1808.

71. Buckingham, *Autobiography*, 170–1. Buckingham spells the impresario's name Salomans.

72. Jerry White, *London in the Eighteenth Century: A Great and Monstrous Thing* (2012), 126; Paul Edwards and Polly Rewt (ed.), *The Letters of Ignatius Sancho* (Edinburgh, 1994), 5 January, 1780, 216 and 7 September 1779, 186.

73. *Royal Cornwall Gazette*, 21 January 1815, 25 September 1813, 9 September 1815, 26 November 1814, 18 & 19 December 1819.

74. *Royal Cornwall Gazette*, 1 October 1814.

75. William Cobbett, *The Political Register*, 16 June 1804, 935–6.

76. *West Briton*, 26 April 1816 quoted in Emidy, *Emidy Family*, 24.

77. *Royal Cornwall Gazette*, 14 December 1822, *Essex and General Advertiser*, 27 January 1843 and *Bradford Observer*, 4 May 1837. See Margery Emidy, *Emidy Family* for a more detailed account of the family.

78. *West Briton*, 24 January 1837 and monument in Kenwyn Cemetery, Truro.

79. William Makepeace Thackeray, *Vanity Fair* (Penguin edn 2001), 240.

80. *Royal Cornwall Gazette*, 26 November 1814, 16 May and 23 October 1835.

81. *Guide to the Parish Churches of Kenwyn and St Allen*, 1 & 5.

82. Emidy's gravestone in Kenwyn churchyard, *Royal Cornwall Gazette*, 25 April 1835 and Buckingham, *Autobiography*, 171.

Chapter 3: George King 1787-1855: A Foundling at Sea

1. Two years after completing this chapter and just before sending my book to the publishers I discovered that Professor Helen Berry had drawn heavily on George

King's manuscript memoir in her excellent monograph *Orphans of Empire: The Fate of London's Foundlings* (OUP, April 2019). However, she uses the material as a 'single, precious thread' running through her study, the emphasis of which is on the foundling experience. George King's story is so remarkable that it's worth telling as a whole, in uninterrupted form, as a rare example of an autobiography written by a common sailor.

2. Jonas Hanway, a governor of the Foundling Hospital and founder of the Marine Society, quoted in Ronald, *Young Nelsons*, 24.

3. Most of the Coram Hospital records are stored now at London Metropolitan Archives. LMA, A/FH/A/08/001/001/017 Petitions 1787–91.

4. See Petitions for record of George's admission aged 3 months and England and Wales Non-Conformist and Non-Parochial Register for his baptism (and that of Henry Rivington) in the Foundling Hospital on 10 November 1787.

5. LMA, A/FH/M/02/17, Facsimile of The Autobiography of George King. Unless otherwise stated all subsequent quotations are from the unnumbered pages of this work, the original manuscript of which is copyright of Coram in the care of the Foundling Hospital. King's words are quoted verbatim but punctuation has sometimes been added for clarity.

6. Sir Thomas Bernard, Treasurer of the Foundling Hospital, 1799, quoted in Gillian Pugh, *London's Forgotten Children: Thomas Coram and the Foundling Hospital* (2007), 67.

7. Quotations from R.H. Nichols and F.A. Wray, *The History of the Foundling Hospital* (Oxford, 1935), 272 & 146.

8. Ruth K. McClure, *Coram's Children: The London Foundling Hospital in the Eighteenth Century* (Yale, 1981), 235.

9. John Hawkesworth, The Foundling Hymn, quoted in Jonas Hanway, *Virtue in Humble Life* (1777), vol 1, 385–6.

10. John Brownlow quoted in Pugh, *London's Forgotten Children*, 66–7.

11. William Blake, *Songs of Innocence and Experience* (first published 1789, Oxford, 1970), 19; White, *London in the Eighteenth Century*, 473.

12. Corporal punishment was not introduced to the Foundling Hospital until the 1830s, when its regime became harsher in line with the utilitarian philosophy reflected in the 1834 Poor Law.

13. Treasurer quoted in Nichols and Wray, *History of Foundling Hospital*, 195. This punishment was not used indiscriminately at this time. Between 1779 and the end of the eighteenth century it was inflicted on seven girls and four boys, most of whom were already apprenticed.

14. NA, ADM 36/6505, Muster Book and ADM 35/2369, Pay Book of HMS *Polyphemus*. See C.P. Hill, *The Oxford Illustrated History of the Royal Navy* (Oxford, 2002), 135–7 for the differences between volunteers and pressed men.

15. See Roy Adkins, *Trafalgar: The Biography of a Battle* (2005 edn), 15.

16. See Rodger, *Command of the Ocean*, 531.

17. T.A. Heathcote, *British Admirals of the Fleet 1734–1995* (2002), 106.

18. Adkins, *Trafalgar*, 46.

19. NA, ADM 51/1544, Captain's Log of HMS *Polyphemus*.

20. Quoted in Adkins, *Trafalgar*, 114 and Tim Clayton and Phil Craig, *Trafalgar: the Men, the Battle, the Storm* (2004), 154 & 223.

21. See Clayton and Craig, *Trafalgar*, 147.

22. Quoted in Adkins, Roy & Lesley, *Jack Tar: The Extraordinary Lives of Ordinary Seamen in Nelson's Navy* (2008), 124.

23. Rodger, *Command of the Ocean*, 542.

24. NA, ADM 51/1544, Captain's Log of HMS *Polyphemus*.

25. Quoted in Adkins, *Trafalgar*, 223.

26. NA, ADM 51/1544, Captain's Log and 52/3852, Master's Log of HMS *Polyphemus*, both 26 October 1805.

27. Several paintings commemorate HMS *Victory* being towed into Gibraltar by HMS *Neptune* eg Stanfield Clark, c.1852 in V & A Museum and William Stuart, mid-nineteenth century in NMM.

28. Clayton and Craig, *Trafalgar*, 357.

29. James Martin, 'Book Concerning the Battle of Trafalgar' quoted in Clayton and Craig, *Trafalgar*, 371

30. *HMS 'Melpomene' Engaged with 20 Danish Gunboats, 23 May 1809.*

31. Adkins, Roy & Lesley, *Jack Tar*, 377.

32. Brian Unwin, *Terrible Exile: The Last Days of Napoleon on St Helena* (2010), 100–1.

33. LMA, A/FH/F/14/001/002, Reminiscences of the behaviour of Governors, Staff and Pupils of the Foundling Hospital by Morris Lievesley, Secretary, 22 & 19. This book was written in about 1847.

34. Letter of Count de Montholon quoted in Emmanuel-Auguste-Dieudonné, Compte de Las Cases, *Journal of the Private Life and Conversations of the Emperor* (ed. H. Colbourn, 1824), vol 3, 250-1

35. Eg On HMS *Owen Glendower* in 1819 George was 'painter of the ship' and on HMS *Windsor Castle* he helped to paint the ship 'inside and out' in 1829. He tried to find work as a painter in Maidstone and in South Carolina. NA ADM 73/59 describes him as a painter.

36. Cobbett, *Political Register*, 11 December 1824, vol 52, columns 661–4.

37. 'The Foundling Hospital' in http://www.british-history.ac.uk/survey-london/vol 24. *The Parish of St Pancras Part 4: King's Cross Neighbourhood*, ed. Walter H. Godfrey and W. McB. Marcham (London, 1952), 10–24.

38. My own search of Roman Catholic church registers for Cork did not reveal George King's marriage. I am grateful to Jennifer Murphy of The Representative Church Body Library in Dublin for looking through the Church of Ireland records for Cork which also yielded no results. Many of the registers have, of course, been lost through the passage of time and Ireland's troubled history.

39. George's status as a Greenwich out-pensioner is verified in NA, ADM 22/294, Pay-Book of Naval Out-Pensions, 1819.

40. This was the time of the Greek War of Independence (1824–9), which sparked off war between Russia and Turkey (1828–9). Britain and Russia along with France intervened in support of Greece but the British were always suspicious about Russia's intentions in this area.

41. Walterborough (now known as Walterboro) was a new settlement of planter families in Hickory Valley. A public library was built in 1820 and several private academies existed by the time George King arrived there.

42. NA, PROB 11/1612/429, Will of Robert Atchison; LMA, A/FH/B/03/033/001, Staff List of wages 1809-13.

43. C.H. Kauffman, *The Dictionary of Merchandise* (Philadelphia 1805), 61.

44. W.H. Hudson, *A Shepherd's Life* (1916), 146.

45. See John Rule and Roger Wells, *Crime, Protest and Popular Politics in Southern England, 1740–1850* (1997), 214; Jenny Hartley (ed.), *The Selected Letters of Charles Dickens* (2015), 325.

46. The Monckton Collection of Deeds of the Maidstone District (Kent Record Office) confirms that the Ellis family owned much land in this area.

47. William Cobbett, *Rural Rides* (first published 1830, New York, 2005), vol 1, 16, 6 November 1821.

48. See Brad Beaven, 'From Jolly Sailor to Proletarian Jack: The Remaking of Sailortown and the Merchant Seafarer in Victorian London' in Brad Beaven, Karl Bell and Robert James (eds), *Port Towns and Urban Cultures: International Histories of the Waterfront, c.1700–2000* (University of Portsmouth, 2016), 160–163.

49. He was so described in *Illustrated London News,* 11 October 1845, 238.

50. NA, ADM 6/296.

51. The Rough Entry Book for Greenwich, ADM 73/59, confirms 49-year-old George King's entry to the Hospital after twenty-three years of service in the Royal Navy.

52. Report by Medical Officer, John Liddell, 1845, quoted by Philip Newell, *Greenwich Hospital: A Royal Foundation 1692–1983* (1983), 161–2.

53. Newell, *Greenwich Hospital*, 153 and 1853 List of Rules on greenwichadmiraltyin pensioner website.

54. A contemporary account from the 1830s quoted in a book published by the Royal United Services Institute in 1908, included in greenwichadmiraltyinpensioner website.

55. Visitor's Guide, 1855 included in greenwichadmiraltyinpensioner website.

56. Royal Commission Report of 1860 and Memo by the Duke of Somerset quoted in Newell, *Greenwich Hospital*, 176 & 260 and Charles Jennings, *Greenwich: The Place Where Days Begin and End* (1999), 25.

57. Quotations from ballads by Charles Dibdin: 'Ben Block', 'In the Wags', 'Royal Reasons for Roast Beef' and 'I was Pressed while A Rowing'; play 'A Sailor's Return' in *The New British Theatre: A Selection of Original Dramas* vol II (1814).

58. *Illustrated London News*, 5 & 12 April 1845.

59. Greenwichadmiraltyinpensioner website, Greenwich Pensioners and the Naval General Service Medal.

60. LMA, A/FH/F/14/001/002, Morris Lievesley's Reminiscences. I owe this reference to a lecture given by Caro Howell, Director of the Foundling Museum, at a Symposium I attended on 10 October 2015: 'Art, Charity and the Navy: Greenwich and Foundling Hospitals'.

61. Census Returns for 1851 and 1841.

62. See England and Wales Non-Conformist and Non-Parochial Death Register which records George's death in Greenwich Hospital, 31 July 1857 and NA, ADM 73/010 which lists him as DD (Discharged Dead), 25 July 1857.

Chapter 4: Othnel Mawdesley 1790–1812: An Adventure in Spain

1. Baptism record in Cheshire Parish Registers, 6 August 1790 at St Martin's church, Chester (Othuel Mawdeslay [*sic*]); https://www.british-history.ac.uk, *A History of the County of Chester,* originally *Victoria County History* (2005), vol 5 part 2.

2. Othnel Mawdesley, 'Private Remarks during the time of being prisoner in Spain' – unless otherwise acknowledged future quotations are from this manuscript, which has no page numbers. It is now in the Caird Library at the National Maritime Museum REG16/000117.

3. Edward Baines, *A History of County Palatine and Duchy of Lancaster* (1836), vol 4, 832; *Brasenose College Register 1509-1909* (Oxford 1909); *Chester Chronicle*, passim.

4. Chester Record Office, WEP 170221111707, Wills of Thomas Mawdesley, 1834 and Frances Mawdesley, 1889.
5. *Brasenose College Register*, 376.
6. https://library.harvard.edu, Giles Shaw, *Historical Notes of the Grammar School, Middleton* (unpublished, 1887), 11-12. An earlier Thomas Maudesley [*sic*] was a master at this school in the sixteenth century.
7. NMM, MRK/104/2/27, Letter from Thomas Mawdesley to Admiral Markham MP, 23 July 1806. I am grateful to Katherine Moulds of the Caird Library, NMM for this reference and for information about Othnel's origins and death.
8. NA, ADM 35/2485, Paybook of HMS *Theseus*, 8 April 1806–30 April 1808.
9. Description of Othnel Mawdesley in *Chester Chronicle*, 5 February 1813.
10. NA, ADM 51/1599, Captain's Log of HMS *Theseus* 8 April 1806–29 June 1807.
11. Rodger, *Command of the Ocean*, 545.
12. John D. Grainger, *British Campaigns in the South Atlantic 1805–1807* (2015), 133.
13. NA, ADM 35/2485, Paybook of HMS *Theseus*, 8 April 1806–30 April 1808; John Masefield, *Sea Life in Nelson's Time (*1972 edn), 33.
14. NA, ADM 51/1738, Captain's Log of HMS *Theseus*, 12 July 1807–10 July 1808, 18 July 1807.
15. Captain's Log of HMS *Theseus*, 31 August and 14 November 1807.
16. Captain's Log of HMS *Theseus*, 1 and 2 November 1807.
17. Mawdesley, Remarks, 28–29 December 1807.
18. Information on Andrew Mitchell from Katherine Moulds and NA, ADM 37/167, Muster of HMS *Theseus*, 12 July 1807–10 July 1808.
19. Rodger, *Command of the Ocean*, 543; Buckingham, *Autobiography*, 119–20. See also Augustin R. Rodriguez Gonzalez, 'The Spanish at Trafalgar' in *Journal for Maritime Research* (April 2005), 41 for 'examples of courtesy and chivalry between English and Spanish sailors'.
20. I am grateful to Paul Cook of the Paper Conservation Studio at the Caird Library, NMM for this information.
21. Richard Ford, *A Handbook for Travellers in Spain* first published 1845 (1966 edn), vol 1, 16.
22. Ford, *Handbook,* vol 1, 69.
23. Quoted in Raymond Carr, *Spain 1808–1939* (Oxford, 1966), 45.
24. Donat Henchy O'Brien, *My Adventures During the Late War: A Narrative of Shipwreck, Captivity, Escapes from French Prisons, and Sea Service in 1804-14* (ed. Charles Oman, 1902), 47.
25. Buckingham, *Autobiography*, 107.
26. Ford, *Handbook*, vol 2, 96.
27. O'Brien, *My Adventures,* 210.
28. See Michael Lewis, *Napoleon and his British Captives* (1962), 45–6.
29. Lewis, *Napoleon and British Captives*, 169.
30. See Francisco Goya's paintings *The Second of May: The Charge of the Mamelukes* and *The Third of May 1808* for a vivid depiction of these events.
31. NA, ADM 37/1189, Muster of HMS *Theseus*, 1 July 1808 – 28 February 1809.
32. If they were preserved they might have been among the other household effects bequeathed by Frances Mawdesley to her friends Letitia and Harriet Hilton. See Will in Chester Record Office.
33. Quoted in Tim Blanning, *The Pursuit of Glory: Europe 1648–1815* (Penguin edn 2007), 660.

34. Rodger, *Command of the Ocean*, 555.

35. Captain's Log of HMS *Theseus*, 11 July 1808–10 July 1809; Rodger, *Command of the Ocean*, 555–6; *The Life of Thomas, Lord Cochrane* by his son (1869), vol 1, chap 1.

36. *Naval Chronicle*, vol 22, July–December 1809, 87; NA, ADM 37/1990, Muster of HMS *Ajax*, 4 June – 30 November 1809; Figurehead of HMS *Ajax* displayed in NMM.

37. NA, ADM 52/4540, Master's Log of HMS *Milford*, 11 August 1811–4 August 1814.

38. Ronald, *Young Nelsons*, 220 & 230.

39. *Chester Chronicle*, 5 February 1813; *Gentleman's Magazine, January–June 1813*, 180. I am grateful to Katherine Moulds for these references.

40. Quoted in Rodger, *Command of the Ocean*, 555.

Chapter 5: William Barlow 1792-1811: Child of the Raj and Sailor

1. OIOC, IOR L/MAR/B/393A, Passenger List of the *Porcher*, 5 February 1800.

2. OIOC, MSS Eur F176/12, Letter from Rev. Thomas Barlow, 4 February 1806 and F176/15, Elizabeth Barlow to her husband, 1 December 1805.

3. CSAS, Macpherson Papers, William Dick to Alan Macpherson, 19 November 1791.

4. *The Memoirs of William Hickey*, ed. Alfred Spencer (1925), vol IV, 321–3.

5. C. Wilkinson, *British Logbooks in UK Archives, 17th-18th Centuries* (UEA, 2006), 29.

6. OIOC, IOR L/MAR/B/359C and L/MAR/B/138/C, East Indiaman Logbooks of *Caledonia* and *Exeter*; *Lloyds Evening Post*, 29 August – 1 September 1800

7. Russell Miller, *The East Indiamen* (Amsterdam, 1980), 155.

8. Quoted in Miller, *East Indiamen*, 134.

9. *London Chronicle*, 15 April and 6–9 September 1800.

10. OIOC, MSS Eur F176/7, William Barlow to his brother, 25 March 1805, 4 April 1804 and 12 April 1803.

11. OIOC, MSS Eur F176/7, 10 February 1803.

12. *Memoir and Letters of the Right Honourable Thomas Dyke Acland*, ed. Arthur Acland (1902), 5–6 and James Milnes Gaskell, *An Eton Boy, 1820–1830* (1939), 5.

13. Iris Butler, *The Eldest Brother, Richard The Marquess of Wellesley, 1760–1842* (1973), 350.

14. OIOC, MSS Eur F176/16, Eliza to her parents, 17 March 1801; F176/66, William to his parents, 8 June 1801; F176/54, George to his parents, 16 January 1806; F176/60, George's account of Eton, June 1809; F176/66, William to his parents, no date.

15. OIOC, MSS Eur F176/66, William to his father, 10 April 1805 & no date.

16. OIOC, MSS Eur F176/7, William Barlow to his brother, 23 June 1803 and 20 October & 29 November 1804.

17. Margot Finn, 'The Barlow Bastards: Romance Comes Home from the Empire' in *Legitimacy and Illegitimacy in Nineteenth-Century Law, Literature and History*, ed. Margot Finn, Michael Lobban & Jenny Bourne Taylor (2010), 31 & 38. Finn's focus is not, however, on the child but on 'the family as a functional socio-economic unit that knitted affines and lineage groups into a seamless garment'.

18. OIOC, MSS Eur F176/3, Sir Robert Barlow to his brother, 7 & 20 December 1804.

19. OIOC, MSS Eur F176/3, 22 December 1804.

20. OIOC, MSS Eur F176/3, 19 February & 27 June 1805.

21. OIOC, MSS Eur F176/66, William to his father, 30 April 1805; F176/3, Robert Barlow to his brother, 27 June 1805.

22. OIOC, MSS Eur F176/67, William to Uncle William, 8 February, 20 May & 25 May 1805.
23. OIOC, MSS Eur F176/3, 17 February 1806.
24. F.B. Sullivan, 'The Royal Academy at Portsmouth, 1729–1806' in *Mariners' Mirror* LXII (1977), 318.
25. OIOC, MSS Eur F176/3, Sir Robert to his brother, 18 February 1806.
26. Sullivan in *Mariners' Mirror*, 324 and John Winton, *The Naval Heritage of Portsmouth* (1989), 53.
27. OIOC, MSS Eur F176/60, George's opinion of Eton, June 1809.
28. OIOC, MSS Eur F176/54, George to his father, 29 April 1806.
29. H.W. Dickinson, *Educating the Royal Navy* (2000), 46.
30. OIOC, MSS Eur F176/7, Uncle William to his brother, 17 September 1807.
31. OIOC, MSS Eur F176/3, Sir Robert to his brother, 6 October 1807; Jane Austen to Cassandra, 24 December 1798 in Deirdre Le Faye (ed.), *Jane Austen's Letters* (1995), 28.
32. OIOC, MSS Eur F176/66, William to his father, Hertford undated.
33. Andrew Hambling, *The East India College at Haileybury, 1806–1857* (2005), 45–6; OIOC, MSS Eur E357, George Yule to his brother, 15 August 1829.
34. OIOC, MSS Eur F176/67, William to Uncle William, 9 December 1807, 22 January, 3 and 10 May, 1809.
35. Hambling, *East India College*, 13; OIOC, J/1/23, Haileybury Records, Petition 13 November 1808; MSS Eur F176/16, Henry to his father, 24 January 1812 and F176/68, East India Company to William, 1809.
36. Private Papers kindly lent by Anthony Barlow, William Barlow to his brother, 8 February, 1810.
37. OIOC, MSS Eur F176/66, William to his father, 23 February 1811; F176/7, Uncle William to his brother George, 10 August 1810; F176/3, Sir Robert to his brother George, 8 July 1810.
38. OIOC, MSS Eur F176/54, George to his father, 17 February and 5 April 1808; F176/ 7, Uncle William to his brother George, 10 February, 1811.
39. OIOC, MSS Eur F176/67, William to Uncle William, 1 and 2 December 1809.
40. OIOC, MSS Eur F176/67, William to Uncle William, 3 January 1810 (wrongly dated 1809); B.F. Coleridge quoted in Rodger, *Command of the Ocean*, 394.
41. OIOC, MSS Eur F176/67, William to Uncle William, 20 May 1810; F176/66, William to his father, 26 December 1810 and 23 February 1811; F176/3, Sir Robert to his brother, 8 July 1810.
42. Private Barlow Papers, Pellew to George Barlow, 18 August 1809 and to Lady Barlow, 15 August 1809.
43. Private Barlow Papers, Pellew to George Barlow, 28 January 1811.
44. OIOC, MSS Eur F176/7, Uncle William to his brother, 10 February 1811; F176/44, Pownoll to his father-in-law, 11 March 1811.
45. OIOC, MSS Eur F1/66, William to his father, 11 April 1811.
46. Private Barlow Papers, Edward Pellew to Sir George, 6 April 1811.
47. Taylor, *Commander*, 219.
48. NA, ADM 53/272, Captain's Log of HMS *Caledonia*.
49. Private Barlow Papers, Pellew to Sir George, 28 June 1811 and NA, ADM 53/272.
50. OIOC, MSS Eur F176/12, Thomas Barlow to his brother, 7 August 1811; Private Barlow Papers, Robert Barlow to Sir George, 24 August 1811; OIOC, MSS Eur F176/55, George to his father, 12 March 1812.

51. Jane Austen, *Persuasion* (Penguin 1965 edn), 76–7.
52. Brian Southam, *Jane Austen and the Navy* (2005), 103–4; NA, ADM 53/272 and Jane to Cassandra, 18–20 April 1811 in Le Faye, *Jane Austen's Letters*, 181.
53. OIOC, MSS Eur F176/7, Uncle William to his brother, 4 April 1804, March 1806 and 12 July 1811; Portrait by John James Halls, 1816.
54. OIOC, MSS Eur F176/16, Eliza to her father, 5 November 1806; F176/12, Rev. Thomas Barlow to his brother, 11 July 1804; F176/47, Sir George to Eliza, October 1816, Eliza to her father, 22 January 1819.
55. Private Barlow Papers, Pellew to Sir George, 28 June, 1811; OIOC, MSS Eur F176/16, Eliza to her parents, 8 April 1806 and William to his mother, 25 November 1806; F176/55, George to his father, 1 September 1815; Taylor, *Storm and Conquest*, 27; OIOC, F176/36, Divorce Papers.
56. OIOC, MSS Eur F176/44, Pownoll to his father-in-law, 11 March 1811.

Chapter 6: Charles Barlow 1800–1805: A Life Lived Through Letters
1. Butler, *Eldest Brother*, 292.
2. OIOC, MSS Eur F176/15.
3. OIOC, MSS Eur F176/36, 19 January 1806, Divorce Papers and Correspondence. Punctuation has been inserted in some letters for the sake of clarity.
4. NA, L/MAR/B/191/A, Logbook of *Surrey*.
5. OIOC, MSS Eur F176/7 and F176/3.
6. Finn, 'The Barlow Bastards', 30.
7. OIOC, MSS Eur F176/54, George to his father.
8. Eg OIOC, MSS Eur F176/54, George to his father 29 April 1806 and F176/16, Eliza to her father, 5 November 1806.
9. OIOC, MSS Eur F176/36, Elizabeth to her husband 17 August 1809 and 54, George to his father, 2 January 1807.
10. OIOC, MSS Eur F176/7, William Barlow to Sir George, 12 August 1807; 16, Eliza and Henry to their father, 10 & 31 August 1807; 15, Elizabeth to her husband, 28 June 1807 and 36, 29 February 1808.
11. OIOC, MSS Eur F176/7, William Barlow to Sir George, 17 September 1807.
12. OIOC, MSS Eur F176/16, 10 September 1808 and 5 February 1811.
13. Thomas Pinney (ed.), *The Letters of Thomas Babington Macaulay* (1974–81), vol. 1, 3 and 6 February, 1813.
14. Mr Okes's name appears on the subscription list for these works.
15. OIOC, MSS Eur F176/8, William Barlow to Sir George, 10 February 1811.
16. Drury Lane Theatre, for example, put on Sheridan's *The Glorious First of June* 'with the stage turned into a sea'. See Uglow, *In These Times*, 65.
17. OIOC, MSS Eur F176/85, 28 October 1813.
18. OIOC, MSS Eur F176/90.
19. NA, ADM 51/2936, Captain's log of HMS *Victorious*, 10 March, 26 April & 6 October 1813 and 8 July 1814.
20. OIOC, MSS Eur F176/95.
21. OIOC, MSS Eur F176/85.
22. Ronald, *Young Nelsons*, 91.
23. OIOC, MSS Eur F176/95, Memoranda relating to Charles.
24. OIOC, MSS Eur F176/85, Letters from Charles as a midshipman.
25. W.M. Thackeray, *Roundabout Papers*, ed. J.E. Wells (1925), 20.
26. Rodger, *Command of the Ocean*, 574.

27. OIOC, MSS Eur F176/95.
28. William Dillon quoted in Ronald, *Young Nelsons*, 95–6.
29. OIOC, MSS Eur F176/85.
30. OIOC, MSS Eur F176/85.
31. Abraham Salamé, *Narrative of an Expedition to Algiers in 1816* (1819), 163.
32. *Trewman's Exeter Flying Post*, 19 September 1816.
33. NA, ADM 51/2720, Log of HMS *Queen Charlotte*, 28 August 1816.
34. Lord Exmouth's Report in *The New Monthly Magazine*, 1 October 1816.
35. NA, ADM 51/2720, Log of *Queen Charlotte*, 6 October 1816.
36. OIOC, MSS Eur F176/85.
37. Taylor, *Commander*, 228–9.
38. Eg NMM, LOG/N/R/36/1&2, 22 June & 19 July,1819, 15 December 1820, 2 & 7 June 1822; William R. O'Byrne, *A Naval Biographical Dictionary* (1849).
39. NMM, LOG/N/R/36/1&2, 18–19 May 1821, 2 May 1819 and 31 May 1821.
40. The letters about this affair are in OIOC, MSS Eur F176/91. William St Clair, *Trelawney: The Incurable Romancer* (1977), 85 confirms that 'Trelawney was in the wrong'.
41. OIOC, MSS Eur F176/93, John Windsor (unclear signature) to Charles, 17 February 1823.
42. OIOC, MSS Eur F176/86, Charles to his father, 12 January 1823, 24 February, 17 and 28 March 1825.
43. OIOC, MSS Eur F176/87.
44. Harold Temperley, *The Foreign Policy of Canning 1822–1827: England, the Neo-Holy Alliance and the New World* (1925), 381.
45. OIOC, MSS Eur F176/90.
46. OIOC, MSS Eur F176/95.
47. OIOC, MSS Eur F176/90.
48. OIOC, MSS Eur F176/87.
49. Jane Austen, *Mansfield Park* (USA, 1964 edn), 198.
50. OIOC, MSS Eur F176/87, 10 February 1834.
51. OIOC, MSS Eur F176/93.
52. Dickens to Forster, 2 July 1837 and 6 December 1839 quoted in Claire Tomalin, *Charles Dickens, A Life* (Penguin edn 2012), 87. Tennyson wrote in similar terms to Arthur Hallam, as did Hurrell Froude to John Henry Newman.
53. OIOC, MSS Eur F176/88 & 90.
54. OIOC, MSS Eur F176/88, 6 May and 1 September 1835, 2 January, 1 February and 9 August and 2 October 1836.
55. Portrait in NMM. See, for example, Charlotte Brontë, *Villette* (first published 1853, Thomas Nelson and Sons, no date), 105, where the doctor hero has a 'full, cleft, Grecian, and perfect' chin.
56. OIOC, MSS Eur F176/89, 9 December 1839 and 16 July 1840.
57. Quoted by Martin Lynn, 'British Policy, Trade and Informal Empire' in Andrew Porter (ed.), *The Oxford History of the British Empire*, vol III (Oxford, 1999), 107–8.
58. Thomas Babington Macaulay quoted in Jasper Ridley, *Lord Palmerston* (1972), 348.
59. Lizzie Collingham, *The Hungry Empire: How Britain's Quest for Food Shaped the Modern World* (2017), 153–4. Collingham herself argues that smoking opium was 'one of the least physically damaging ways of taking any of the recreational drugs available at the time' and that the crusade against it was 'absurd propaganda'.
60. Julia Lovell, *The Opium War: Drugs, Dreams and the Making of China* (2011), 110–1.

61. OIOC, MSS Eur F176/90.

62. OIOC, MSS Eur F176/89.

63. O'Byrne, *Naval Biographical Dictionary*.

64. OIOC, Mss Eur F176/89, 5 May 1841.

65. Lovell, *Opium War*, 159 & 221.

66. OIOC, MSS Eur F176/89, Charles to his father, 5 and 16 March 1846.

67. OIOC, MSS Eur F176/96, August 1846; F176/90, 13 March 1843.

68. NA, PROB 11/2225/229.

Chapter 7: Sydney Dickens 1847–1872: A Life Illuminated by his Father's Fiction

1. C[harles] D[ickens] to W.C. Macready, 19 April 1847 and Mrs Sydney Smith, 7 September 1847 in *The Letters of Charles Dickens* vol V (ed. G. Storey & K.J. Fielding, Oxford, 1981), 58 & 180.

2. Quotations from Lillian Nayder, T*he Other Dickens, A Life of Catherine Hogarth* (Cornell, 2011), 155 and R. Gottlieb, *Great Expectations: The Sons and Daughters of Charles Dickens* (New York, 2012), 90.

3. Charles Dickens, *David Copperfield* (first published 1849–50), passage from Chapter 1.

4. Charles Dickens, *Dombey and Son* (first published, 1847), end of Chapter 1 and passages from Chapters 8, 16, 22 & 41.

5. Quotations from Arthur A. Adrian, *Georgina Hogarth and the Dickens Circle* (Oxford, 1957), 28 and Michael Slater, *Charles Dickens* (Yale, 2011), 305–6.

6. CD to his brother Alfred, 7 September 1847, *Letters,* vol V, 160 and CD to Miss Burdett Coutts, 13 January 1852, vol VI (ed G. Storey & K. Tillotson, Oxford, 1986) 574.

7. Henry Fielding Dickens, *Recollections* (1934), 44 and *Memories of My Father* (1928), 14, 19 & 25.

8. Slater, *Dickens*, 312.

9. *Letters,* vol VI, 161–2, CD to his wife, 3 September 1850.

10. Charles Dickens, *Great Expectations* (first published 1860–61), passage from Chapter 2.

11. Charles Dickens, 'Our French Watering-Place' in D. Pascoe (ed.), *Selected Journalism 1850–1870* (1997), 153, 154 and 162.

12. CD to J.T. Delane, 12 September, 1853, *Letters,* vol VII (ed. G. Storey, K. Tillotson & A. Easson, Oxford, 1993), 145; CD to E.F. Piggott, 17 January 1856 vol VIII (ed. G. Storey & K. Tillotson, Oxford, 1995), 26–7; CD to Hon Mrs Richard Watson, 14 September 1860, vol IX (ed. M. House, G. Storey & K. Tillotson (Oxford, 1997), 308.

13. *Letters,* vol V11, 678, CD to Rev. Gibson, 18 July 1855.

14. H. Dickens, *Recollections*, 11–12 and CD, *Selected Journalism*, 154.

15. Wilkie Collins quoted in Nayder, *The Other Dickens*, 245; *Selected Journalism*, 152; CD to Catherine, 7 September 1853, *Letters,* vol VII, 137 and CD to Mark Lemon, June 1853 quoted in Lucinda Hawksley, *Dickens's Artist Daughter Katey: Her Life, Loves and Impact* (2007 edn),123.

16. CD to Henry Austin, 6 September 1854 and CD to Mrs Gaskell, 31 July 1854, *Letters,* vol VII, 410-11 & 383.

17. CD to Mrs Brown, 5 July 1856 and CD to Miss Burdett Coutts, 15 July 1856, vol VIII, 145 & 165.

18. CD to Catherine, 25 August 1856 and CD to Miss Burdett Coutts, 10 July 1857, *Letters,* vol VIII, 178–9 & 372.
19. *Selected Journalism, 3,* 10 & 61; CD to Cerjat, 3 January 1855, *Letters,* vol VII, 496
20. CD to Hon Mrs Richard Watson, 7 October 1856 and review in *Maidstone, Rochester, Chatham & Canterbury Journal,* 26 December 1857, vol VIII, 202 & note 3, 496.
21. Charles Dickens, *A Christmas Carol* (first published 1843), passage from Stave 2.
22. CD to Charley, 10–12 July 1858, *Letters,* vol VIII, 602.
23. Katey quoted by Fred Kaplan, *Dickens, A Biography* (1988), 399.
24. CD to Miss Burdett Coutts, 8 May & 23 August 1858, *Letters,* vol VIII, 559 & 632.
25. Helen Thomson to Mrs Stark, 30 August 1858, *Letters,* vol VIII, 749 and H. Dickens, *Recollections,* 19.
26. Passage from Dickens, *David Copperfield,* Chapter 8.
27. CD to Rev. Gibson, 6 November 1858, *Letters,* vol VIII, 697.
28. *Selected Journalism,* 'Chatham Dockyard', 229 and 'Where We Stopped Growing', 34; *Letters,* vol VIII, 247 and vol X, 356.
29. CD to Bulwer Lytton 6 January 1859, Rev. Ashton Burrows, 22 January 1859 & Rev. Gibson, 11 May 1859, Letters vol IX, 5, 14–15 & 64. The naval school run by Joseph Ashton Burrows was not the same establishment as Eastman's Naval Academy set up by Thomas Eastman in 1855 and subsequently run by George Spickernell.
30. CD to Rev. Brewsher, 14 March 1860, Rev. William Bell, 21 April 1860, Cerjat, 3 May 1860 & Rev. Ashton Burrow, 30 June 1860, *Letters,* vol IX, 225, 238, 247 and 269.
31. CD to Mrs R. Watson, 14 September, 1860, *Letters,* vol IX, 309.
32. CD to Cerjat, 1 February 1861, W.H. Wills, 8 December 1861 & Miss Mary Boyle, 28 December 1861, *Letters,* vol IX, 383, 535 and 554.
33. CD to Mary Dickens, 23 September 1860 & John Forster, 4 October 1860, *Letters,* vol IX, 315 & 320.
34. CD to John Leech, 18 January 1861, Letters vol X (ed. M. House, G. Storey & K. Tillotson, Oxford, 1998), 16.
35. Passage from Charles Dickens, *Little Dorrit* (first published 1855–7), chapter 7.
36. Passage from Dickens, *David Copperfield*, chapter 32.
37. Quoted in Amanda Foreman, *A World on Fire* (2010), 179–82.
38. Adrian, *Georgina Hogarth,* 171.
39. Charles Dickens, *Dombey and Son* (first published 1848, Chapman & Hall edn, no date), 395–6.
40. Dickens Museum, Ouvry Papers, Messrs Banton & Mackrell Solicitors to Sydney Dickens, 27/1-8.
41. Quoted in *The Dickensian,* 1 August 1914.
42. Passage from Dickens, *Great Expectations,* chapter 34.
43. CD to Cerjat, 16 March 1862 & 28 May 1863, *Letters,* vol X, 53 & 253.
44. *Selected Journalism,* 230 & 232–3.
45. CD to E.S. Dallas, 12 November 1864, *Letters,* vol X, 453.
46. Dickens Museum, Carlton Papers, Catherine Dickens to Clara Macirone, 12 June 1872 and XB326, Last Will and Testament of Catherine Dickens.
47. NA, 196/36/920, Service Records; CD to Miss Coutts, 12 February 1864, *Letters,* vol X, 356.
48. *All the Year Round,* 24 December 1864, 468–9.
49. CD to Lord John Russell, 16 August 1865 *Letters,* vol XI (ed. M. House, G. Storey & K. Tillotson, Oxford, 1999), 82.

50. Arthur Adrian in *Dickensian*, Spring 1992.

51. NA, ADM 101/136/1A, Medical and Surgical Journal of HMS *Antelope*; Anthony Bower, 'The Little Admiral: Sydney Dickens from *Britannia* to *Topaze*', Part I in *Dickensian*, Summer 2013.

52. NA, 196/17/73 and ADM 11/83 (latter quoted in Bower, 'Little Admiral'); CD to W.H. Wills, 2 September 1867, *Letters*, vol XI, 417.

53. 'Where we Stopped Growing' in *Selected Journalism*, 30.

54. Charles Dickens, *Barnaby Rudge* (first published 1841), passage from chapter 15.

55. Tomalin, *Charles Dickens*, 366.

56. CD to Rev. Bewsher, 14 March 1860, *Letters*, vol IX, 225.

57. Quoted in Bower, 'The Little Admiral' Part II in *The Dickensian*, Winter 2013.

58. Frederick William Fisher, *Reminiscences of Admiral Sir Frederick William Fisher* (1938), 53–4.

59. Dickens Museum, Ouvry Papers, Sydney to his father, 19 March 1869 and Banton & Mackrell, 27/12-15 & 15/55.

60. CD to Alfred, 20 May 1870, *Letters*, vol XII (ed. G. Storey, Oxford, 2002), 530.

61. Dickens, *Dombey and Son*, passage from Chapter 47.

62. Charles Dickens, *The Life and Adventures of Martin Chuzzlewit* (first published 1844), passage from chap 14; Dickens, *Great Expectations*, end of chapter 19; quotation in Gottleib, *Great Expectations*, 239.

63. Dickens Museum, Ouvry Papers, 27/10 & 17/63.

64. Dickens Museum, XB 326, Will of Catherine Dickens. This photograph was left in Catherine's will to her granddaughter, Sydney. A copy of it is now held by the Royal British Columbia Museum.

65. Bower, 'Little Admiral', Part 2, 6 and Dickens Museum, Ouvry Papers, 15/44.

66. Quoted in Bower, 'Little Admiral', Part 2, 9.

67. Dickens Museum, Ouvry Papers, 14/31 and Carlton Papers, B366 2014.3.1

68. CD to Miss Coutts, 12 February 1864, *Letters*, vol X, 356.

69. Dickens, *Barnaby Rudge*, passages from chapter 30.

Chapter 8: Ada Southwell 1875–1953: Child Migrant

1. Henry Mayhew, *London Labour and the London Poor* (ed. Rosemary O'Day & David Englander, 2008), 177–80.

2. Kay Moloney Caball, *The Kerry Girls: Emigration and the Earl Grey Scheme* (Dublin, 2014), 63, 87 & 152–5. Mayhew came across the same prejudice against Irish immigrants among London costermongers. See Mayhew, *London Labour*, 85–120.

3. Dr Barnardo quoted in Philip Bean & Joy Melville, *Lost Children of the Empire* (1989), 41.

4. Arthur A. Adrian, *Dickens and the Parent-Child Relationship* (Ohio, 1984), 59.

5. From 'The Departure of the Innocents' in The Children's Society, *Our Waifs and Strays*, August 1887, 3.

6. Jerry White, *London in the Nineteenth Century* (2007), 216. Such 'deaths by despair' are again on the increase according to Angus Deaton's current investigation into inequality in Britain, as reported in the *Guardian*, 14 May 2019.

7. Barnardo's Archive, Macpherson Report on Alfred Southwell and Governor's Report on Henry and Ada Southwell, 1883.

8. Maud Pember Reeves, *Round About a Pound a Week* (first published 1913, 1979 edn), 76.

9. A.S. Jasper, *A Hoxton Childhood* (2013 edn), 73; Charles Booth, *Life and Labour of the People in London* (1902), final volume, 62.

10. Barnardo's Archive, Governor's report.

11. www.findmypast.co.uk, Admission Register for Hammond Square School, 1875.

12. The price of *cartes de visite* ranged from around 10*s* to 2*d* by the 1890s. See R.W. Rimmer, 'Poverty: A Subject for Photography' in *The Historian*, Sept 2003, 5–7.

13. Arnold Bennett's Journal quoted in White, *London in the Nineteenth Century*, 436.

14. Library and Archives of Canada, Passenger List for Home Children; Roger Kershaw & Janet Sacks, *New Lives for Old: The Story of Britain's Child Migrants* (National Archives, 2008), 28 and Joy Parr, *Labouring Children: British Immigrant Apprentices to Canada, 1869–1924* (1980), 31.

15. Roy Parker, *Uprooted: The Shipment of Poor Children to Canada, 1867–1917* (Bristol, 2008), 69.

16. Marriage certificate from St Giles church, 8 July 1884, by permission of Chris Beldan.

17. Parr, *Labouring Children*, 62 & 71. Parr estimates that one in four girls' relations received no news at all.

18. Letter written by Emily, 12 November 1886, by permission of Chris Beldan.

19. Report by Andrew Doyle, *Emigration of Pauper Children to Canada* (Local Government Board, 1875), 16–17.

20. Parr, *Labouring Children*, 111.

21. The Allan Line, https://personal.uwaterloo.ca

22. Edward Rudolf of the Waifs and Strays Society quoted in Kershaw & Sacks, *New Lives for Old*, 88.

23. Quotations from 'The Departure of the Innocents' in *Our Waifs and Strays*, 1887; letter of Home Secretary, Lord Harcourt, 1884 quoted in Parker, *Uprooted*, 199.

24. Doyle Report, 11–12 & 35.

25. Letter written by Marie Parker, Ada's granddaughter, to Shirley Gettler, Bessie's daughter-in-law, 24 April 2001; letters from Harriet Southwell, undated and 8 May 1884; letter from Emily Southwell to Mrs Morrow, 12 November 1886, all by permission of Chris Beldan.

26. https://spitalfieldslife, The Commercial Directory 1885 shows that the address Harriett gives, 62 Commercial Road, was in fact the Boundary Tavern (research by Jackie Millen).

27. Harriett to Emily, 12 December 1886, by permission of Emily's granddaughter, Pat Gillibrand.

28. Quotation in Parker, *Uprooted*, 138.

29. The drawing was clearly sent with a letter of which only the last page survives.

30. This was the Sebright Public House, which operated twice weekly as a music hall and hosted one of Marie Lloyd's first appearances.

31. https://www.reynolds-lake-ca-genealogy; Harriet Southwell to 'Mrs Eastling', 8 May 1884, by permission of Chris Beldan.

32. Barnardo's Archive, Macpherson Documents.

33. Emily Southwell to Mrs Morrow, 11 November 1888; death certificates of Harriett and George Southwell supplied by Chris Beldan.

34. Barnardo's Archive, Macpherson documents and 1891Canada Census.

35. Parr, *Labouring Children*, 115-6.

36. IICSA, *Child Migration Programmes: Investigation Report* (March 2018).

37. Undated letter by permission of Pat Gillibrand.

38. Parker, *Uprooted*, 212.
39. Their story is told in Christine Kinealy, Jason King & Gerard Moran (eds), *Children and the Great Hunger in Ireland* (Quinnipiac,1918).
40. Kershaw & Sacks, *New Lives for Old*, 88.
41. Barnardo's Archive, Ledger, 26 April 1888.
42. Doug Gelbert, *A Walking Tour of Montreal – Golden Square Mile* (ebook). Fashionable portraits of the Stevenson family by William Norman & Son are housed in the McCord Museum, Montreal.
43. Testimonial by G. Stephenson by permission of Pat Gillibrand.
44. Census Canada 1891 where Ada's age is given as 15 and Thomas Kitching & Mavelle (Kitching) Beldan, 'I Remember', 18.
45. See Parr, *Labouring Children*, 127 and Mark G. McGowan, 'Rethinking the Irish Famine Orphans of Quebec, 1847–1848' in Kinealy, King & Moran, *Children and the Great Hunger*, 96-7.
46. Quoted in *Forgotten*, produced by Eleanor McGrath for TVO, 2018.
47. Kitching & Beldan, 'I Remember', 5-6.
48. *Forgotten*, 2018.
49. Emily to Mavelle Beldan, 28 March 1954, by permission of Pat Gillibrand; Marie Parker to Shirley Gettler, 24 April 2001; Pat Gillibrand to Chris Beldan, 13 October 1996.
50. Canada Census 1901.
51. 'I Remember', 4 & 8.
52. Research done by Chris Beldan in *Auburn Citizen*, 27 August & 11 September 1906, 3 September 1907, 14, 16 & 18 November 1908.
53. 'I Remember', 20; photograph by permission of Chris Beldan and death certificate of Henry Southwell.
54. 'I Remember', 12 & 18–21.
55. 'I Remember', 22–3; emails from Chris Beldan (Winnie's son), 6 February & 4 March, 2018.
56. Quotations from 'I Remember' and 'The Departure of the Innocents'.
57. See Parr, *Labouring Children*, 137 and Caball, *Kerry Girls*, 144.
58. 'Departure of the Innocents'; Harriet Southwell to Emily, 12 December 1886; Chris Beldan email, 6 February 2018.
59. The words of Kevin Rudd, Prime Minister of Australia in November 2009. There is currently pressure on Prime Minister Trudeau of Canada to make a similar apology.
60. See Report by Human Rights Council, 16 August 2016 and Mona Mahmood in the *Guardian*, 6 May 2016.
61. See League of Nations Declaration, 1924 and United Nations Declarations, 1948 & 1959.

Chapter 9: Sea Fever: Lives Changed by the Sea

1. John Gabriel Stedman, 'An Elegy on my Sailor' quoted in S. Thompson (ed.), *Journal of John Gabriel Stedman 1744–97* (1962), 375–6.
2. Thompson, *Journal of Stedman*, 309–10, 313, 327, 333–6 & 369. Johnny's story is partly told in Anthony Fletcher, *Growing Up in England: The Experience of Childhood 1600–1914* (2008), which does not mention his slave background.
3. Quotations from Stedman 'Elegy'.
4. Letter to Elizabeth Robins quoted in Constance Babington Smith, *John Masefield: A Life* (1978), 15.

5. Masefield's letters quoted in Babington Smith, *John Masefield*, 27–8 & 31–2.
6. Babington Smith, *John Masefield*, 97–8.
7. From 'Sea Fever' (1904) in Philip W. Errington (ed.), *Sea Fever: Selected Poems of John Masefield* (2005), 10.
8. John Masefield, *A Tarpaulin Muster* (1907), 196 & 49.
9. 'The Tarry Buccaneer' in *Selected Poems*, 12.
10. John Masefield, *Sea Life in Nelson's Time*, 82 & 54–5.
11. 'Hell's Pavement' in *Selected Poems*, 4.
12. *Selected Poems*, 46–7 & 39.
13. Quotations from 'The Emigrant' and 'Sea Fever' in *Selected Poems*, 24 & 10.
14. Doyle Report, 3, 18, 24, 21, 35, 25, 22.
15. Interview with Margaret Humphreys in the *Guardian*, 20 February 2010.
16. John Catlin, *Family Quartet: Vera Brittain and her Family* (1987), 140; Shirley Williams, *Climbing the Bookshelves* (2009), 32; Lord Montagu of Beaulieu, *Wheels Within Wheels: An Unconventional Life* (2000), 36.
17. Ann Thwaite, *Passageways: The Story of a New Zealand Family* (Otago, 2009), 264.
18. Lynn Smith, *Young Voices: British Children Remember the Second World War* (2007), 319–20.
19. Alistair Horne, *A Bundle from Britain* (1993), 211, 152, 318 & 307.
20. P. Linn, 'National Identity and Social Mobility: Class, Empire and the British Government Overseas Evacuation of Children during the Second World War' in *Twentieth Century British History*, 1996, vol 7, 312 & 333.
21. Quoted in Jessica Mann, *Out of Harm's Way: The Wartime Evacuation of Children from Britain* (2005), 319 & 307.
22. D. Foster, S. Davies & H. Steele, 'The Evacuation of British Children during the Second World War' in *Aging and Mental Health*, vol 7, 2003, 404–5.

Select Bibliography

This book is largely based on original sources, which are listed below and cited in the endnotes. I also consulted many books and articles for background material but have listed only those which are especially relevant to the history of children and of the sea, as well as to the circumstances in which my particular 'children at sea' lived.

Archive Collections

Barnardo's Archive
Macpherson Report on Alfred Southwell
Governor's Report on Southwell Family
Ledgers concerning Ada Southwell

British Library, Oriental and India Office Collections
Barlow Collection, MSS Eur F176
Records of East Indiaman ships, IOR L/MAR/B, *Porcher, Caledonia, Exeter, Surrey*

Cambridge South Asian Studies
Macpherson Papers

Chester Record Office
Wills of Thomas Mawdesley, 1834 and Frances Mawdesley, 1889 WEP 170221111707

Dickens Museum, London
Ouvry Papers
Carlton Papers
Will of Catherine Dickens

Isles of Scilly Museum
Family and Shipping Archives

London Metropolitan Archives
Staff List of wages 1809–13, A/FH/B/033/001
Petition of Mary Miller, A/FH/A/08/001/017
Autobiography of George King Facsimile A/FH/M/02/17
Governor's Reminiscences, A/FH/F/14/001–2

Morrab Library, Penzance
Joseph Emidy material

National Archives:
Muster Books, Captains' and Masters' Logs, Paybooks of HMS *Gorgon*, HMS
 Indefatigable, HMS *Impetueux*, HMS *Polyphemus*, HMS *Theseus*, HMS *Caledonia*,
 HMS *Ajax*, HMS *Milford*, HMS *Victorious*, HMS *Queen Charlotte*, ADM 36, 37,
 51, 52 & 53
Medical and Surgical Journal of HMS *Antelope*, ADM 101/136
Pay-Book of Naval Out Pensions ADM 22/294
Service Records of Sydney Dickens, 196/36/920 & 196/17/73
Wills of William Furzer, Robert Atchison, Charles Barlow PROB 11

National Maritime Museum
Letter from Thomas Mawdesley to Admiral Markham, MRK/104/2/27
Logbook of Henry James, Midshipman, LOG/N/R/36

Private Papers
Anthony Barlow, Family Letters
Chris Beldan, Family Letters and Documents
Pat Gillibrand, Family Letters
Bridget Somekh, Journal of Othnel Mawdesley, subsequently donated to the National
 Maritime Museum

Royal Cornwall Museum, Truro
Royal Cornwall Gazette
West Briton

Online Archives
Old Bailey Proceedings Online www.oldbaileyonline.org
Trials of Mary Branham, John Owen, George Robinson et al, Francis Gardener &
 William Tuckey, James Pulet et al, Joseph Tuso, Ann Mather

State Library of New South Wales https://www.sl.nsw.gov.au
Arthur Bowes Smith, A Journal of a Voyage from Portsmouth to New South Wales and
 China in the Lady Penrhyn, Merchantman, 1787–89, MS fair copy compiled c.1790
Ralph Clark, Journal kept on the Friendship during a voyage to Botany Bay and Norfolk
 Island, and on the Gorgon returning to England, 1787–92
John Easty, Journal 1786–1793
David Collins, An Account of the English Colony in New South Wales

Published Works
The place of publication is London unless otherwise stated

Adkins, Roy, *Trafalgar: The Biography of a Battle*, 2004
Adkins, Roy & Lesley, *Jack Tar: The Extraordinary Lives of Ordinary Seamen in Nelson's
 Navy*, 2008
Adrian, Arthur A., *Georgina Hogarth and the Dickens Circle*, Oxford, 1957
— *Dickens and the Parent-Child Relationship*, Ohio, 1984
Atkinson, Alan, *The Europeans in Australia: A History*, Oxford, 1997

Austen, Jane, *Mansfield Park*, 1814
— *Persuasion*, 1817
Babington Smith, Constance, *John Masefield: A Life*, 1978
Bateson, Charles, *The Convict Ships*, 1969
Bean, Philip & Melville, Joy, *Lost Children of the Empire*, 1989
Berry, Helen, *Orphans of Empire: The Fate of London's Foundlings*, Oxford, 2019
William Blake, *Songs of Innocence and Experience*, 1789
Blanning, Tim, *The Pursuit of Glory: Europe 1648–1815*, 2007 edn
Booth, Charles, *Life and Labour of the People of London*, 1902
Bower, Anthony, 'The Little Admiral: Sydney Dickens from *Britannia* to *Topaze*' in *The Dickensian*, Summer & Winter, 2013
Buckingham, James Silk, *Autobiography*, 1855
Bundock, Michael, *The Fortunes of Francis Barber: The Story of the Jamaican Slave who became Samuel Johnson's Heir*, Yale, 2015
Carr, Raymond, *Spain 1808-1939*, Oxford, 1966
Catlin, John, *Family Quartet: Vera Brittain and her Family*, 1987
Chapman, Don, *1788: The People of the First Fleet*, Sydney, 1988
Clayton, Tim & Craig, Phil, *Trafalgar, the Men, the Battle, the Storm*, 2004
Cobley, John, *Sydney Cove 1788*, 1962
Colley, Linda, *Captives: Britain, Empire and the World*, 2002
Collingham, Lizzie, *The Hungry Empire: How Britain's Quest for Food Shaped the Modern World*, 2017
Conrad, Joseph, *Youth: A Narrative and Two Other Stories*, 1902
Conrad, Robert Edgar, *Children of God's Fire: A Documentary History of Black Slavery in Brazil*, 1983
Coote, John, *The Faber Book of the Sea*, 1980
Damousi, Joy, *Depraved and Disorderly: Female Convicts, Sexuality and Gender in Colonial Australia*, Cambridge, 1997
Dickens, Charles, *A Christmas Carol*, 1843
— *Barnaby Rudge*, 1841
— *David Copperfield*, 1849
— *Dombey and Son*, 1846
— *Great Expectations*, 1860
— *Letters*, Pilgrim edition, vols V-XII, Oxford 1981–2002
— *Little Dorrit*, 1855
— *The Life and Adventures of Martin Chuzzlewit*, 1843
— *Selected Journalism 1850–1870*, ed. D. Pascoe, 1997
Dickens, Henry Fielding, *Memories of My Father*, 1928
— *Recollections*, 1934
Dickinson, H.W., *Educating the Royal Navy*, 2000
Doyle, Andrew, *Emigration of Pauper Children to Canada*, 1875
Edwards, Paul, (ed.), *The Life of Olaudah Equiano*, 1988
Eliot, George, *Adam Bede*, 1859
Emidy, Marjorie, *The Emidy Family*, privately printed 2000
Errington, Philip, *Selected Poems of John Masefield*, 2005
Flannery, Tim, *Watkin Tench's 1788*, Melbourne, 2009
Fletcher, Anthony, *Growing Up in England: The Experience of Childhood 1600–1914*, 2008

Forester, C.S., *Mr Midshipman Hornblower*, 1950

Forster, John, *The Life of Charles Dickens,* Memorial edn 1911

Fryer, Peter, *Rhythms of Resistance: African Musical Inheritance in Brazil*, 2000

— *Staying Power: A History of Black People in Britain*, 1984

Gillen, Mollie, *The Founders of Australia: A Biographical Dictionary of the First Fleet*, Sydney, 1989

Gottlieb, R., *Great Expectations: The Sons and Daughters of Charles Dickens*, New York, 2012

Hambling, Andrew, *The East India College at Haileybury*, 1806–1857, 2005

Hayward, Jennifer & Caballero, M. Soledad, *Maria Graham's Journal of a Voyage to Brazil*, Anderson South Carolina, 2010

Hawksley, Lucinda, *Dickens's Artist Daughter Katey: Her Life, Loves and Impact*, 2018

Hickey, William, *Memoirs,* ed. Alfred Spencer, 1925

Historical Documents of New South Wales, Sydney, 1892

Holden, Robert, *Orphans of History: The Forgotten Children of the First Fleet*, 2001

Horne, Alistair, *A Bundle from Britain*, 1993

Hughes, Robert, *The Fatal Shore*, 1987

Jasper, A.S., *A Hoxton Childhood*, 1979

Jennings, Charles, *Greenwich: The Place Where Days Begin and End*, 1999

Kaplan, Fred, *Dickens: A Biography*, 1988

Keneally, Tom, *The Commonwealth of Thieves*, 2006

— *The Playmaker*, 2014 edn

Kershaw, Roger & Sacks, Janet, *New Lives for Old: The Story of Britain's Child Migrants*, 2008

Kinealy, Christine, King, Jason & Moran, Gerard, *Children and the Great Hunger in Ireland*, Quinnipiac, 2018

Le Faye, Dierdre (ed.), *Jane Austen's Letters*, 1995

Lovell, Julia, *The Opium Wars: Drugs, Dreams and the Making of China*, 2011

Macaulay, Thomas Babington, *Letters*, ed. Thomas Pinney, 1974–81

Mannix, Daniel P., *Black Cargoes: A History of the Atlantic Slave Trade 1518–1865*, 1963

Masefield, John, *Sea Life in Nelson's Time*, 1905

Mayhew, Henry, *London Labour and the London Poor*, eds Rosemary O'Davy & David Englander, 2008

McClure, Ruth K., *Coram's Children: The London Foundling Hospital in the Eighteenth Century*, Yale, 1981

McGrady, Richard, *Music and Musicians in Nineteenth Century Cornwall*, Exeter, 1991

Moloney Caball, Kay, *The Kerry Girls: Emigration and the Earl Grey Scheme*, Dublin, 2014

Montagu, Lord, *Wheels Within Wheels: An Unconventional Life*, 2000

Nayder, Lilian, *The Other Dickens: A Life of Catherine Hogarth*, Cornell, 2011

Newell, Philip, *Greenwich Hospital: A Royal Foundation, 1692–1983*, 1983

Northup, Solomon, *Twelve Years a Slave*, 2013 edn

O'Brian, Patrick, *Master and Commander*, 1971 edn

O'Brien, Donat Henchy, *My Adventures during the Late War*, 1902 edn

Oxley, Deborah, *Convict Maids: The Forced Migration of Women to Australia*, Cambridge, 1996

Parker, Roy, *Uprooted: The Shipment of Poor Children to Canada, 1867–1917*, Bristol, 1998

Parr, Joy, *Labouring People: British Immigrant Apprentices in Canada, 1869–1924*, 1980

Pember Reeves, Maud, *Round About a Pound a Week*, 1913

Porter, Andrew (ed.), *The Oxford History of the British Empire*, 1999

Pugh, Gillian, *London's Forgotten Children: Thomas Coram and the Foundling Hospital*, 2007

Rodger, N.A.M., *The Command of the Ocean: A Naval History of Britain, 1649–1815*, 2004

Ronald, D.A.B., *Young Nelsons*, Oxford, 2009

Slater, Michael, *Charles Dickens*, Yale, 2011

Smith, Emma, *The Great Western Beach: A Memoir of a Cornish Childhood Between the Wars*, 2008

Smith, Lynn, *British Children Remember the Second World War*, 2007

Southam, Brian, *Jane Austen and the Navy*, 2005

Taylor, Stephen, *Commander: The Life and Exploits of Britain's Greatest Frigate Captain*, 2012

— *Storm and Conquest: The Battle for the Indian Ocean, 1809*, 2007

Thomas, Hugh, *The Slave Trade: The History of the Slave Trade, 1440–1870*, 1997

Thompson, S. (ed.), *Journal of John Gabriel Stedman 1744–97*, 1962

Thwaite, Ann, *Passageways: The Story of a New Zealand Family*, Otago, 2009

Tomalin, Claire, *Charles Dickens: A Life*, 2012 edn

Uglow, Jenny, *In These Times: Living in Britain Through Napoleon's Wars 1793–1815*, 2014

Wagner, Gillian, *Children of the Empire*, 1982

Williams, Shirley, *Climbing the Bookshelves*, 2009

White, Jerry, *London in the Eighteenth Century: A Great and Monstrous Thing*, 2012

— *London in the Nineteenth Century*, 2007

Index